Taming the Lion Tamers:

The Inside Story of a landmark Sex Abuse Case

By David Flowers

To the 1982 Student

ACKNOWLEDGEMENTS

This story exists because of a small group of thoughtful, committed people. To Gregg Meyers, lawyer extraordinaire, it was a genuine privilege to be beside you in the trenches on this case and so many others. Guerry Glover bristles when called a hero but there is no more apt term to describe his singular acts of courage and his perseverance to do what was right, even in those moments when it seemed no one else cared to. To the young man known here as Kevin Dunn, his strength and willingness to confront Porter-Gaud School and its arrogance will forever be an example for all who come forward in the future. The true number of victims of Fischer and his abettors, James Bishop Alexander, and Berkeley Grimball, will never be known, but to those who did help in exposing these criminal acts you should know that many, many people owe you an eternal and immeasurable debt of gratitude.

My children lived this case in a way that others never think about. Louie, Sarah, and Amy lived firsthand the effects this case and others had on their Dad. I hope this book might help them understand, maybe just a little, why I was so sad and mad a lot of the time and why I wasn't the father they were hoping I might've been. To them I say that I regret that you witnessed what this work did to me, but just know that I hate the impact it had on your lives and I love you all more than you can imagine.

In bringing this book to its present form, I've been fortunate to have the invaluable aid of many people. To the numerous readers who all offered something worthwhile, I thank you. Rosemary Karalius did the sketches of the scoundrels on the cover and I offer her my sincere thanks. Thanks also to Beck Sipes for creating the book covers, front and back. Soren Velice's edits and suggestions helped to sculpt an unwieldy mess into its final form and for that I am, and will be, eternally grateful. My Kauai o'hana saved my life and gave me my voice back. Mahalo a me ka nui ke aloha.

To Natalie, who brought me out of darkness, encouraged me to tell this story, and then gave me the space to do it: Always.

INTRODUCTION

This is a true story. I was one of the lawyers.

I wrote the first draft of this manuscript shortly after the events occurred almost twenty years ago. I wanted to record a contemporaneous factual account of this remarkable story. It then lay dormant for many years until a confluence of recent events compelled me to dust it off and publish it.

Those recent events began with the release of an Emmy-nominated documentary film based on this same story entitled *What Haunts Us*. Filmmaker Paige Goldberg Tolmach created a powerful vehicle for raising awareness about how childhood sexual abuse thrives when bad people value the reputation of institutions more than they value innocent children and when good people choose to not get involved.

After the release of the film, Porter-Gaud School mounted a public relations campaign to continue old false narratives and create new ones about this story to deflect from their continuing refusal to accept responsibility for what they allowed to happen on their premises and to dozens of students, including many of their own. The current chairman of their board of trustees (Hank Cheves) and their current headmaster (DuBose Egleston) sent a letter full of lies to a group of alums who wanted answers to some questions raised by the film. It was very similar to a press release that a previous headmaster of the school issued more than 20 years ago which is an integral part of this story. Also, while they were publicly expressing regret and feigning apologies, Headmaster Eggleston was privately spreading a vile lie about one of the heroes of this story, saying this hero spit on one of the Porter-Gaud representatives in the courtroom at the trial, in an attempt to attack the character of that hero and cast doubt on the truth of the story as depicted in the film. When confronted about the lie, Eggleston acknowledged that he didn't believe the lie was true but did not apologize for spreading it. The school still employs him as the head of the school even though they know about this conduct. The school also hurriedly changed the name on a student award, a fundraising level and a building named after one of the men you will read about in this story who demonstrated an appalling lack of concern for the safety of children and was one of the administrators responsible for dozens of children being sexually molested. It is interesting to note that the building named after Berkeley Grimball was given his name *after* the events you will read about here. It is also interesting that the school only changed these things when the public discovered their existence in an effort to make it look like they were contrite. What the board of trustees doesn't get is that they had twenty years to change those things but chose to do so only when confronted with their inappropriateness by others. They want credit for acting expeditiously but waited almost twenty years to do what was right even back then. In response to the group of alums' concerns about the school receiving over $500,000.00 from its insurance company in a lawsuit, the school agreed to pay some Indulgences in an effort to absolve themselves of responsibility for their sins, including the fact that the school profited monetarily from their shameful behavior. Even after the Indulgences are paid, the school will retain some of that money. Because of the actions and words of the current administration of Porter-Gaud, a true account of what really happened is necessary to counter the false narrative and lies that continue to be spread by the school and to give true meaning to "the supreme importance of the truth", a phrase found in the mission statement of Porter-Gaud School which has no meaning to past or current administrators of that school.

I was asked to appear at a number of film festivals around the country where the film was shown, along with the director and other participants. I was struck by the overwhelming effect it was having on audiences. First, the film did exactly what Ms. Tolmach hoped it would do: start a conversation about childhood sexual abuse. Second, the countless questions we got after each showing demonstrated the thirst for answers not only to the larger questions raised by the film, but also for more information about this particular case.

I practiced law for about twenty years before walking away in 2011. Most of my career was spent representing victims of sexual abuse in civil litigation. I handled cases against most major religious denominations and all types of other organizations from the Boy Scouts of America to the CIA. I dealt with things that should only be in nightmares yet are all too real for far too many people. I also encountered the most absurd and lame excuses offered up by the enablers, protectors, and facilitators of serial pedophiles. From all of those cases, one stands alone as the worst example of institutional arrogance and lack of caring for children and that is the one you will read about here. Porter-Gaud School distinguished itself through its own words, actions, and utter lack of concern for kids as the single worst example of institutional callousness, arrogance, and deceit I encountered in my career. Their recent reaction to *What Haunts Us* reinforces that conclusion.

AUTHOR'S NOTES

Much of what you will read herein is actual transcripts of the legal proceedings. Where I did not have permission to use their true identities, I changed the names of some of the victims to protect their privacy. Some of the court proceedings, including depositions, have been condensed for brevity and readability. I strove to maintain the essence of the words of those whom I have condensed and offer humble apologies to any who think I missed that mark. I also made minimal changes to punctuation and syntax in the transcripts.

I chose to present one part of the story out of chronological order: the guilty plea of the pedophile. I did so to give the reader a sense of the horror that is a direct result of the behavior of the school officials which fills the rest of the pages. I included the words of the victims as they spoke at the plea hearing, so the reader will have the appropriate context within which to gauge the behavior and words which compose the rest of the story.

"Falsehood is cowardice, the truth courage."

Hosea Ballou

The prey was so plentiful here.

It had always been available in his old territories, but his previous handlers didn't seem to like it when he sated his urges with the prey in their domain. They always cast him out whenever he got caught hunting on their watch.

But here, it was different. His new handlers were different. He was invited here by one of his new handlers and he quickly came to know that these new handlers were unlike any he had seen before. Yes, there was the mild slap on his paw the first time he went after one of their charges, but he understood it to be a warning to be more discreet rather than a prohibition against hunting in their domain.

And they had allowed him to stay. They not only made more and more of their charges available to his ever-increasing urges, they even steered some of the most vulnerable ones right into his clutches.

Over the years he came to learn that he had free run and free reign over the prey in this new domain. His handlers allowed him to hunt as much as he wanted, until his bottomless hunger was sated. Even as his urges increased, they continued to make the prey available to him.

He liked this territory because his handlers here allowed him to become one of the worst lions of all.

PART 1 – THE LION

Courtroom C was packed that Friday morning, April 23, 1999. The victims, their families, and members of the news media squeezed into every available seat. There was considerable apprehension in the room about whether Eddie Fischer would get any jail time. Many in the room were aware that at least five Catholic priests had recently pled guilty in Charleston to molesting young boys and not a single one went to jail. Most feared that Fischer would get the same preferential treatment. Others expressed concern about the judge's age. The Honorable Gerald Smoak, known to be fair, was not a young man, and some feared he might identify with Fischer's advanced years and give him probation.

Hurricane Hugo had badly damaged the downtown courthouse in September 1989, and due to insurance squabbles and red tape, ten years later the court system was still in temporary quarters. Courtroom C was the largest courtroom in the temporary court building. It was a spacious courtroom with the judge's bench in the front left corner, set at an angle. On that day, Judge Smoak was assigned to hear guilty pleas in General Sessions Court, which is criminal cases in South Carolina. He was not a resident of Charleston. He was a visiting judge from another part of the state and likely had not seen any of the media coverage about Eddie Fischer.

I had arrived early, and after a few handshakes and greetings, found a spot in the farthest corner. I brought only a legal pad. This was not a day for lawyers. This day was for 'the guys' – the victims of Eddie Fischer. I recognized some of the victims in the courtroom. I guessed some of the

1

other men I didn't know were on 'the list.' The courtroom was unusually quiet for the number of people in attendance. Right before the judge entered, Fischer came in through a side door with his lawyer, Lionel Lofton. They took their seats at one of the tables in front of the bar to the judge's right. Debbie Herring was already seated at the other table. She handled most of the sex crime prosecutions in Charleston. Though diminutive in stature and soft-spoken, she was and is one of the best anywhere on child sexual abuse cases. Lionel greeted her, came over to her table and spoke briefly with her.

The door from the judge's chambers opened and the bailiff announced, "All rise, The Honorable Gerald Smoak presiding."

The judge took his seat and began the proceeding. His voice conveyed the authority of the black robe he wore. "Be seated. Ladies and gentlemen, before we start, number one, there will be no filming of the victims in this matter that we're going to take up this morning, and there will be no sound recordings in the courtroom. And I hope that's clear with everyone here. Solicitor call your first case."

Debbie rose and said, "The State versus Edward Fischer."

"Mr. Lofton. would you and your client come forward, please?" The judge said and then paused while the two men came around from behind their table and stood right in front of the judge. "Thank you, sir. Solicitor, how many indictments are there?"

"He's pleading guilty to 13 indictments."

"And as I understand it the -- which one of the indictments is going to be an Alford plea; would you tell me that?"

"The first indictment, indictment number 97-GS-10-7161." An Alford plea is a special plea derived from a U.S. Supreme Court case that allows a defendant to maintain his innocence but concede that the evidence is strong enough that he would be convicted. When a defendant enters an Alford plea, he is sentenced as if he had pled guilty.

"Would you go through them and tell me what they are and what the punishment is, Solicitor, please?" The judge pulled a note pad closer and prepared to write.

"Yes, your honor. Lewd act upon a minor. That was ten years. Lewd act, that was ten years at the time. Buggery, that was five years. Lewd act upon a minor, which was ten years at the time. Criminal sexual conduct with a minor in the second degree, which is 20 years. Criminal sexual conduct with a minor, which is 20 years. Criminal sexual conduct with a minor, which was 20 years. Criminal sexual conduct with a minor, which is 20 years. Assault and battery of a high and aggravated nature, ten years. Criminal sexual conduct with a minor, second degree, 20 years. Criminal sexual conduct, third degree, ten years. Assault and battery of a high and aggravated nature, ten years. Criminal sexual conduct with a minor in the second degree, 20 years." The reason the crimes were called different things is the offenses spanned almost 40 years. The laws changed during that time and Fischer could only be charged with what was against the law at that time, using that era's nomenclature.

"Alright. Thank you, ma'am." The judge looked right at Fischer, "You are Edward Mein Fischer?"

"Yes, your honor." Fischer sounded scared.

"Alright, sir. Would you raise your right hand, please?" The accused complied. "Do you solemnly swear to tell the truth and nothing but the truth, so help you God?"

"I do, your honor."

The judge then turned to Lionel Lofton. "Mr. Lofton, do you represent the defendant?"

"Yes, your honor."

"Have you explained to the defendant the charges contained in the indictments, the possible punishment and his constitutional rights, including the right to a jury trial?"

"I have."

"And in your opinion does the defendant understand the charges, the punishment and his rights?"

"Yes, he does."

"How does he wish to plead, guilty or not guilty?"

"Guilty as to all, with exception to the one we mentioned earlier where we have the Alford plea, indictment number one."

"And do you agree with that decision to plead guilty?"

"Yes, I do, your honor."

The judge looked at Fischer. "How old are you, sir?"

"Seventy-one, your honor."

"And what education do you have?"

"I have a college degree and a master's degree."

"And what kind of work do you do?"

"I'm a retired schoolteacher."

"Now, you are pleading guilty to 13 counts, and the first indictment, as I understand it, you're going to enter an Alford plea; do you understand that, sir?"

"Yes, your honor."

"An Alford plea simply means that you do not admit anything, but that you feel that if you were tried, that the proof is such that you would probably be convicted so you're going to enter this plea; do you understand that?"

"Yes."

"Alright. Then you're going to enter pleas straight up on --that was on lewd act, the first indictment. Now, the second one is also lewd act, which carries ten years; do you understand that, sir?"

"Yes."

"Then we've got buggery, which carries five years; do you understand that?"

"Yes."

The judge restated each crime and the respective punishment and got Fischer to acknowledge that he understood each. The judge then resumed his questioning of Fischer with a litany of questions that are pretty standard in every guilty plea across the country.

"Understanding the nature of the charges against you and the consequences of a guilty plea, how do you wish to plead to these charges, guilty or not guilty?"

"Guilty, your honor."

"Do you understand that when you plead guilty that you admit the truth of the charges that are made against you?"

"Yes."

"Did you commit these offenses, sir?"

"I did, your honor."

"Alright, sir. Solicitor have there been any plea negotiations in this case?"

Debbie Herring responded. "Your honor, that all of these will run concurrent." This meant that any sentences that the judge rendered would be served simultaneously, instead of one after the other. It made sense in this case because if Fischer got jail time, given his age and his allegedly poor health, no one expected him to last long in prison.

"Alright."

Debbie pointed out that the South Carolina legislature had recently enacted a law which stated that for any violent crime, the criminal must serve 85 percent of the sentence given before being eligible for parole. Sexual crimes against minors were all considered violent crimes by this new law. While all the other sentences were important, the last indictment was covered by this law and any sentence on that charge would likely determine how long Fischer stayed in jail, if he went to jail at all.

"That's the criminal sexual conduct with a minor, that's the 20-year?"

"Yes, your honor." This meant that if the judge gave Fischer the maximum sentence on this charge, he would be required to serve 17 years in prison before he would be eligible for parole. At Fischer's age it would be a life sentence.

"Alright. Solicitor, I would like to hear the facts before I accept the pleas."

Debbie then gave a brief description of each of the thirteen victims who were pressing charges against Fischer, including the circumstances of their abuse.

John Doe 1 was first molested by Fischer in 1960 when Fischer was a teacher at a Catholic school in Charleston. The abuse began in the library at the school. It also occurred in Fischer's car.

John Doe 2 was molested in 1961 when Fischer was a teacher at Sacred Heart Elementary School, also a Catholic school in Charleston. The molestation occurred at Fischer's house.

John Doe 3 was assaulted from 1972 until 1975 when Fischer was a teacher at Porter-Gaud School, a private school affiliated with the Episcopal church in Charleston. Like many of his other victims, Fischer offered to help this boy with weight training to build his muscles. He also took photographs of this young man, as he did with many of the other victims.

John Doe 4 was in the eighth grade at Porter-Gaud School when Fischer first got to him. The boy had suffered an injury on the athletic field and was sent to the training room on the campus where Fischer molested many of his victims, including this one. He was also assaulted later at Fischer's home.

John Doe 5 was molested from 1977 until 1979. He was a student at Porter-Gaud. Fischer plied this young man with alcohol and drugs before assaulting him at his home. Fischer also ingratiated himself with this boy's parents, having dinner at their home and telling them that he could tutor their son. This was also a common ploy by Fischer.

John Doe 6 was another Porter-Gaud victim. It began when he was in the seventh grade in 1977. Fischer provided him alcohol and drugs.

John Doe 7, Guerry (pronounced "Gary") Glover, was a student at both Porter-Gaud and College Prep schools. The assaults on him began when he was nine years old. The first assault occurred at the Glover's home and then subsequent assaults, over many years, occurred at Porter-Gaud school and at Fischer's home.

John Doe 8 was a physician at Johns Hopkins. He was in the ninth grade at Porter-Gaud when he was assaulted. Fischer claimed to be a licensed driving instructor and he persuaded this boy's parents to let him teach their son to drive a car. The assault happened at Fischer's house after he plied the boy with alcohol and drugs.

John Doe 9 was also in the ninth grade at Porter-Gaud in 1980. Fischer took this boy to the beach and then back to his house where he told the boy he knew a group of women who would pay the boy to have sex with them. This was one of Fischer's most common ploys.

John Doe number 10 was 14 years old when Fischer first molested him in 1989. By this time, Fischer had moved on to teach at James Island High School, a public high school in Charleston. Fischer persuaded this boy's single mother to let him take her son on trips away from Charleston. He also tutored the boy.

John Doe 11 was also a student at James Island High School. He was not a student in any of Fischer's classes. Fischer targeted him and flattered the boy about how intelligent he was and got him to his house where the assaults occurred throughout the summer after the boy graduated from high school.

John Doe 12 was also at James Island High School. He was in the eleventh grade when Fischer met him passing in the hall. Fischer told the boy he seemed to be a loner and he could help the boy build relationships.

The assaults occurred at Fischer's home.

At the time of the hearing, John Doe 13 was still a child. It happened in 1996 and 1997. The boy was not a student at any school that Fischer taught in. He was Fischer's paper boy. All of the assaults occurred at Fischer's home.

Debbie paused before continuing, "Your honor, as you see, there are many victims here and many lawyers, but I would like to make a brief statement to the Court. As you've seen, these victims were not abducted in alleyways by strangers, but really what happened to them was worse, because the most important figure in a child's life besides that of a parent is a teacher. And this relationship was abused in the most horrific way in this case. You may have noticed that the ages of these children varied from elementary to high school, depending solely on the access of Mr. Fischer and who he could get in his grip. In May of '97, it became clear that this was going to be investigated, as one of these young men had reported to it to the school board. After that he still had this other young child, victim number 13, coming over to his home. And he has proven that he has the ability to gain access to children even if he is not a teacher. He stands before you, I know, as an elderly man, but what is unfortunate is that he has lived already the best years of his life, but they were lived and enjoyed as he was inflicting such pain and humiliation and horror upon so many children in Charleston County. I don't say that he's ruined their lives, but as you will see them coming in here today, most of these young men, while all of them are brave and have made successes in their life, but that has been in spite of what Mr. Fischer has done to them. And finally, he stands before you as a serial rapist, and the State would just ask that you consider him as such."

The judge held up his right hand. "I'm going to accept the plea at this point. I find that there is a substantial factual basis for the plea and I find that the defendant's decision to plead guilty is freely, voluntarily, knowingly, and intelligently made and that the defendant has had the advice and counsel of a competent attorney with whom he says he's satisfied, so I will accept the plea. You may proceed."

At this point in the proceeding, the 13 victims were given an opportunity to describe to the judge the effects that Fischer's crimes had on their lives. Some appeared in person, some wrote letters, and lawyers spoke for a couple of them.

Debbie began with a letter from John Doe number one. "*Your honor, Edward Fischer's crimes go beyond the act itself. Every day for the past 30-odd years I have lived with this terrible secret deep within myself. The results have been devastating and it will take a lot of time for me to heal. Once your childhood is lost, you never get it back. Feelings of anger, fear and mistrust dictate your life. All of these lead to broken relationships and lost friendships. This is not just about me; it is for all of his victims. Mr. Fischer's crimes took a toll on the victims and their families and their friends. The effects are far reaching. Also, I would like you to know that this is not a case of one or two victims, that would be bad enough. But please look at the number of victims and the length of time that these crimes went on; children stripped of their youth by someone who is charged with their care and development, an authority figure who abused his power and his victims. And now, decades later, we must deal with this again, but this time so that we may heal. Hopefully justice will be served today so that we may heal and have a happy life and hopefully have closure to this dreadful matter."*

"Your honor, John Doe number two will address the Court in person."

"Alright, Sir," the judge said as he nodded respectfully to John Doe 2, who was very nervous. He was 51 years old and had spent his adult life in retail sales. He wore his best suit to the hearing. He had spent many days writing and rewriting his remarks. He told the judge about his early life and how he came into contact with Fischer at Sacred Heart elementary school. "Being from a broken family, I immediately enjoyed the special attention that he gave to me. I enjoyed riding in his Cadillac, and I felt that I was the envy of my classmates. I didn't like being deemed a teacher's pet, but at the same time, I felt special, because he seemed to like me more than he did the other kids, a fact that I very much regretted later." He described how Fischer targeted him and ingratiated himself with the young boy's mother and offered to help the boy develop his muscles. He had the boy spend the night at his house and sexually assaulted him. The assaults continued on a weekly basis for some time. "The mind has a unique way of blocking out things that it doesn't want you to remember. There are many, many times that I do remember, and I also remember that control and manipulation that he had over me was not imaginary. My mother looked at it as favors by him to give me rides to school, to the doctor, to the dentist, and going to get a haircut. He would take me to the fair and we would go to Folly Beach and play bingo and eat hot dogs at Pete's Hot Dog Stand on the beach. He would take me to Robinson's Cafeteria on Wentworth Street and show me off to all of his friends. He would call me his boy. I felt like he was calling me his prize. I felt like a puppet on a string and he was the puppeteer manipulating and controlling my every move. I remember him teaching me what to say in confession, so the preacher would give me absolution for my sins." The assaults continued even as the boy entered high school. At one point, his mother became suspicious of Fischer's interest in her son. She asked her son about it and when he asked her why she wanted to know, she replied, "because if I find out that he is doing something to you, I'll kill him." At that time, the boy realized he could not tell his mother what Fischer was doing because he did not want to see her go to prison. When the boy finally mustered the courage to tell Fischer that the abuse was going to stop, Fischer "told me that he had emphysema and that if I left him, he would die. I can still remember me beating on the back of his car, a black 1957 Ford, and I told him that was his problem, not mine." The abuse caused this man many physical injuries, including shingles, throwing up blood, ulcers, and anxiety. He was hospitalized and medicated for these conditions for years without ever telling anyone about the abuse. He also struggled with addiction to alcohol. "At a time in my life when I should have been building self-esteem and building self-confidence, Eddie Fischer had stripped me of any chance I had to lead a normal, healthy, prosperous, and productive life. All of my life has been nothing but menial jobs, disastrous relationships, and unfortunate situations. To this day I find it extremely difficult to get close to anyone. I've tried my best to cover up my psychological problems with alcohol and drugs, never knowing that eventually the alcohol and drugs would compound my problems even more. I had sought help through counselors, psychiatrists, psychologists, and medical doctors, never once discussing the facts about my teenage years." After he got away from Fischer, he would often see the teacher out and about in Charleston, always accompanied by a young boy. He finally started putting his life together when he was 44 years old. "This recovery and healing process are still going on to this day, a process that I thank God for. I know that I have an awful lot to heal and I know that my journey will take a long time, but at the same time, I feel grateful that at least I had the opportunity to heal. For at this moment, I no longer consider myself a victim of Eddie Fischer, but a survivor. Who knows how many people have not had this opportunity. I am now 51 years old and I live by myself, this is my choice. For any relationship I've ever been in has ended in disaster and the pain of separation for me is not worth trying to start another one. I isolate myself because I choose to. It's easier this way. I do not feel depressed, nor do I feel I have excess energy at the end of a long day. I seldom laugh, and I don't know how to cry. It seems the only emotion that I can show well and often is anger. And I seem to be a master at that, because I show it often. I don't know what part the sexual abuse by Eddie Fischer has played in my life's problems, but I do know this, it played a major, major role. Your honor, I have been asked to state how the long-term sexual abuse by Mr. Eddie Fischer has affected my life. There are many more instances that I can tell you and many other situations that happened, and there is much more detail that I could go into, but I choose not to. Whether or not Mr. Fischer gets his due justice in this courtroom remains to be seen. But at least this is one way that I myself had to put some closure to it and my life's nightmares. Through all of the pain, through all of the heartache, through all of the living hell he has put me through, I forgive him for what he's done to me. But I forgive him not because it's going to help him, but because it's going to help me. Sooner or later Eddie Fischer will have to pay for the horrible things that he has done, whether it is on this earth or not. May God have mercy on your soul. Thank you, your honor."

Debbie rose again. "Your honor, John Doe number three is not here. I will read the letter that he has written. '*I would like to explain that those of us who have suffered at the hands of the accused have been sentenced for life. Nothing is more personal than sexual abuse. Nothing will ever make it go away. Sexual abuse transgresses the body, the mind, the heart, and the soul. The acts of Mr. Fischer against young adolescents should be punished in the severest manner. I, on the other hand, have to live with images of him performing oral sex on me until my penis bleeds. Remembering the pain of him trying to enter me anally. My sentence is for a lifetime. I hope that the public record of this case is clear, clear to those who stand up to pedophiles, that they will be supported. Clear to those that commit these crimes, that they will be punished. Clear to all schools that programs should be put in place to combat this behavior. Lastly, and most importantly, I urge that the sentence given in this case to be protective of an unknown number of adolescents from this horrific experience. I ask for the maximum allowed by law.*'

"Your Honor, John Doe number four is here to speak."

John Doe number four was a successful businessman in his mid-thirties. "I think everybody came here for their own reason. I came here today to see you, Mr. Fischer, to see my nightmare, to face you; to look you in the eye and tell you what you did to me had a tremendous impact on my life." He said he felt "different" from his first day at Porter-Gaud because he was Jewish attending the Episcopal school, but he praised the education he got there. He described an experience in the eighth grade when he tried out for the soccer team. He hurt his leg and was sent to the training room to see Fischer for treatment. While icing his leg, Fischer's hands went up under the boy's towel to his genitals while other people were nearby. Fischer told the boy to return the next day for more treatment. On the second day, Fischer masturbated the boy in the training room at the school. It continued for most of that school year. "What was really interesting is that everyone at that school knew what was going on and no one did anything to stop it. Coach Brian told Mr. Fischer that he was not allowed to be with me in the training room anymore with the door closed. So, Mr. Fischer told me that we would continue, but we'd have to be more careful and we'd have to leave the door open." In the ninth grade, Fischer got the kid to come to his house, where one assault occurred, and the boy decided to stop it from happening again. He talked about the next couple of years in school being difficult for him, but he managed to stay away from Fischer's clutches. Then, in his senior year, he woke up one morning to find Fischer in his home, talking with the boy's parents. In that conversation, Fischer persuaded the parents to allow the boy to come over to his house that day, which the boy did. At Fischer's home, he put his hand down inside the boy's pants and the boy made him stop. He went to college out of state, but the difficulties continued. "I left Charleston shortly after to go to college haunted by my experiences with this man. I don't live in Charleston today, maybe because of what this man did to me. Coming home holds pain for me. Going down Beaufain Street, Mr. Fischer, and seeing your home holds pain for me. My heart beats faster as I get near it even to this day. I went to college. I started to call Mr. Fischer at four in the morning, five in the morning, and just hang up. I wanted him to have some sleepless nights, because I was having them. I figured if I'm up and I can't sleep because of what this man did to me, I don't want this man sleeping. I never told a soul. I couldn't tell anyone. Harboring the secret and carrying the shame was the worst part of the whole thing." He moved out of state but was still having difficulty dealing with this secret. "And I met a woman who was my first psychologist. And at age 25 I was finally able to tell someone the secret that I had now kept for 13 years. I told her that I felt guilty, that I felt ashamed because I had participated. And she said, 'you were 12'. She said, Mr. Fischer was a grown man, approximately 50 years old. You had no responsibility at 12. She said, 'if you had begged him to have sex with you when you were 12, it was his responsibility as an adult to say no. It was not yours.' So, the process started where I could feel no guilt or shame for what had happened." As part of his healing process, he asked around about Fischer and learned he was still teaching. He called James Island High School to inform them "you have a molester working for you . . . they mentioned his age. I said, 'if he's there, he's molesting.' And they said, well, they hadn't had any problem. And I said, 'I'm telling you, you have a problem there.' They said, 'Porter-Gaud recommended him.' That infuriated me." He then called Porter-Gaud and said, 'how could you have recommended this man to go on anywhere? You all knew what he was doing all along.' Every one of them knew, teachers, principals. Major Alexander would probably be here, living today, if it wasn't for this case. And I said, 'how could you have recommended him on? He molested me when I was there, and he molested a lot of kids when I was there.' At that point I thought I had done what I could do. Guerry Glover did the bravest thing in the whole world, I'll respect him . . . I don't know him, but I'll respect him for my whole life. Because how he got the courage to come forward to do this in Charleston, South Carolina, I don't know. Between the intimidation that Mr. Fischer places and the intimidation that the Charleston society places on this whole kind of thing, it took an amazing amount of courage to come forward. I've harbored guilt for years that I didn't stop this from happening to some other child." He finally told his family when he was 34 years old what Fischer had done to him. "And then I thought it was over. I thought I had told my family, I can go on with my life now. I can hold my head up high. I have nothing to be ashamed of. I did nothing wrong. And then six months later I'm home and it's a fluke that I'm home, I don't come home a lot. The night that Guerry Glover's statement came out was also Rosh Hashanah and I'm watching ER in bed and I see what the story's going to be on the late news, and I hear, and I think of my mother in the other room; did she hear? And I knew . . . I felt that God had sent me home to hear this so that I would corroborate Guerry's story, I would finally come up and face it. I have been so scared of Mr. Fischer my whole life. I think that this man is going to hurt me. I literally have told my therapist in the last month, I am scared that he's going

12

to hurt me just for speaking here today. That's how much intimidation he carried. And I called Debra Herring the next day. I told her that I would corroborate the story. I asked her what would be involved. I had no idea that he would stay at home for two years, not in jail. I had no idea that just because he's 71 he might not go to jail. I was 12, your honor. Seventy-one? Fine. Fine time to go to jail in my opinion. He had emphysema. He's had emphysema since I've known him. He can't walk upstairs, he has to go to the bathroom a lot at night or something, I think a jail cell is the perfect place for him. I think he should get the maximum sentence for what he did. You don't mess with children. The children are the future. I don't have to tell you that. I have two nieces now and a nephew, and I look at them every day and I just pray that they'll get through their life and that no one will get in there who's not supposed to get in there and do something that could change the path, the natural path of their life. And I hope they don't have to go through the obstacles. I don't think that there's anything else to say."

The judge gave this gentleman the same respectful nod that he gave the earlier speaker. "Thank you for coming, sir."

Debbie stood and read a written statement from John Doe number five. "*This is not an easy topic or an easy letter for me to write, but it is something that I must do. When I read that someone had come forward to expose Mr. Fischer for what he really is I knew that I too had to let my experience be known to support Guerry's courageous efforts. I wish that I was personally here today reading this letter, but I just did not feel that I could do it.*" He met Fischer for the first time as a 13-year-old student at Porter-Gaud. "*I didn't know much about him at the time, other than he was the school disciplinarian, and that he was admired by most of his students. So, when he picked me, I felt special. As a teenager, I was having some trouble at home, nothing serious, but enough to warrant the concern of my parents. Mr. Fischer's offer to my parents to help me was met with some reservations. "Who was this man?" they wondered, "What were his credentials?" They asked Porter-Gaud School about him and he was given a glowing recommendation. Fischer himself boasted about his training as a guidance counselor and of his wealth of experience helping young boys.*" Fischer would come to the boy's home for dinner. He came so often the boy's parents became comfortable with him and decided that Fischer could help their son. Fischer persuaded the parents to let their son start coming to his home for dinner occasionally. At one of these dinners, Fischer introduced the boy to alcohol. "*Several drinks later I was light-headed but enjoying the attention and the feeling of maturity. We talked for a few hours and he started to ask me questions*

13

about sex and told me how handsome I was and how he knew women who would pay me money to be with them. And did I have a place where I could hide a lot of money where no one could find it. And did I like sports cars and how he had given one boy or helped one boy get a sports car and anything else that he could think of to tell a 14-year-old boy that would excite him and whet his appetite. As my brother, who was also molested by Fischer would say, he knew all the right buttons to push and the things to say to get you sucked in. The next week I couldn't wait to go to his house, cars, money, women, sex and getting to drink alcohol, these were the things that made up the dreams of a 14-year-old. After dinner he offered me a drink, which I was ready for." On the second visit, Fischer offered the boy a Quaalude and marijuana. *"Needless to say, I was more than relaxed and remember very little of the night except that he started to show me pornographic movies, and how they made me feel. I had passed out, but I knew that something that was wrong had happened to me that night. Fischer later called my parents to say things were going well and he wanted me to spend the night so that we could make more progress. I felt very strange the next day as he told me to put on a hat and pull it down over my face. He claimed to know people who would kill their own mother for five dollars. I was scared and ashamed and felt like I had done something wrong."* The assaults then became a regular thing and Fischer kept the boy supplied with plenty of drugs. Fischer also became a regular presence at the boy's home, including most holidays and special occasions. *"When I would tell Fischer that what was happening was wrong, he would answer it was okay. One time, he said that he really cared for me, that I should not cross him because something bad would happen to me. And once he even told me that in the Bible Jesus Christ said it was alright about what we were doing."* The boy began to realize how wrong all of this was. *"My senior year I tried even harder get away. My senior advisor was Major Skip Alexander, and I kept trying to turn to him for help. He always acted uneasy around me and when I tried to tell him what was happening, he said, 'Mr. Fischer is helping you. He's a good man and you should be thankful he has taken a special interest in you. You should be grateful for his help'. I always thought the school must know what was going on, and I thought the other men at the school must be doing the same thing. Major Alexander committing suicide, I know for sure now, that he was aware of what was going on and that he was covering it up."* The boy chose a university far away from South Carolina to be as far away from Fischer as he could be. *"I am now 35 years old, and since meeting Mr. Fischer I have had a drug and alcohol problem, I've had feelings of worthlessness and despair, I've had counseling about my experiences, and today know that I was a victim and should not feel shame and guilt for what happened to me, but it is these feelings which are keeping me from coming forward; as I'm sure similar feelings keep others silent today. Guerry and everyone who has come forward should be commended for their courage. For me, I feel nothing but guilt for not coming forward sooner. I feel as if I had the last 20 years of my life stolen from me and I sought comfort in drugs and alcohol to ease the pain caused by Mr. Fischer. Too many of the 20 years my fantasies had been twisted by him as I thought of ways to get even with him; how I would run him over when I saw him walking, how I wish he would die a terrible death. Only now I'm starting to get over it, but new fears and thoughts have replaced the old. As a married man with children, I am less and less fearful that I am homosexual or that other people would think that I am, but the worry has plagued me for all of my life. And now I fear that I will turn into a child molester. As studies have shown, some people who were molested as children grow up to be child molesters. Knowing what I am and feeling how I feel, if I lived next-door to myself, would I want my children around a man like me? There is no dispute that Eddie Fischer is guilty. He's pleading guilty. He says he was sick and after going to get help for the last 18 months he's getting better; so, go easy on him in sentencing. Besides, he's an old man who will probably die in prison if he gets a long sentence. Your honor, he should die in prison. He should have been locked up long ago. His is a lifelong, evil sickness, which no amount of psychiatric help could cure. He's a liar, a self-proclaimed king of the B.S.'ers, a killer of innocence, a corruptor and a thief of my life. My life has been stolen by this man. Although I am still alive, many, many times I've thought of suicide, and tried on several occasions. Intentional high-speed car races, motorcycle accidents, drug overdoses, severed arteries that left me in a hospital for the loss of four pints of blood. Through this, God has kept me alive for some reason; perhaps if only to expose this man? What about those that have actually committed suicide or died because of him? He may say he's sorry, he may be on his way to being cured; how can I believe the man who has lived the life of a lie and boasted of it? People steeped in evil and sickness do not change. Thank you, your honor."*

"John Doe number six is here to speak."

John Doe number six was a thirty-something who had had many jobs in his life. "Good morning, sir. I ask for the maximum sentence to be imposed. When an adult takes advantage of a child, it is a heinous crime. When that adult is placed in a position of authority and abuses that position, it is all the more egregious. Edward Fischer did so repeatedly. His crimes will affect my family and me for the rest of my life. Once again, I ask for the maximum sentence. I also would like to say, thank you, Guerry."

The judge thanked him for coming and looked at Debbie.

"John Doe number seven is Guerry Glover. He's here to speak."

Spontaneous applause broke out in the courtroom. Some in the gallery even stood to show their admiration as they applauded.

The judge was not as quick as most judges would normally be to restore order and his words sounded almost apologetic, "Alright. Let's have order in the court. Yes sir."

"Your honor, there is no way that I can convey to you in this short period of time the full impact on my life of my being molested by Edward Fischer. Twenty-three years of my life have been severely harmed as I have dealt with the long nightmare of childhood sexual abuse, surviving the traumatic effects of that abuse, and the legal proceedings that have been necessary to get to today. Mr. Fischer began sexually abusing me when I was an innocent, prepubescent, vulnerable sixth grader and he snared me in his web of manipulation and control. That is unspeakable. My middle and high school years were burdened with shame and fear, resulting from my innocence being stolen from me. Repeated assaults continually added to the harm. The mental and emotional manipulation, which it took me years to realize Mr. Fischer was so good at, and which as a child I was unable to counteract, made it impossible for me to escape his trap. A child is no match for a pedophile such as Mr. Fischer. Finally, during the summer after I graduated from high school, in a stupor after having taken three Quaaludes that Mr. Fischer had given to me, I came to momentarily and said, 'This has to stop.' I was terrified to quit using alcohol and drugs because I was afraid that I was not going to live through feeling the pain that I had tried to avoid on a daily basis. It has taken 15 years of grace and hard work to get where I am today. There were so many times along the way that I truly believed I was not going to make it. I do not minimize Mr. Fischer's responsibilities for his actions at all, but I wish that Berkeley Grimball and Gordon Bondurant from Porter-Gaud were being sentenced along with Mr. Fischer. The sense of inevitability that he so accurately portrayed because he was able to get away with this for so long, added to my sense of hopelessness. That hopelessness was a dark cloud that has affected the very fabric of my life. The emotional and physical rape of a child has horrific consequences. I have sat in a car with the exhaust coming in on many occasions over the last 23 years. Without the love and support of so many people in my life, I am absolutely sure that I would be dead today. The damage done by Mr. Fischer to my family has been devastating. My parents are in their seventies, and the last two years have been devastating. Mr. Fischer's betrayal of our entire family has caused immeasurable pain. I wish that it could be made easier for children to speak out. For the last two years Gregg Meyers has been so kind, as he has helped me through the emotional roller coaster of these legal proceedings. Hopefully this sentencing hearing will show that going through this was worth it. I'm very grateful too and deeply saddened by the number of victims who were willing to stand up with me to end Mr. Fischer's reign of terror." Guerry turned toward the gallery and addressed the other victims directly. "Thank you all. I would not have made it through the last 18 months without . . .." He could not finish the sentence. He looked down, composed himself, and turned back to the judge. "Mr. Fischer's lawyer says his client is extremely sorry and very remorseful. I so badly want to believe that. However, those are empty words to me unless backed up by action. It is with true sadness that I ask you to put a human being in prison. But I do. I hope that Mr. Fischer will be an example to us all that someone who rapes children is severely punished. I hope that people will learn from what they see today and be more willing to protect children. I desperately want good to come out of these experiences. Mr. Fischer's actions shook my faith in people. Today the Court has the opportunity to restore some of that faith. I wish Mr. Fischer had been stopped earlier at any of the many junctures where that should have happened. To those who maliciously try and blame the victims of childhood sexual abuse for what happened to them, a serious jail sentence for Mr. Fischer's crimes will demonstrate clearly that it is not the child's fault. Please, your honor, show me that this legal system works. Thank you."

The judge thanked Guerry and gave him a genuine smile. Everyone in the room, including the judge, knew that the only reason the hearing was taking place was because of this courageous man. The courtroom was unusually quiet as Guerry returned to his seat.

Debbie waited until Guerry was seated to proceed. "Your Honor, victim number eight cannot be here today. He lives in Maryland." She picked up a letter from the table and read it aloud. "*I am happy for you for you to use my name for the public record in the hopes that it will be easier to take someone like Mr. Fischer out of the flow of society more quickly in the future so that he might obtain the help he needs, but more importantly, before the spirits and minds of so many young people can be damaged the way E.M. Fischer damaged so many. I know that to this point many of the 12 or 13 people who have come forward have been referred to only by a number for their protection. I want the people who will hear this and read my name*

17

to think of why people want to be given anonymity when they have to come forward in a case like this. I hope that you, the reader, will not contribute to the need to protect people who come forward in a case like this. I hope that this can be seen as the case of a sick man who the system in our lives could not handle in an appropriate way. I think I am weak to fear talk about me when I am trying to do the right thing, but I am also pragmatic. Please, reader, don't blame the ones who were little more than children when this man came into their lives. This man, what I can only think of as sick and depraved, changed the world for at least the 12 or 13 people who have admitted to have had encounters with him. Some speculate that the actual experience of this man and the crimes he is now admitting to occurred on a very different scale. Don't blame young people, even if they are older now. Be thankful Guerry Glover had the guts to come forward and reveal to the world a very private pain that should never have happened. In short, I have thought a lot about my brief experience with E.M. Fischer. I have thought about it not infrequently for years. It is very hard to think about something you definitely didn't understand at the time, something you really can't talk about, something that turns out to be given names like molestation or crimes against nature, and not admit it played a profound role in your development. That just may be an easy way of putting it. I believe with all my heart, all my soul and all my mind that Edward M. Fischer should be put behind bars with the sickest and the most depraved of the criminal population. I think he will find what he needs there. I don't think he should ever be released."

She laid the letter back on the table, and said, "Your Honor, victim number nine is here to speak."

Carlos Salinas worked for Amnesty International and was an extremely eloquent speaker. "Like a perverse ripple, the defendant's crimes created a series of secondary, more subtle wounds that will undoubtedly outlast any sentence he could be given. Not only were the lives of children severely damaged, but other not-so-visible, but equally insidious, wounds were inflicted as well. I, like so many others, did not tell anyone about this crime for the shame, for the fear, for the confusion and for the guilt I felt. But I was not the only one that was hurt. My relationship with my parents hurt. What had once been an extremely open and communicative relationship with my parents, especially my mother, suddenly was changed. I now harbored a horrible secret that as much as I wanted to, I could not share with her. I felt removed from her. I felt alone. I felt estranged from the rest of my family. I also did not tell our second layer of protection, our friends. I didn't even tell my closest friends. I was removed from them in a similar way. I don't think my friends had the slightest suspicion that something had gone terribly wrong. And thus, I lived with this painful secret, or rather the secret would take over my life. And the more I realized that my friends and my parents and my family really didn't know, the safer I felt, yet, in that much more pain. The contradiction itself was very painful. I so badly wished that nothing had ever happened, that at some point I'd wake up and realize that it had all been a strange and twisted nightmare. But instead another day and another night would follow, and a sick, sinking feeling that somehow, I was permanently dirty, that I was corrupt, that I was spoiled, that I was no good, would persist. There was no turning back, and yet, the road ahead was dark and full of twisted shadows and canned laughter and complete uncertainty. For years I felt like this. And for years everything around me seemed alien, seemed like a terribly perverse joke and was completely pointless. Clearly there is no way I will ever get that back, those years that could have been so different, that could have been the best years of my life. That time, that anguish, that desperation is now history. I can't change that. None of us can. But we can confront it and try to change what follows. And so, I confront the fact that the defendant befriended me, carefully, over the space of a few years, only to manipulate me masterfully into being naked in front of him while he kissed my back and fondled me, and later manipulated me into allowing him to masturbate me. Your honor, I mean no disrespect to you and the Court, but I think it is important that you catch a glimpse of what I lived so that you can understand why I say what I say. With your permission, I would like to inform you and the Court that when the defendant masturbated me, that was the first time I ever consciously ejaculated. I had no idea what was going on. Not only would I be confused about my sexual identity, an issue that was handled even worse back then than it is now, because we still have a long way to go, but every time I would ejaculate after that, I would remember the defendant. I would see his face. I would hear his voice and smell him. I would see him lamely repeating that sex is just touch and feel. He would repeat that over and over again. So, by the time he was through with me, I had no idea what was what, which way was up, who I was, or how it was that I had been so masterfully manipulated. Indeed, it took me many years to realize this. But in addition to the pain he inflicted and the alienation that he forced and thrust into my life, the defendant also violated one of the most important principles for a healthy society, and that is of trust. Between children and adults, and children and parents, between students and teachers, quite

19

simply, the trust that must exist between all of us. Your honor, given what I have seen, how will I handle the occasion when an adult is friendly to my kids or those of my siblings or friends? What should I tell them? Should I say to parents who want to ensure their children do not descend into this nightmare that they should avoid kindness? Avoid generosity? Random friendliness is just a betrayal waiting to happen? This is not the world in which we want to live. And yet, this is just a world that the crimes of the defendant and his accomplices would have us create. We have to resist the temptation to build even more walls around us. Shutting ourselves off from one another even further is not the answer. Part of the answer, your honor, is in your hands. And so, I am here before you and I humbly ask you for justice. Justice can help us recapture the hope of what can be. Justice will not reverse time, it will not make our pain disappear, it is not a magical formula that will make everything alright. I know that. But justice is the way by which we as a society can confront those who, like the defendant, take advantage of the trust that we give each other, of the friendliness that we cherish, of the human bond that enriches our days and nurtures our souls and makes life worth living. Justice is the way through which we, as a society, reject the notion that because of these crimes, we have to grow colder, and our hearts have to grow harder and our doors have to be shut even more tight. Through justice we can mete out a punishment to state clearly and unequivocally that this type of crime will not be tolerated. That, first and foremost, we will defend the most vulnerable among us, our children. To parents, we should tell them not to reject generosity or friendship. We have to urge them to communicate closely and frequently with their children, to listen carefully and actively to what the children are saying and what they're not saying. We have to remind them not to take anything for granted so that such crimes can be detected, and action can be taken. Our parents must create safe spaces for communication. We must create safe spaces, especially during those not so easy years we know as adolescence. Your honor, never in a million years would my parents have imagined that something like this could have happened to one of their children. Nor did I think that ever in a million years something like this would happen to me. And yet, here I am before you. I believe that a strong and unambiguous sentence from you can be an important lesson to the parents. It can be a message to them that the State will act. It will be a message that the State will fully engage and fully protect children. I will be forever grateful to Guerry for his courage to come forth. I had hidden the secret deep, deep inside me. But at some point, I knew that I would someday talk. And I thank Guerry for making this moment happen. This defendant will be punished. And that takes care of one person. But we cannot lose sight that there is a systemic failure, there is an institutional failure that also needs to be addressed. The defendant was able to engage in this activity due to the act of omission and actual complicity of school officials, from what we thought was the best school in the area, Porter-Gaud. I urge you to mete out a strong and unambiguous sentence and I hope this is the first in a series of judgments and or actions that will ensure children do not have to be traumatized like this again. And if it does happen, it's not because of criminal negligence by our school officials. I also hope a strong and unambiguous sentence can signal to those who are still silently suffering that they can and should come forward, that they are not at fault, as some irresponsible Porter-Gaud official seemed to have suggested during the course of these recent events, A strong and unambiguous sentence can tell people that the State will ensure that the victim will not be re-victimized, that the victim will indeed be a survivor. The victim is not who is at fault or the one who should feel any shame or embarrassment whatsoever, as difficult as these topics are. That disgrace belongs to the defendant and his accomplices. And so, I hope a strong and unambiguous sentence from your honor may encourage others to confront their past and understand where blame should truly fall. This is important not only for their peace of mind, but also to prevent more victims. Many years ago, I made the bad decision not to tell anyone about what had happened. And look what happened, I'm barely at the midpoint of the defendant's criminal career. Friends after me were also victimized. It is hard for me to face that. Of course, I wish I had said something then, but how could I, given that this is such a taboo? A strong and unambiguous sentence can help us provide a safe space, even in spite of this taboo, so that when someone is victimized as if they were robbed, as if a relative had been murdered, they feel as compelled and as comfortable and as supported by all in denouncing this criminal activity so that the criminal can be prosecuted. In closing I would like again to thank Guerry Glover for his perseverance and his singular courage. I am thankful for the work of the Assistant Solicitor, Debra Herring, my attorney, and the organization People Against Rape. I thank all of the other victim/survivors who have come forward while not losing hope that others will follow. I thank my parents, my mother who's here with me, my siblings, my friends, and my wife. And I thank you, your honor, as I urge you to issue a strong and unambiguous sentence."

"Thank you, sir."

Debbie introduced the next speaker who was very soft spoken. "Your Honor, I'm 26 years old. For me to be able to stand here and relate to you what has happened to me in my life is impossible right now. I have tried for the past week to come up with a statement and have simply been overwhelmed with the depth of the scars that this man has left. Before I came here today, I was told not to expect justice because our justice system is about moving cases, that each case has a number and that's the extent of the depth. But I ask you to please, after seeing the emotion that you see from all of these victims, to make the sentence mean something, to give it the maximum that you possibly can so in the future other victims will not be so scared to come forward. That's all I have to say."

"Thank you, sir."

Debbie then introduced John Doe Eleven, Kevin Dunn. "Your honor, before I begin, I want to thank all the victims that have come forward. I also want to thank Guerry Glover, because I really believe that he has saved my life by coming forward. I have told him that. He knows that." He turned and looked straight at Guerry and smiled. "Thanks, Guerry." He paused before turning back to the judge. "Your honor, Mr. Fischer molested me and indeed he admits to molesting me some 10 years ago while I was a student at James Island High School, and he was a teacher. I cannot begin to tell you how pervasive and destructive this one single event has been in my life. And the life of my family and my friends. You cannot know the hell that I have been through for the past ten years. The memories and the nightmares of what Mr. Fischer did to me are just as fresh and just as vivid now as they were ten years ago. There isn't a day in the last thirty-two hundred days that I have not been haunted or in some way affected by the visions of Mr. Fischer molesting me. Your honor, you know the old saying time heals all wounds? I can say for me that is not true. Time has not healed my wounds. Time will not heal the wounds inflicted on me by that man. I could identify a whole host, a whole litany, of the negative effects and negative impacts sexual abuse has had on my life at the hands of Mr. Fischer. In fact, I do not believe there is one single aspect of my life that this man has not infected. I could describe for you in some detail, for instance, the problems that I have had and have with drug abuse, sexual identity issues, relationship issues, control issues, boundary issues, lack of self-esteem, anxiety, depression, suicidal thoughts, guilt, and shame. And this would just be naming a few. In the interest of time, I won't go into the details of these things, with one exception. I mentioned just a moment ago: trust. I would like to focus for a moment and bring your attention to that word, that subject, trust. Your honor, I first met Mr. Fischer in either the tenth or eleventh grade, I don't remember when. From the very first time that I met him, he stressed to me honesty and trust. On many occasions, in fact, every occasion that I can recall, Mr. Fischer would tell me, 'You've got to trust me. I'll never do anything to hurt you. You have got to trust me.' But Mr. Fischer told me lots of things back then. For instance, he told me that one time he was married and that his wife was deceased. He told me that he had a son; he even had a picture of a young man in his house that he showed me and told me was his son. Mr. Fischer also told me that he was a retired Colonel in the United States Air Force. These are just some of the things Mr. Fischer told. True? In fact, I didn't know that they were not true until last year. Mr. Fischer always emphasized trust. The first time he molested me, the very day of, he emphasized trust. 'You've got to trust me. I'll never do anything to hurt you. You've got to trust me.' There were times after that, after the molestation, that I began trying to avoid Mr. Fischer. I avoided him for a number of reasons. I avoided him because I was shocked by what he had done to me, that I was still in a state of disbelief and confusion. But most of all, I avoided him because I was afraid of him. I was truly afraid of him. I thought that if I didn't have to see him or talk to him, if I could avoid him at school or if I could avoid talking to him on the phone, I wouldn't have to go to his house. And that worked sometimes, but it didn't work all the time." He talked about how Fischer would contact him and persuade him to come back to Fischer's house and how the teacher would promise that the molestation would not happen again. But it did happen again. "At this point I was devastated. I lost all trust in anyone and anything. 'Trust me', he said. 'I'm sorry. It won't happen again.' Your honor, Mr. Fischer is going to try and convince you today that he is sorry for what he has done, that he is remorseful, and he's going to tell you that he won't do it again. This man is sorry for one thing. He is sorry he got caught. This man is remorseful for one thing, and that is he will not be able to molest children, hopefully, again. Mr. Fischer is a master of deceit. He is a liar. He lied to his victims to have sex with them. He lied to the parents, many of the parents, so that he could have access to their children. And, your honor, he will lie to you. Because he wants you to give him a light sentence, so he can go on molesting children. Please do not believe him. In this courtroom there are victims from the age of 50 to 15. Several of them were molested before I was born, by the same man. From 1960 to 1997, September 1997, Mr. Fischer has been molesting kids for at least 40 years. There is no reason to believe that he will stop, that he will ever stop. I believe it is your responsibility, it is your duty, to see to it that this man does not hurt any children again. I am asking that you please do the right thing, the just thing, and sentence this man to the maximum allowable in this court. He is a monster. He is the epitome of evil, and he should not walk free amongst us. Thank you."

"Thank you, sir."

Debbie rose, "Your honor, victim number 12 is also here to address the Court."

John Doe Twelve was a friend of Kevin's in high school. Neither knew that the other was a victim of Fischer until they got to this hearing. It was a very emotional moment for both. He spoke with no notes. "Your honor, I met Mr. Fischer as a junior in high school. Just like all the other children, he said he'd help me with women. He was successful, a lifestyle with money, cars. He said could help me with my personal life. And being a young man not being in the 'in group', I believed him. Just like John Doe number 11 said, trust is the basis for anything in this world. 'Trust me', he says. So, I did. And being in the position he was, he had every availability to use his position to his best means of molesting these children. Not only do I blame him, I blame the school system. I blame the school system for letting that bastard around children for the last 40 years. And to this day I've tried to block it out. I've never told a soul, out of shame. I felt I was dirty. I never told a soul until about a month and a half ago, to my brother. He was furious. My dad died about two years ago and he went to his grave not knowing. It's probably a good thing. It's probably a good thing that he went to his grave not knowing, because I come from Italian background, and that's one thing he would not stand for, people harming his kids. I can tell you right now I had a little boy that I gave up for adoption. I was married at one time and I gave him up to my ex-wife. I think subconsciously it's because of this reason, this man right here. But I can't see him. He's moving away. I haven't seen him in about two years. And that's probably one of the most painful things in my life. About five years ago I got out of the Air Force. I was a troop leader in the Air Force. I got divorced, and ever since then . . . I've been in relationships, I have no problem meeting women, fine, but I've pushed every single one away. Because once they start getting close, I push them away. And up until about two months ago, three months ago, when I saw this on the news, actually awhile back, about a year and a half ago, when it all came out, I never knew Guerry, but it dawned on me why I push people away now, why I don't trust nobody. It's because of him." He raised his voice and pointed at Fischer. "He was in a position to be around children. He put this act on where he's Mr. Go Lucky, Mr. Rich, Mr. Fantasy. Always a smile on his face. Everyone, all the kids, wanted to be like Mr. Fischer, nice car, nice house downtown, knows everything about women, so we thought." He looked right at Fischer. "All you are is a big fake." He stared at Fischer. Fischer did not look at him. He paused a moment before looking back at Judge Smoak. "And I can tell you right now, your honor, even to this day, if anything happened to my son, he wouldn't be here today. There would be no court here, because I would have provided my own justice to him. If anybody would have hurt my boy, I probably would be the one over there for murder. He didn't have a chance in the world to be here today to represent himself. I think losing my son is probably the worst thing that's ever happened in my life. I've never been to therapy. I've never even talked to anybody until a month and a half ago, and that's my brother. My mom doesn't know. None of my sisters know. I've got a big Italian family. Like I said, my father don't even know. He's in the grave now. And he will . . . well, he will never know." He looked back at Fischer, with tears welling up in his eyes. "He is probably looking down cursing you out right now, Mr. Fischer. I know if he could, he'd take care of business. If he couldn't, he'd find somebody who would. But he died at 71, your age, almost 72 years old. My mother and father were married for 48 years, great marriage. And I know if I had told him he would feel like he didn't do the right thing with raising me. But, in the same aspect, he'd be furious. Not with me, but with you, because of the position you held in the public-school system, that they trusted you with us and our future and what we had going for us in our lives. Our time to explore this world, expand our lives, and you took that away from us. Even to this day, I think I can speak for everybody here, all the victims, we can't have the opportunity, like a normal child should have, out playing, you know, Army, riding bikes, going to the pool, and playing in the pool, going to summer camps, not a care in the world but to catch fireflies, you know, doing the things that boys do, flirt with girls and all that stuff. Have a good time, hang out in the mall, talk. I never had the opportunity. I pushed everyone away because of you. Pushed my mother and father away. I had a bad problem with my mom because of you. Always fighting, and she never knew why. I couldn't tell her. And I'm so ashamed. And I think after this, I am going to tell her, because I'm not ashamed no more. I did nothing wrong. You took advantage of 30-plus, I don't know how many kids, simply because we did not know. We had not lived on this earth long enough to know better. And you knew that." Again, he paused for some time before he looked back at the judge. "Your honor, I hope all the victims today, myself, and all the letters that the victims have sent you today have proven to you for future use that this should not be tolerated. Now or the future, because it disrupts so many lives. Not only the victims, the friends, the family. The victims' future. And I hope to God he does not get parole. I hope you put this man behind bars. I hope he gets in a jail cell with the biggest man in jail. And I hope he does to you what you did to us, Mr. Fischer. I hope he gets a good time with you. That's all I have to say, your honor."

We learned after the hearing that the reason this young man voluntarily relinquished his rights to see his son was his fear that as a victim of sexual abuse that he might one day become an abuser himself. He did not want that to happen to his son. It was truly one of the most tragic stories I heard in my entire career.

After a short break, Debbie told the judge that John Doe number thirteen was still a minor and a local attorney was present to speak on his behalf. "I will be brief. I try to make my living being eloquent, but I am very humbled today by all of the victims who have come forward, their eloquence to the court. On behalf of victim number 13, I just want to go to a couple of items that I know will also be considered by a court and address them specifically. Mr. Fischer is an old man now, and he will be thought of as being vulnerable if he gets time in jail. But the young people that he pursued were vulnerable, and it would be the ultimate paradox if the vulnerability of age, which was the heart of the repeated crimes he committed now became the shield that gave him an avoidance of justice. We know that he is a sick person, because only a sick person would do this. But it's a sickness that despite his training he has appeared to embrace over a generation of lives. He's like a doctor who's hooked on drugs but commits malpractice every day on his patients and goes and shoots up the next day and butchers the next victim. He's supposed to know. He did know the impact that it had on the victims in this case. And he never stopped. He never tried to stop. From what we know, he never gave a second thought or a moment's notice to anything but to continue on to what satisfied him at the expense of everybody else. Because of the number of people, the amount of time, the sensitivity of the position he was in, this is a benchmark case. They don't get any worse than this. They don't last any longer. They don't represent any worse betrayal of trust on every kind of conceivable level. My victim was not a student. It was because of friendships, connections with his parents, that he became a victim. And because it's a benchmark case, the eyes of all the community are on it. It's not just the citizens of Charleston whose eyes are on this, but it's other people who are sick. Logic doesn't convince these people to go get help. And if Mr. Fischer receives anything but a substantial sentence, then others like him will breathe a sigh of relief. And they will go on about their business with the belief that not much will happen to them either, because they know that whatever they get caught for, it won't be as bad as what Eddie Fischer did. And the tragedies that you have heard of today will be compounded a hundredfold. There is little good that comes from situations like these. But on behalf of my client, we ask that you not compound them anymore. We ask for the maximum penalty allowed by law, because we believe it is the only way that this court can send a strong message and a just message to people like Mr. Fischer to stop, that it will matter, that it's worth it. And that, in fact, some little good, the only good that can be salvaged by these tragedies will be salvaged. We appreciate your consideration."

"Thank you."

"Your Honor, you've now heard from all of the victims," Debbie said and then sat down.

The judge looked at the defense table, "Alright. Mr. Lofton?"

"If the court please, Your Honor, I'll be very brief. I know you've heard . . .."

"No sir, take your time, sir," the judge interjected.

"Judge, this is a tragic case, no question about that. It's tragic from the standpoint of the victims who are here, and it's tragic from the standpoint of Mr. Fischer. Your Honor, the real tragedy is that Mr. Fischer suffers from an illness, and he's suffered from an illness for a long period of time. Eighteen months ago, Mr. Fischer started receiving treatment for that illness. And as a result of that, he has made great progress, as you can see from the doctor's report, which we submitted to the Court earlier."

"Yes sir, I've read the report."

"Your Honor, some of the victims made reference to this and I too would like to mention it. It's a real tragedy that there were people in the past, 15, 18 years ago, that were aware that Mr. Fischer had an illness. And rather than stepping up and trying to help with that problem, they allowed it to continue. And as a result of that, other victims were a part or party to Mr. Fischer's illness." This was an obvious reference to the officials at Porter-Gaud School which no one in the room expected. "Judge, the easy thing to do in this case is to lock Mr. Fischer away for the rest of his life, that's the easy thing to do. And that's what we used to do. In ancient history when we didn't know why a person was sick or why a person had a disease, we just locked them up. Get them away from everybody. But, Judge, that won't solve the problem. That won't cure the sickness. As I indicated, he's been in treatment for 18 months. The doctor tells you in his report that he has made great progress, but that he is going to require intense treatment. There isn't any place that I'm aware of in the Department of Corrections where he will receive that kind of treatment. So, if the Court's only concern is punishment, then you just lock him up. If the court's concern is that he receive some punishment and some treatment, then I would respectfully ask you to fashion a sentence wherein he isn't locked up for the rest of his life, where he is treated, where he is given a chance to recover from this illness. You've heard the bad side of Eddie Fischer today. During the period of time that I have represented Mr. Fischer, I've received numerous phone calls as well as personal visits from a number of very prominent and not so prominent members of our community. And while all of the things that you have heard today have been bad, all of the years that Eddie Fischer taught in the schools of this county were not all bad. Eddie Fischer touched the lives of a number of people in a very positive way. And he assisted a number of people in a very positive way. And had he not been sick, his entire teaching career would have been a positive part of the lives of these victims, as well as the others that he taught during that career. So, we ask you this morning to be as merciful as you can, understanding that he does suffer from an illness. And understanding that until 18 months ago, no one, no one, attempted to treat that illness. Mr. Fischer has just a few brief words to say to the court."

"Yes sir."

Fischer rose and cleared his throat. "Your Honor, I realize now that I did hurt these people and I'm humbly sorry. I apologize to each one of them and I hope that one day they can forgive me. That's up to them. I didn't realize how much I had hurt them. But with that I put myself to the mercy of the Court."

After a brief pause, Lofton spoke again. "That's all we have, Your Honor."

"That's all you have?" The judge was genuinely surprised.

"That's all we have. We just ask you to take into consideration the doctor's report as well as the letters from the doctor."

"Yes sir, I have read the letters and the reports. I really have. We'll take a short break and let me think about this a few minutes, please." The judge left the bench and exited the courtroom. There were a lot of tears during the brief break. I did not leave my seat.

When the judge returned to the bench, he had a very stern look on his face. Fischer and his lawyer stood. The judge looked straight at Debbie, "Solicitor, the only agreement would be that the sentences would be concurrent; was that it?"

"Yes, Your Honor."

"Alright. Thank you very much. On this indictment, number 97-GS-10-7718, is that under the new . . .."

"Yes sir, that's under the 85 percent rule," Debbie responded.

"Alright. Alright, Mr. Fischer." The judge paused for some time and then looked right at Lionel. "Mr. Lofton, I don't think I've ever had a worse case since I've been on the bench or since I've been practicing law, sir. I really don't." He let his comment hang in the courtroom, stared at Fischer for several minutes, and then looked down before continuing. When he began speaking again, it was a very solemn voice. "Alright, Mr. Fischer. On 97-GS-10-7718, you're confined to the State Department of

Corrections for a period of 20 years." That was the '85% case'. Fischer would have to serve at least 17 years before being eligible for parole. The judge paused for a brief moment as if acknowledging the impact of that sentence, and then announced the sentence on all of the other cases. "Number 97-GS-10-0576, assault and battery of a high and aggravated nature, you're confined for a period of ten years, concurrent. On 97-GS-10-7171, criminal sexual conduct in the third degree, ten years concurrent. On 97-GS-10-7215, criminal sexual conduct second degree, that's 20 years concurrent. 97-GS-10-7165, assault and battery of a high and aggravated nature, that's ten years concurrent. 97-GS-10-0578, criminal sexual conduct with a minor, second, 20 years concurrent. 97-GS-10-7157, criminal sexual conduct with a minor, second, that's 20 years concurrent. 97-GS-10-7164, criminal sexual conduct with a minor, second, 20 years concurrent. 97-GS-10-7163, criminal sexual conduct with a minor, second degree, 20 years concurrent. 97-GS-10-717, lewd act upon a minor, ten years concurrent. Buggery, 97-GS-10-7159, five years concurrent. 97-GS-10-7169, lewd act, ten years concurrent. And, 97-GS-10-7161, lewd act, ten years concurrent. Good luck to you sir."

The judge left the bench immediately. He had given Fischer the maximum sentence on every charge. The courtroom was quiet as Fischer was led away by the deputies. After he was gone, there was more hugging, some smiles, and more tears. As I sat in the corner trying to write down the sentences, my notepad was smeared by the tears that were falling from the tip of my nose.

As belated as it was, Fischer's plea and his acceptance of responsibility for his actions was a profound moment for the victims. None of them ever imagined that he would do so. However, as several of the speakers noted, there were others who bore responsibility for Fischer's reign of terror. Getting them to accept any responsibility was to be another matter altogether.

PART II – THE LION TAMERS
CHAPTER 1

Porter-Gaud School is a prestigious private school in Charleston, formerly affiliated with the Episcopal Church, situated on 70 acres of prime real estate on the harbor. Its sprawling campus and perfectly coifed grounds seem an unlikely place for horror. It was the place that everyone who was someone, or wanted to be someone, sent their children to school. It was less about the education -- although the education was very good -- than it was for the students and their parents to have a chance to be in The Club. A significant percentage of the doctors, lawyers, business people and other influential citizens in Charleston sent their children there.

It was the modern incarnation of three former schools in Charleston: The Gaud School, the Watt School and Porter Military Academy. The merger occurred in 1964, the same year the Civil Rights Act was passed by Congress. Private school enrollment in South Carolina and the rest of the South increased in 1964 even though the Charleston County public schools had largely ignored the United States Supreme Court ruling in *Brown v. Board of Education*, requiring the racial integration of public schools across the country. Just the year before, in 1963, a federal court in Charleston had ordered the school district to admit eight black students to a formerly all-white public high school in downtown Charleston.

Some families from outside of downtown Charleston and its blueblood society sent their children to Porter-Gaud to raise their station in life. These folks and their children were known at Porter-Gaud as "Aways" because they were from outside downtown Charleston, and far removed from those who considered themselves better than the rest. It's often said that downtown Charleston is one of only two places in the world -- Boston being the other-- where from sea level the residents look down on the rest of the world.

Guerry Glover began attending Porter-Gaud in 1972. He was nine years old the first time Fischer assaulted him, at Guerry's home on Johns Island, one of the barrier islands that protect Charleston. He was the youngest child of Harold and Evelyn Glover, who owned a tomato farm on the island. Fischer was a guest at the Glovers' home that night. He knew the Glovers because Guerry and his older siblings attended Porter-Gaud School, where Fischer taught. Fischer had ingratiated himself with the family and was an occasional visitor at their home.

Eddie Fischer was hired to teach at Porter-Gaud in 1972. He had been volunteering there the previous year to help with the football team. The first complaint about him came during his first semester at the school. He had invited Ronnie Hammond, a young male student, to sneak out of his house one evening to meet at a local drugstore by enticing the boy with tales of older women who pay teenage boys for sex. Fischer told Ronnie to not tell his parents, and that he was not to masturbate before the meeting. He promised Hammond he would "go in a boy and come out a man." As instructed, the boy didn't tell his parents; instead, he told his older brother, who went to the drugstore at the appointed hour and saw Fischer looking around. The older brother went home and told his parents the whole story. Mr. and Mrs. Hammond called their friend Berkeley Grimball, headmaster of Porter-Gaud at that time, and complained about Fisher.

Although Grimball promised the Hammonds he would do something about the incident, he later said Fischer denied it, so Grimball went no further. He merely told Fischer that if he did anything like that again, he would have to resign. He also claimed to have put Fischer "on probation." Grimball never talked to the boy, Ronnie Hammond, about the incident.

Grimball did not tell the Glovers, or anyone else, about Fischer. Nobody did anything to monitor him or protect Porter-Gaud's students. No written documentation of the incident was created. No faculty members were alerted or asked to report anything they saw; in fact, in the ensuing years Fischer received annual raises and was appointed disciplinarian of the school.

By the time Fischer got to Guerry, he had been molesting young boys in Charleston for more than a decade at schools in Charleston. He had been dismissed by a Catholic high school and a Catholic elementary school after short stints at each, but the Diocese of Charleston claims to have no record of the reasons for his dismissals. It is known that he molested students at each school. After the first assault, Fischer had Guerry in his clutches because the boy was paralyzed with fear. Over the years to come, the assaults increased in number and severity. The assaults continued through the tenth grade at Porter-Gaud. Like so many victims of sexual abuse, Guerry sought relief with alcohol and drugs, much of which Fischer provided.

When he was in the tenth grade in 1982, Guerry decided he needed to escape. The only way he figured he could do that was to get out of Porter-Gaud; he had asked his parents several times to let him change schools. Harold and Evelyn knew something was going on with Guerry, but they felt Porter-Gaud was the best place for him; Guerry's siblings had graduated from there. It was where their friend, James Bishop Alexander, the assistant headmaster, could keep an eye on Guerry and help him with his difficulties. Alexander was so close to the Glovers that he was a groomsman in Guerry's older brother's wedding. The Glovers also knew Fischer and thought he was a good teacher and good role model for their children, including Guerry. He was already going to the best school in Charleston, so they didn't want to send him somewhere else; Guerry could never give them a good enough reason to change schools. He would have to disclose what was happening to him, which Guerry felt was impossible at the time.

So, he decided to get kicked out of the school. After a few unsuccessful attempts, in the Spring of 1982 for a school assigned project, he brought a commercially built dollhouse to class and claimed to have built it himself. It was a flagrant case of cheating that was sure to get him expelled. No one could understand why Guerry, who used to be a good student, would do such a thing. But late in the 1981-1982 school year, Guerry got his wish and was expelled. Porter-Gaud allowed him to finish his final exams off-campus, but he would have to enroll elsewhere for the next year.

Guerry's parents enrolled him at College Preparatory School, another private school in Charleston. Guerry thought his long nightmare was over and he was finally free from Fischer.

A few weeks after Guerry was expelled, a parent called Alexander and told him Fischer had sexually assaulted her son, another student at Porter-Gaud. Alexander had been a well-known figure at Porter Military Academy before the merger and stayed on at Porter-Gaud afterward, rising eventually to the positions of assistant headmaster and principal of the Upper School. He was known to the students there as Major Alexander, one of many monikers that stayed with him for the rest of his life. He was also known as "Bishop," "Maj," "Skip," and "Skipper." Alexander had never married, and by all outward appearances had dedicated his life to educating and helping young people. He was universally adored by students and parents throughout his time at the school and thereafter. Alexander met with the boy and his parents and confirmed that the assault had occurred. Fischer had taken the student to his house where the assault took place. In response to this allegation, Grimball and Alexander allowed Fischer to resign quietly.

Unbeknownst to Guerry, Grimball and Alexander then went to work assisting Fischer which would make his nightmare worse than he had dreamed possible.

Fischer applied to teach at College Preparatory School. Somehow, Alexander learned of this and made a personal visit to the headmaster at College Prep. Instead of telling the headmaster what he knew about Fischer, or why he left Porter-Gaud, Alexander gave a favorable recommendation for Fischer. Due in large part to this visit by Alexander, College Prep hired Fischer.

On Guerry's first day of school in the fall of 1982, thinking he had escaped his nightmare, he saw Fischer in the hallway at College Prep, and was horrified. Fischer's abuse continued throughout Guerry's junior and senior years. As did the drugs and alcohol.

After he graduated two years later, Guerry went to college and eventually earned a master's degree in historical preservation from the University of Georgia.

In 1986, Fischer applied for a job with the public-school district in Charleston. He listed Alexander as a reference. The district sent a document to Porter-Gaud addressed to Alexander for him to fill out. The document was entitled Reference Blank. It had Fischer's name and social security number on it, as well as an indication that Fischer was applying to be considered for a position teaching "history (social studies)". The main body of the form had 14 specific areas for Fischer to be evaluated on and Alexander was to check boxes for each category to indicate his belief that Fischer was Inferior, Below Average, Average, Above Average, or Superior for each respective item. There was also a box for Not Observed. On the form, Alexander rated Fischer Average in Tactfulness. He rated him Above Average in Scholarship, Character, Personality, General Intelligence, Initiative, Skill in Teaching, Professional Growth, Social Qualities, and General Rating. He rated Fischer Superior in the areas of Health, Personal Appearance, Student Control, and Cooperation. Below that section of the form were three questions that sought comments about the applicant. In response to the question *"Any physical defects or mental peculiarities?"*, Alexander hand wrote, "none known". To the question *"What opportunity have you had to observe the candidate's work?"*, he wrote, "taught with him for many years". And, the third question was, *"In your judgment is the above candidate well fitted for the above position?"*. Alexander wrote, "yes". There was a space for any additional remarks, but Alexander left it blank, and then signed it as J. Bishop Alexander and listed his position as Principal.

When Guerry returned home to Charleston after graduate school, he still could not escape the specter of Fischer's abuse. In 1988 he went to Porter-Gaud to set the record straight about Fischer. He met with Alexander to discuss why he had gotten himself expelled from Porter-Gaud. It was a matter of self-respect for Guerry, who had been labeled a troublemaker there. Alexander heard what Guerry had to say but didn't seem surprised by Guerry's allegations. He offered no assistance of any kind and advised Guerry not to tell his parents.

In 1994, while walking in downtown Charleston, Guerry saw Fischer driving with a young boy in his car and immediately sensed that Fischer was probably molesting the boy. By then Guerry was in the process of reclaiming his life after years of drug and alcohol abuse; he didn't know who to turn to about the boy in Fischer's car, so he went to see a cleric.

Guerry figured the cleric, an Episcopal priest and friend of his parents, would know what to do. Guerry didn't know it at the time, but this priest was on the board of directors of Porter-Gaud School. The priest listened carefully to Guerry's story. He told Guerry he needed to take this story to Porter-Gaud and "lay it on Gordon Bondurant's desk."

Porter-Gaud had hired Bondurant as the headmaster in 1988 when Grimball retired. Guerry had never met him, but on the advice of the cleric, made an appointment to see him. Although Fischer was no longer teaching at Porter-Gaud, he was at that time teaching at a public high school in Charleston, James Island High. Guerry hoped Bondurant could help him get Fischer out of teaching for good. It was a cordial meeting and Bondurant seemed to listen to Guerry's story. Guerry told him that Alexander knew of Fischer's history and of his sexual interest in students and suggested Bondurant talk to Alexander to verify the story. By that time, Alexander had also retired from Porter-Gaud. Guerry told Bondurant that he would give him a week to verify the information.

Bondurant called Guerry a week later, as they agreed. He told Guerry he'd seen Alexander on campus only a couple of days after their meeting, and that he had asked Alexander about Guerry's claim. Alexander had confirmed Guerry's story about Fischer, but that's where Bondurant ended it. He told Guerry that the school would not help him get Fischer out of teaching, and that the school could not publicly support Guerry if he decided to go to the police. He also said it was not Porter-Gaud's problem that Fischer was still teaching.

Guerry felt betrayed. He expected Bondurant and others to be outraged about Fischer. He could not fathom why they would not help him protect students.

Three more years passed and on May 4, 1997, Guerry drove uninvited from his family's farm in the vegetable farming country on Johns Island to Bondurant's office at Porter-Gaud. Guerry knew that without the school's support, he could not go to the authorities. He knew intuitively and from personal experience that children don't win when they tell a different story than adults. He knew the truth, but he also knew convincing the police and prosecutors of it was going to be very difficult. Without corroborating evidence, his telling of events was unlikely to overcome the legal hurdle of beyond a reasonable doubt. Fischer's denial would probably be enough to establish reasonable doubt.

Bondurant had never supervised Fischer; he came to Porter-Gaud after Fischer had left. In fact, before Guerry had gone to see him in 1994, Bondurant could not recall ever hearing Fischer's name. He had turned Guerry away in 1994, and he did so again in 1997. He believed Guerry's issue with Fischer did not involve Porter-Gaud, since Fischer was no longer on the Porter-Gaud faculty. Bondurant declined Guerry's request to jointly report Fischer to the police and hoped that was the end of it.

Three days later, on May 7, Guerry reappeared at the school, again unannounced. This time he was more determined. He was shown into Bondurant's office and immediately began forcefully telling Bondurant he needed help. Bondurant told Guerry he was busy and didn't have time to meet, so Guerry asked for an appointment. Bondurant told him his schedule was full, and he would not have time to meet. Guerry crossed the room to Bondurant's desk and began flipping pages on a desk calendar to find an open date. May 19 was clear. Guerry said, "This is when I'm coming back." Bondurant acquiesced, sensing that Guerry wasn't going to leave until he got an appointment. They agreed to meet at Med Deli, a nearby restaurant.

The next day, Guerry's optimism was shattered. He received a card in the mail from Bondurant: "Dear Guerry, I shall be unable to meet with you on May the 19th. I honestly have nothing else to add to what I said before. Sincerely, Gordon Bondurant." Guerry was angry, disappointed, and disgusted.

A couple days later, however, Guerry got another note from Bondurant saying the headmaster had changed his mind and would meet with Guerry, but only at the school and that he wanted to have a friend present. Guerry immediately called Bondurant to see who the friend was; Bondurant admitted his friend was a lawyer. Guerry asked if he should bring a "friend" too. Bondurant told him he could bring a friend.

After the call, Guerry wondered why Bondurant had changed course and why he wanted a lawyer present. The meeting never occurred. Guerry decided to hire a lawyer.

Because so many of Charleston's lawyers were affiliated with the school, Guerry's initial attempts to find a lawyer to represent him against the school were unsuccessful. The first lawyer he went to see was one of the most successful and connected lawyers in the town: Gedney Howe. Howe didn't actually see Guerry, but a lawyer in his office gave Guerry a little time and told him the statute of limitations would bar any civil lawsuit Guerry might want to file and that he was going to have a hard time finding a lawyer in Charleston who would take on Porter-Gaud.

"You're going to need a brass-balled motherfucker," the lawyer said.

Guerry tried another lawyer and got the same response as at Howe's office: that the statute of limitations would be an insurmountable hurdle and that they would not take a case against Porter-Gaud.

Both of these lawyers had ignored Guerry's actual request; he wasn't interested in a civil lawsuit -- he wanted to get Fischer out of teaching. Guerry felt lonelier and more discouraged than ever. As he was griping to his roommate one night about how impossible it seemed to find a lawyer to help him take on Fischer and Porter-Gaud, the roommate told Guerry he had heard a local lawyer who was not a native Charlestonian speak about sexual abuse, and suggested that he give the lawyer, Gregg Meyers, a call.

CHAPTER 2

"Your life is about to change," Guerry said to Gregg Meyers. It was mid-May of 1997 and Guerry was sitting uncomfortably on a couch in a spacious office in downtown Charleston. The office of Pratt-Thomas, Pierce, Epting & Walker was in a house built in the 1830's with brick walls more than a foot thick.

Meyers wondered to himself how many times he had heard that; every client thinks his or her case is going to change the world. All Gregg could say was, "Yeah, right."

"I'm not kidding," Guerry said, concerned that this lawyer was not taking him seriously.

"Why don't you tell me why you're here," Gregg said. He was a tall, curly haired former athlete who had acquired a quiet, professorial affect as he aged. His thick glasses did nothing to diminish that persona. Born in New Orleans and raised near Pittsburgh, then Minnesota, he attended law school in Minnesota before going to work for seven years for the United States Department of Justice in the Civil Rights Division. Described by many as "scary smart", his early legal work was handling school desegregation cases around the country, mostly in the South, which brought him to Charleston. His innate brilliance coupled with his genuine love for the law made him an exceptional advocate for whatever case or cause he took on. He had been at the firm for seven years and had one of the ground floor offices that was about twenty feet square. He didn't have a

39

conventional desk; instead, he had an enormous double-sided standup desk that took up a good part of the room. In one corner near a large window, he had a couch, two chairs and his favorite rocking chair.

He primarily handled construction cases at the firm, but he also had a persistent interest in trying to change the law in South Carolina to make justice more attainable to victims of sexual abuse. Too often, victims are denied justice for reasons that have little to do with what happened to them. Legal technicalities, especially statutes of limitations, decided far too many of those cases, and Gregg was interested in eliminating some of those technicalities.

He began working on these cases almost by accident; his wife at that time was a therapist who had several patients who were victims of sexual abuse. She had been trying to find a lawyer in Charleston who would help one of her patients with a lawsuit against the perpetrator of his abuse, but each lawyer the patient went to declined to get involved, saying that the events happened too long before the victim sought help.

Guerry spent about two hours telling Gregg the long and detailed story of his life. He described the abuse by Fischer and his own attempts to get Porter-Gaud to help him do something about the teacher. It took a while because Guerry's mind is usually two sentences ahead of his mouth and he often does not finish a sentence before moving on to the next one. He had a hard time telling the story in a linear fashion because it had so many tangents and digressions. He had also assumed too much about Gregg's knowledge of downtown Charleston society; he dropped several names that he thought Gregg would know, then had to explain that person's position in the blue blood society.

He finished by telling Gregg that he was not interested in money. He wanted Fischer out of teaching.

When Guerry finished, Gregg thought about what he had heard and said, "Let me see what I can do." He didn't consider himself to be a brass-balled motherfucker, but he never shied away from a tough case, and this case appeared to be very tough indeed. The fact that Guerry only wanted to get Fischer out of teaching struck Gregg as a noble and worthwhile goal that initially seemed within reach.

Gregg served on the board of trustees of the public-school system in Charleston. He knew Chip Zullinger, the superintendent of schools, and believed this relationship would help. Zullinger did not tolerate sexual abuse of students and would handle the situation in a responsible and appropriate way. Gregg wrote a letter to the superintendent, not as a board member, but as a private lawyer representing Guerry. The superintendent immediately sought to ascertain whether the Eddie Fischer at James Island High School was the same one who had taught at Porter-Gaud in the 1970s and had one of his staff call the principal at James Island. The principal, a personal friend of Fischer's, told Fischer questions were being asked about him, and Fischer decided to retire immediately.

Guerry had achieved his goal of getting Fischer out of teaching. The fact that it was accomplished with a single letter astonished Guerry and made clear to him what the powers that be at Porter-Gaud could have done if they had cared enough to try. It made him angrier at their inaction than he already was.

CHAPTER 3

The story contained an element Gregg had not seen in any of the cases he had handled in the past: Guerry said Fischer told him Porter-Gaud officials knew about Fischer's sexual interest in students yet recommended him for employment at other schools. Porter-Gaud officials had never reported Fischer to law enforcement or warned their own students or parents about the sexual predator freely roaming the school. They had not warned prospective employers of Fischer's predatory habits. This failure to do the right thing with the information they knew about Fischer seemed to Meyers to be a new way to attack the problem. He performed a conflict of interests check, a standard procedure in most law firms, and his firm had no formal conflict that would prevent him from suing Porter-Gaud.

In May 1997, Guerry knew Fischer had abused him, and he knew Fischer had abused other students, because Fischer had often bragged to him about other victims he had molested. He knew Porter-Gaud administrators had refused to help him on three separate occasions when he reached out to them. The school, whose mission statement contained a lofty reference to the "supreme importance of the truth," seemed to have a hard time living up to that ideal when it painted the school in an unfavorable light.

However, for all that Guerry knew in May 1997, there was much more he did not know.

After doing his due diligence, on August 10, 1997, Gregg wrote a letter to Gordon Bondurant inviting a dialogue to see if the school was interested in resolving Guerry's potential legal claim without resort to litigation, known as a demand letter. Gregg pointed out to Bondurant that litigation would not be a good thing for either the school or Guerry. He did not include a monetary demand, which is unusual for such a letter. Gregg never got a response.

When Bondurant got Gregg's letter, he realized Guerry was not going to just go away. He charted a course of conduct that continued, and in fact exacerbated, the cover-up that Grimball and Alexander had begun so many years before. First, he had his "friend", Charleston attorney Bill Craver, inquire whether Porter-Gaud School was required to tell law enforcement authorities what they knew about Fischer. South Carolina, like many states in 1997, had a law that required certain public officials, including teachers, to report any information they had about child abuse. Craver did some legal research but was not able to find a definitive answer, since as he later stated, "Bondurant's not a teacher." He also felt that since the conduct occurred so long ago, the school did not have to report it. He then called the local prosecutor, David Schwacke, to ask about it. Craver later testified under oath that he called Schwacke to relay all of the information the school had about Fischer. Schwacke denied under oath that Craver ever told him anything about Fischer. He said Craver only inquired about whether the school had an obligation to report an allegation about conduct that occurred many years prior.

In an attempt to intimidate Guerry, Craver then went further. He faxed Gregg's demand letter to a Porter-Gaud alum, Jack Sinclaire, a prosecutor in Schwacke's office. Craver suggested Guerry and Gregg were trying to extort money from Porter-Gaud. He apparently felt that if he could get the two charged with a crime, Guerry would finally leave the school alone. His strategy assumed Sinclaire would be loyal to Porter-Gaud and go along with it in order to protect the school. Craver later claimed to have related the entire story about Fischer to Sinclaire, which Sinclaire later denied under oath. Craver claimed under oath that he wanted to give the prosecutor's office all of the information about Fischer that the school had so prosecutors could act if they felt it was warranted; Sinclaire and every other employee of the prosecutor's office who testified or was asked stated that their office had no information about Fischer until Guerry Glover came

43

and reported it later in 1997. Craver was lying and was now part of the cover-up.

Between May 1997, when Craver claims to have told the prosecutor's office about Fischer, and September 1997, when Guerry actually did tell them, Fischer was continuously molesting at least one young boy. Craver had joined a long list of supposedly smart, educated people affiliated with Porter-Gaud who could have spared dozens and dozens of boys from abuse. Later, instead of acknowledging what he did, he falsely blamed the prosecutor's office for not properly handling the information he had lied about giving them.

Also, in August 1997 Guerry wrote a personal letter to all 23 members of Porter-Gaud's board of trustees. In it, he told them in great detail about Fischer and that he wanted the school's assistance in dealing with him. Not a single member of the board responded in any way to Guerry's direct appeal.

With Gregg by his side, Guerry finally felt confident enough to go to the authorities.

Rather than have Guerry tell his story multiple times, Gregg hired a court stenographer to come to his office and record Guerry's story under oath. After swearing to tell the truth, Guerry gave a detailed statement about what Fischer had done to him and his knowledge of other victims. Gregg asked the questions and Guerry told his story in response. Gregg paid the bill to create the transcript, then took Guerry and his sworn statement to meet with Debbie Herring on October 1, 1997. Gregg knew assistant solicitor Debbie Herring from prior cases and knew she was the right person to go after Fischer. During that session, Debbie asked Guerry for the names of all the victims Fischer had ever mentioned to him. The handwritten list, when completed, had 42 names on it, and most of them were Porter-Gaud students.

The next day, a local judge signed a warrant to search Fischer's home. During the search, the police found several items of interest, including a couple of pornographic eight-millimeter films, a film projector, condoms, lubricants, a vibrator, pornographic magazines, a Polaroid camera, and a children's guide to the internet. They also found hundreds of photographs of young people, but all were clothed. A warrant was issued for his arrest that day.

The local media was immediately all over the case. A reporter knocked on Fischer's front door. Fischer, surprisingly, spoke. "I've had a rough time." he said. "I'm really hurt by the allegations. There will be a time when I can talk, but my attorney has told me not to answer any questions. People who know me, I have no problem with. But it's the people who don't know me where the problem comes from. It's very embarrassing; you just don't have any idea. I am very hurt. You never know – life's going along good, then bam . . ." He never spoke to another reporter.

Porter-Gaud decided to get out in front of the story and deflect attention from itself. Bondurant sent a letter to the parents of all Porter-Gaud students. It said allegations had been made against a former teacher of the school, and further stated that the school was cooperating with the criminal investigation. Not a single parent called Bondurant to express concern or ask questions about their child's safety. He later said three or four parents told him they thought it was a good letter.

Craver, meanwhile, inserted himself deeper into the cover-up when he drafted a press release which was approved by Bondurant and given to the press. Craver and Bondurant both knew it was false when they sent it to the local media. Their attempt to protect the school's image would soon come back to haunt them.

Fischer was arrested on October 7, 1997. Other victims started coming forward.

CHAPTER 4

After meeting with Guerry and checking for conflicts, Gregg began to discuss with other lawyers in his firm that he may have a new abuse case against a local school and worked with one of them to develop the legal theories. Gregg called a former student of Porter-Gaud to confirm part of Guerry's story. He did some legal research and developed what he believed to be a viable argument to overcome the statute of limitations.

Porter-Gaud's lawyers stalled in responding to his demand letter and Gregg became concerned that they were dragging their feet, completely unaware they were actually trying to have him and his client arrested. He filed a very simple lawsuit which was captioned *John Doe vs. Unnamed Private School*. He filed it merely to stop the legal clock; he knew he would have to deal with the statute of limitations in the future and did not want a judge chiding him for waiting too long to file after Guerry first came to see him. The lawsuit did not mention Porter-Gaud School or any of its officials by name.

Meanwhile, a supporter of Porter-Gaud heard on the street that Gregg Meyers was representing someone against the school; she knew Gregg was competent handling abuse cases and she did not want him handling one against Porter-Gaud. She complained to Trenholm Walker, one of Gregg's partners, who then raised the issue with one of the senior partners, Douglas Pratt-Thomas. On a Friday afternoon, Pratt-Thomas and Walker strolled into Gregg's office and told Gregg that the firm made about $300,000 a year in fees from one of Porter-Gaud's supporters. They went on to tell him the firm would not handle a case against the school. Gregg was surprised by their assertion that they did not know about the case. He had been openly discussing the issues and theories of the case, but since there was no legal conflict, he did not recall if he had mentioned the name of the school. They insisted he drop the case.

Walker then quizzed Gregg about his legal theories. After hearing Gregg's thoughts, Walker said it was a weak case. Walker then searched the firm's computer and questioned at least one lawyer in the firm to see if Gregg had been intentionally concealing the case from the partners. The lawyer denied it and Walker, who later became a lawyer for Porter-Gaud, found nothing on the computer to support his accusation.

The firm's demand that he withdraw from the case bothered Gregg. He understood the firm's point of view, but he had never backed away from a case because it was controversial, and he wasn't inclined to start now. At the same time, he had young children and didn't want to be impulsive. He needed time to think about his future.

I had also been handling abuse cases for a number of years, and Gregg and I had recently worked together on a particularly difficult case against the Catholic Diocese in Charleston. Though we are polar opposites in many ways, we discovered that our respective strengths and weaknesses dovetailed quite nicely, and as he liked to tell people, "together, we make one pretty good lawyer." To buy himself the time he needed, Gregg called me and asked if I was interested in taking the case. He was thinking about leaving his firm, but he wanted the litigation to proceed while he thought through what he should do. If he left the firm, he wanted an agreement from me that we would handle the case together. Of course, I agreed.

While Gregg was making sure Guerry would have someone to help him continue the fight, his partner Douglas Pratt-Thomas went to work for Porter-Gaud, beginning with a visit to the courthouse to voluntarily dismiss the suit Gregg had filed. He then met with A. Victor Rawl, the Senior Circuit Court Judge in Charleston County. Only those two men know what words they exchanged that day, but the result of the meeting was that the judge signed an order, which was very unusual, and potentially criminal, to have the lawsuit removed from the public files. To this day, the lawsuit Gregg filed against Porter-Gaud on behalf of Guerry Glover cannot be found at the courthouse in Charleston. Pratt-Thomas wrote a letter to Craver letting him know that the suit had been dismissed and the matter was over.

Pratt-Thomas and another partner later explained to Gregg why the firm could not handle a case against Porter-Gaud and complained about him having done so even though there was no formal conflict. Gregg understood their point, until late in the meeting when Pratt-Thomas said, "I do not care what happened to a bunch of kids a long time ago."

Gregg had no visible reaction, but he knew in that moment he could not practice law any longer in that firm. He left the firm August 18, 1998, and resumed representing Guerry, the two of us working together.

CHAPTER 5

Kevin Dunn was different from Guerry. He attended James Island High School, the school where Fischer ended up after Alexander's provided a written recommendation to the public-school district in 1986. Kevin had no idea Fischer used to work at Porter-Gaud, and he had no way of knowing Alexander had recommended Fischer for employment at the public school. Therefore, from a legal standpoint, Kevin was in a much different position than any of the Porter-Gaud victims, especially Guerry. Gregg and I thought we could successfully argue that it was not possible for Kevin to know any of the information about Fischer's tenure at Porter-Gaud or his departure until it became public knowledge through the news media that Fischer had been arrested. The school's fraudulent press release helped us, because we argued that even if Kevin had filed a lawsuit many years before, Porter-Gaud would have lied about what they knew and when they knew it, and that point was confirmed by their press release. It was what the law recognizes as an act of fraudulent concealment by Porter-Gaud.

Kevin was a serious, quiet, reserved, yet very warm Korean-American who spent his entire life in Charleston. He was from an upper middle-class family in which religion played an important role. He was a senior at James Island when he first met Fischer and was a member of the Young Republicans. He didn't have Fischer as a teacher, but Fischer nonetheless targeted Kevin. He struck up conversations with Kevin in the hallways of the school and eventually convinced Kevin to come to his home for dinner and intellectual conversation. The assaults on Kevin began almost immediately, and like so many other victims of abuse, it changed his life profoundly.

Kevin was also different in another way. The first assault on Kevin occurred when he was 18 years old. Porter-Gaud would later argue that because he was legally an adult, that any sexual contact between Fischer and him was consensual.

Kevin was one of the first to call the solicitor's office after Fischer's arrest. He had wanted to do something about Fischer for a long time. When he heard another man had come forward, Kevin's only thought was that he needed to step forward to corroborate the story. In the world of criminal prosecution of sexual offenders, especially teachers, a second victim coming forward is critical. When only one victim is pursuing charges, it is usually a child against a well-respected teacher. He said-she said cases are tough for prosecutors to win. However, if more than one victim pursues charges, especially if their stories are similar, the case instantly becomes more credible and the perpetrator is more likely to be prosecuted.

CHAPTER 6

In any potential civil lawsuits, we knew the statute of limitations was our biggest hurdle. The law in South Carolina at that time was that a victim had three years to file a lawsuit against Fischer and/or his employer. The Porter-Gaud victims had a very difficult hurdle, because even though they did not know what Grimball and Alexander knew, they knew Fischer worked at the school. The law presumed that if they had filed their lawsuits within three years of what happened to them or by age 21, whichever was later, they could have learned what Grimball and Alexander knew, and therefore could pursue their claims. Since Kevin did not have this particular barrier, we decided to lead with his case.

On January 28, 1998, we filed Kevin's case, *John Doe vs. Porter-Gaud School, Berkeley Grimball, James Bishop Alexander, and Edward Fischer*. It was based in large part on the recommendation made by Alexander to the public-school district in 1986. When the suit was filed, everyone on our side knew we were in for a long, tough fight. The social, emotional, and legal issues were daunting, but Guerry and Kevin were committed to exposing the truth.

Shortly after we filed Kevin's case, Gregg met with Guerry's father, Harold. Harold had asked for the meeting because he wanted to find out what was going on with Guerry and offer his help if we could use it. Harold was small in stature and wiry with leathery skin from his years of growing tomatoes under the Lowcountry sun. He was born and lived his entire life on Johns Island. Though only 20 miles away from Charleston, it was worlds away from the hustle and bustle and bluebloods of the peninsula city. Harold was taciturn, and when he spoke, it was always prudent to listen. Guerry described his father as "the most decent man I have ever met." Anyone who ever met Harold would have a hard time disagreeing.

Guerry finally told his father about Fischer in 1997, just before Fischer's arrest. He knew the story was about to be public and wanted to warn his father. He tracked his dad down on the farm and got in Harold's pickup truck. As Guerry started telling the story, Harold pulled onto the shoulder of the road and parked. Guerry then told his Dad the whole story, including his recent visits to Bondurant. "You mean they knew, and did nothing?" It was a feeling Harold would never come to grips with.

A couple days later Harold asked to meet with Gregg. As they chatted, Gregg was struck by Harold's quiet rage about what this school had done to his son and his family. Alexander had been a friend of the Glovers, and when Guerry was having so much trouble during his teen years, Alexander advised the Glovers to send Guerry away to boarding school. He never mentioned to the Glovers what he knew about Fischer or warned them not to leave Guerry alone with him. Harold wondered aloud to Gregg if there was anything he could do to help with the litigation. The offer caught Gregg off guard, but for the first time caused him to think about the case from a parent's perspective. He realized that parents like Harold paid a substantial amount of money to this elite school and should have been secure in knowing the school would do everything possible to provide a safe environment for children. Some of the parents, like Harold, had worked themselves ragged to pay the tuition. Gregg's first thought upon hearing Harold's point of view was that it might be a breach of contract case. The parents had paid money and the school had breached the contract. He did some research that night and decided a claim on behalf of a parent was certainly innovative, and might be successful, but that a breach of contract was not the way to file it. In a contract case, if Harold won, the damages awarded would probably only be the amount of tuition he had paid over the years. Gregg knew Harold was not interested in money; for Harold, Guerry, and Gregg the case was orders of magnitude beyond a refund of tuition.

Breach of fiduciary duty is a legal principle that recognizes that in some circumstances, actors may have an obligation to act in the best interest of someone other than themselves. Gregg thought it made sense that when it comes to the safety of children in a school, administrators' primary responsibility is students' safety rather than their own or the school's interests.

Loss of consortium is a legal concept recognizing that an injury to one person may impact another person or, more precisely, the relationship between two people. The traditional paradigm is when a married person is severely injured and rendered unable to perform everything from housework to childrearing to their intimate relationship, it can profoundly a spouse as well. It is rare for the law to recognize that the relationship between a parent and a child can be affected in a similar way, but Gregg knew a parent is adversely affected any time a child is harmed. He also knew that when a child is victimized in the manner that Fischer hurt Guerry, it could affect a parent profoundly. In his research, Gregg discovered that in South Carolina the parent-child version of a consortium claim was called "loss of services." The parent loses the services of a child due to the interruption caused by the injury. It is an explicit legal fiction developed in the 1600s, modeled on injury to a servant.

Gregg learned from his conversations with Guerry and Harold that their relationship had been severely impacted for more than 22 years: the wrecked cars, difficulties at school, the alcohol problems, Guerry repeatedly removing the wires on his braces with pliers. Finally, it occurred to him that Harold never knew the reason for that gulf between him and his son until October of 1997, when Guerry first told him about Fischer's years of abuse. This meant Harold may not have any problem whatsoever with the statute of limitations. Gregg called me that night and we decided to file a case on behalf of Harold Glover, which we did on February 1, 1998. No one on either side knew that filing would alter the litigation -- and the community of Charleston -- forever.

CHAPTER 7

In every civil lawsuit, the parties, through their lawyers, engage in a
lengthy process known as discovery. The court rules require the parties to
exchange information prior to trial. The reasons for this are sound: if a trial
is really about finding the truth, anything that helps to find that truth is
preferred. Exchanging documents and having the opportunity to question
witnesses allows each side to better prepare for a trial. Some cases involve
thousands and thousands of pages of documents. We knew early on that
these cases were not going to be document cases. Sure, there would be
some documents involved, like the recommendations and Fischer's
employment file, but these cases were going to depend mostly on
testimony.

The way you find out what witnesses know about a case and what they
are going to say in court is through depositions. A witness is usually
subpoenaed to a lawyer's office. There, a court reporter, the lawyers, and
the parties gather to hear the witness answer questions under oath. It is
treated exactly as if the witness were testifying in court, except that in a
deposition, if an objection is made to a question, the witness usually has to
go ahead and answer because there is no judge present to rule on
objections. Objections are made in depositions merely to preserve the
argument for later. Generally, the purpose of the deposition is to find out
what the witness knows. However, a deposition can be used for other
purposes. Sometimes it is necessary to lock a witness into his or her story,
so you can be assured that their testimony is not going to change before

trial. Lawyers are bound by a code of ethics to only use depositions to gather information. Unfortunately, unscrupulous lawyers sometimes use depositions to intimidate a witness. We expected that in this litigation, so we tried to prepare our clients and witnesses accordingly.

After we filed the cases, the first formal response we got came from Wells Dickson, a lawyer hired by Eddie Fischer. Dickson was a very likeable and capable lawyer in Charleston with a solo practice who shared office space with Lionel Lofton, the lawyer who represented Fischer on the criminal charges.

Dickson knew a free exchange of information in the civil lawsuits would probably not help his client while the criminal charges were pending. This was especially true since we wanted to take Edward Fischer's deposition as soon as possible to find out what he would say about Guerry, Kevin and Harold's allegations against him.

In a criminal case, the accused has a Fifth Amendment constitutional right to not testify against himself, and if he invokes that right, it cannot be held against him. However, in some states, a civil case is different. When testifying in a civil case in South Carolina, a witness may "assert the Fifth", but it can be used against them in a very damaging way. If a witness like Fischer refuses to testify in a civil case pursuant to the Fifth Amendment, the jury is instructed by the judge that they may presume the response to any question he refused to answer would be adverse to his interests.

Dickson knew this was likely, so he attempted to stay or suspend all activity in the civil cases until the criminal cases were concluded. Fischer and Porter-Gaud filed motions to delay any discovery in the cases. A hearing took place in Moncks Corner, about 30 miles from Charleston, before Markley Dennis, a very fair and well-respected judge. It was at this hearing I first met Laura Robinson. She was a young associate with the firm of Glenn, Murphy, Gray & Stepp, in Columbia, S.C. The school's insurance company had hired the firm to defend the cases against Porter-Gaud, Grimball and Alexander. I knew Robinson was not going to be their lead counsel, but I presumed she would be doing most of the work. I didn't know at the time that she was a graduate of Porter-Gaud. I also did not know then that her mother was in the senior administration at Porter-Gaud, or that she used to be the law clerk for Judge Rawl, who had already helped

Porter-Gaud and would attempt to do so again and again.

Robinson was indignant that we had sued her alma mater. She assured me the school and its officials had not done the things we accused them of; before long, it was clear that her loyalty to Porter-Gaud clouded her judgment, and it also became apparent that she was in way over her head in this litigation.

Dickson argued at the hearing that discovery, especially depositions, would prejudice his client's interests and should be suspended so the criminal case could proceed without complications from the civil case. Porter-Gaud predictably joined this effort and attempted to thwart the normal discovery process. I argued that stalling discovery would harm the plaintiffs' interests and the cases should move forward because a great deal of discovery was needed. I suggested that Fischer could invoke his right not to testify pursuant to the Fifth Amendment if he chose to and pointed out that the case also involved the school and its role, not just Fischer. The judge agreed and refused to postpone discovery.

We experienced some difficulty scheduling the first depositions. We had already filed formal notices requiring Grimball, Alexander, and Bondurant to appear for questioning. Finally, we were able to schedule several depositions for the first week of May 1998. We were to begin with Fischer on Monday, then Alexander, Grimball and Bondurant on Tuesday. We intended to make these men answer some very tough questions.

CHAPTER 8

Suicide is an ever-present specter in many sex abuse cases. Too often, the victim or victims see it as the only escape from their demons. Eventually, we learned about approximately 15 Porter-Gaud students or former students who committed suicide during Fischer's tenure at Porter-Gaud and since, including six members of Porter-Gaud's class of 1979, which had only a total of 49 boys. The suicides continue many years after Fischer's incarceration and death.

Occasionally, the perpetrator is also a suicide risk. Many people thought Fischer might take his own life. No one expected someone else affiliated with the school to do it.

On April 30, 1998, James Bishop Alexander left his home on the Isle of Palms late in the afternoon. He had spent a considerable amount of time putting labels on various items in his house indicating who was to get furniture and various possessions. He left several stacks of papers on the bed in his spare bedroom which were labeled, for example, "car insurance." He had sat at his kitchen table and wrote a note to his brother, Tom. He tore up a draft of the note and left it in his trash can. He also left two .22 caliber bullets, a small can of WD-40, a note pad and a pen on the table.

In the note to his brother, he said, in part: "I am truly sorry that my actions have put the family through grief and I would do anything to go back and undo anything that have [sic] done wrong. The support of all of you is what has kept me going this long as I see trials and civil cases going on for years and drawing national attention. I feel that this action may diminish the attention on me just a little as it might otherwise go on and on. I find it, after much thought, best to end this life."

He asked his brother to call a member of the clergy in Maryland to go to the family farm and be supportive of a former Porter-Gaud student who was living there. It is interesting to note that in the draft that was torn up, he included the following words, which did not make it into the final draft: "I know it is hard to believe that I truly believe I am trying to minimize the hurt that I have and will cause by having written." Later, when we formally requested copies of these notes from Porter-Gaud and Alexander's estate, Laura Robinson told a judge that Alexander's suicide and the notes were personal and had nothing to do with the litigation. It was to be only the first time of many that she misrepresented something to a court.

Sometime after he finished the note, he drove to his brother's house and taped it to the door. He then drove north, which would not have been unusual for him. He and his brother owned the farm in Maryland, and he went there often. This trip was to be different, however. In Whiteville, North Carolina, a small town just over the state line with no apparent connection to Alexander or the litigation, he turned onto Alligator Run, a dead-end dirt road that was close to, but secluded from, the main highway. It was also, perhaps coincidentally, right across the highway from a cemetery. He turned his white Honda Accord around, so it was facing toward the highway. After parking on the side of the road, he put his wallet in a plastic bag along with another note he had written. This note said, "I am James Alexander and have ended my life due to personal problems that could go on for years without a finite ending." It instructed whoever found him to call his brother. He then covered himself with a blue blanket he had brought along and shot himself in the chest. It is hard not to wonder whether his last thoughts were of Fischer, or of the many Porter-Gaud students that he had 'helped' over the years, or something more sinister. Perhaps he hoped that his knowledge of Fischer's conduct, and his own participation in helping and protecting Fischer had died with him.

I was attending a legal seminar in New Orleans the next morning when I got a call telling me the news. My first emotion was anger. I was mad at Alexander for not having the guts to answer some questions and maybe take responsibility for his role in protecting and advancing Fischer's career. I was mad that some of the story likely died with Alexander. And I was mad that Guerry, Kevin, and the rest of the victims had been victimized yet again.

I talked with Laura Robinson that morning. We initially agreed to postpone all of the depositions that had been scheduled for the following week. Laura called back later and suggested that we go forward with Fischer's deposition. She pointed out that both sides really needed to know what he was going to say. She also said a memorial service for Alexander at Porter-Gaud and his funeral would take place over the weekend and would not conflict with Fischer's deposition.

We agreed it was in everyone's interest to get Fischer under oath and testifying as soon as possible. With a quick round of calls, we were able to resurrect Fischer's deposition for the following Monday.

CHAPTER 9

In preparing for Fischer's deposition, we anticipated that he might assert his constitutional protection against self-incrimination. Therefore, I prepared two sets of questions. The first was a normal set of questions to be asked if he chose to answer freely, even if not truthfully. The other set was specifically designed to use if he asserted his constitutional right not to testify against himself.

Wells Dickson was a part-time judge and was scheduled to hold court in Kingstree, South Carolina on that Monday, so he asked if we would agree to come there to do the deposition. Everyone agreed. Kingstree is a typical small Lowcountry town about ninety minutes from Charleston with huge live oaks draped with Spanish moss surrounding the courthouse. The deposition was conducted in the court annex, a small white building that held some of the county's administrative offices. The room we were provided was tiny and we were quite cramped. It had a single table and one bookshelf with some law books. We had to scavenge chairs from nearby offices to accommodate everyone who showed up. Wells Dickson and Lionel Lofton were there representing Fischer. Bobby Stepp, a partner at Laura Robinson's law firm and her supervisor, was there on behalf of Porter-Gaud and the individual defendants, Grimball and Alexander. Another lawyer, Carol Ervin, had been hired by Porter-Gaud to attend and monitor the insurance company's handling of the case.

The atmosphere was tense. I shook hands with everyone in the room except Fischer. Throughout my career, I refused to shake hands with, or even be cordial to, anyone who harmed children. The deposition was significant for several reasons, but one stood out above the rest. I had the list of 42 names that Guerry created that we believed were all victims of Fischer. I had put them on one sheet of paper and numbered them down the left side of the page. I asked the defendants' attorneys to agree to use the numbers instead of the names in the deposition in order to protect the privacy of those men. All the lawyers agreed. This list of names was thereafter referred to as The List.

With introductions and preliminaries out of the way, the court reporter instructed Fischer to raise his right hand and swear to tell the truth. He complied. Before I could ask the first question, Wells Dickson, in his thick Charlestonian brogue, read a statement: "As discussed prior to us beginning the deposition, Mr. Lofton and I have discussed with our client, that because of the pending criminal charges, his right to remain silent pursuant to the Fifth Amendment of the United States Constitution and the corresponding Article of the South Carolina Constitution, and he has elected to do so, and he will be exercising that right probably 98 percent of the time if I have to put a percentage on it. He is going to answer his name, his address, and his age, and other than that, we have advised him that because of the pending litigation that we have no way of selectively claiming that right under South Carolina law as we understand it. I would also like to state for the record that failure to answer is not to be taken as an admission of guilt, and we are only proceeding because of the denial of our motion to stay at least the discovery aspect of these three civil cases as they apply to Mr. Fischer."

My questions were short, concise, and intended to be devastating to Fischer and Porter-Gaud if they were used in the civil trials. That was their purpose. They included:

After you left Porter-Gaud, persons at Porter-Gaud did recommend you for employment to subsequent employers, didn't they?

Isn't it true that Mr. James Bishop Alexander provided a letter of recommendation or a form recommendation for you to be employed by the school district?

Were these recommendations part of any agreement or plan related to your resignation from Porter-Gaud?

Do you have any knowledge while you were employed at Porter-Gaud whether James Bishop Alexander ever had any sexual contact or sexual relationship with a student at Porter-Gaud?

Have you ever provided alcoholic beverages to a student under the age of 18?

Have you ever provided marijuana to a student?

Have you ever provided Quaaludes to a student?

Are you a pedophile?

Have you ever had sexual contact with a student while they were your student?

Have you ever taken any photographs of young males under the age of 15 where they didn't have any clothes on?

It is true that you have actually molested children of friends, isn't it?

He pled the Fifth to every one of these questions. I concluded the deposition with the following questions:

Would you like to take this opportunity to apologize to John Doe, the plaintiff in one of these lawsuits?

Would you like to take this opportunity to apologize to Mr. Harold Glover for what you did to his son?

Would you like to take this opportunity to apologize to any of the victims or their families?

He pled the Fifth to these questions as well. Notably, when it was their turn, Porter-Gaud's lawyers didn't ask any questions. The deposition concluded much earlier than any of us had expected, but I was satisfied with the outcome. The transcript, in effect, was an admission by Fischer that he had molested students and that the Porter-Gaud officials were complicit in his behavior.

CHAPTER 10

It wasn't until the first week in July that we were able to find dates open on everyone's calendars for the other depositions. We were to question Grimball and Bondurant first in the same day, then the defense lawyers would have an opportunity to question Guerry and Kevin. They wanted a full day for each.

July 1 was a typical summer day in Charleston. It was hot and humid that morning as Gregg, Guerry, Kevin, and I walked to Bill Craver's office, where the depositions were to be conducted. The conference room was at the end of a short, narrow brick alley.

Grimball arrived with Porter-Gaud's lawyers. He wore a dark suit and horn-rimmed glasses; his most notable feature was his unnaturally white hair. He was an arrogant member of an old Charleston family who believed, without evidentiary support, that he was superior to most people and could recognize not only other superior people, but especially inferior people. I refused to shake his hand.

We wasted no time. I asked the court reporter to swear him in. She instructed him to raise his right hand and swear to tell the truth, the whole truth, and nothing but the truth. He did so.

The deposition began slowly with him recounting his educational and professional background. He began teaching in 1945, and was in the education field until 1988, when he retired from Porter-Gaud. He testified about the merger of the three schools to form Porter-Gaud in 1964, and that he was appointed headmaster of the new school; headmaster was the only position he held during his 24-year tenure.

My first questions about the case concerned his preparations for his deposition. He told us about a meeting at Gordon Bondurant's house before the first case was filed, which he, Bondurant, Alexander, and at least four lawyers attended. He also said they had had another meeting the very day of Alexander's suicide to prepare for the depositions that had been scheduled, but that Alexander did not show up.

I then turned to the events leading up to Eddie Fischer leaving Porter-Gaud.

Grimball testified that Fischer's proposition to Ronnie Hammond happened in the '80-'81 school year, not 1972. He claimed he had confronted Fischer about it and Fischer denied it. "I told [Fischer] at that time that if I heard anything more from this parent about his actions with his son, that I would ask for his resignation." He then testified that Alexander came to him toward the end of the school year in 1982 and told him he had received a phone call from a parent alleging, in Grimball's words, that "Fischer had taken his son to his home, Fischer's home, shown him pornographic material and made a pass at him." Grimball said he told Alexander to ask Mr. Fischer to resign. "So, as a result of that, Mr. Fischer resigned, and Mr. Alexander was the one who brought me the letter."

After he acknowledged that the first call came from Ronnie Hammond's father, I asked him more about the call, and if he'd taken notes of the call or put anything in Fischer's personnel file. He said he hadn't.

"It just never occurred to me," he said.

He said he did not talk to the student or do any other investigation beyond asking Fischer about it. I asked why he chose not to ask the student about it.

"Because I felt like that I . . . my job was to find out from the teacher, the faculty member, who was accused of the . . . of sexually abusing or becoming . . . I would say . . . using the term 'too intimate' with this man's child. I didn't see any point in talking to the student about it."

Grimball's timeline between the two calls was always very curious to us. He maintained that the Hammond call was the academic year before the 1982 call and flatly denied that it could've been ten years before.

I then asked him about the call in 1982. He testified he did not confront Fischer about this allegation. When I asked why not, he replied, "Because Fischer had been put on probation. I'm trying to make this clear. I'm sorry if I'm not. He was, in a sense, put on probation after the first call, was told that if I heard anything more about it, he'd be asked to resign. So, he knew that. So, he knew he had to resign. Mr. Alexander said, 'Well, he's resigned.'"

I asked a follow-up question, "And once the allegation was made without ascertaining whether it was true or not, you asked for his resignation?"

"Exactly, because I felt that Mr. Alexander had told me that a parent had called. I didn't think a parent would call with an allegation like that if it weren't true."

"What was different about that allegation and the first call you got?"

"The first call that I got had to do with Mr. Fischer allegedly helping this kid with his lessons at a drugstore, a public drugstore, not taking a kid to his house and performing any sex acts on him. There's a big difference."

I asked if he or Alexander did any investigation to ascertain the truth of the new allegation. His reply was interesting. "Because the parent had called. A parent would not make up a story like that and call a school to put his child in that position, or the family in that position, if it weren't true. That's what I assumed."

"Did you contact the police?"

"It didn't occur to me. I mean, it wasn't anything that . . . for example, I don't know what the laws are now regarding this thing because this has been 10 years since I was even in the school business, so maybe the whole thing has changed. I had no obligation to report anything to police.

The way I looked at it at that time, this was a school problem."

"Okay, Mr. Grimball. In 1982, if you witnessed someone breaking into the house across the street from your home, would you call the police?"

"Yes, certainly. The same way right now, if I saw anybody breaking into the house, I would call the police."

"Why would you do that?"

"Because they're breaking the law and breaking into the house, and I see the guy breaking into the house."

"Do you think you have any legal obligation to do that?"

"No."

"But is it fair to say that you would feel some moral compunction to do that?"

"Yes."

"In 1982, did you feel any moral obligation to contact the police about this allegation against Ed Fischer?"

"No."

"Why not?"

"Because, in the first place, this was something that was . . . it was brought to my attention; an action was taking place in Fischer's house. It was certainly an immoral situation, but I saw no reason to report that situation to the police."

I asked him whether he did anything to find out if Fischer had done similar things to other students. He said he didn't. When I asked him why and suggested in my question that he wanted to protect the school's reputation or was afraid of Fischer suing the school for slander, he got angry and defensive.

"I wasn't afraid of anything. I was doing what I thought was the best thing to do as the headmaster of the school, period, at that time. And it never occurred to me that this whole thing was . . . I was supposed to notify the students we had a possible pedophile on the staff? I mean, that would be ridiculous."

Grimball then testified that he did not inform other faculty members about why Fischer resigned because everyone resigns for different reasons. He also admitted that he took no notes of the events surrounding Fischer's resignation and did not put any documentation in Fischer's personnel file. He did not create any document whatsoever related to the resignation.

"Do you think that would be important information for subsequent employers, the reason why a teacher was fired or resigned?"

"I don't think it would have any particular . . . I don't think any . . . the successor to my position would have any reason to know why a certain teacher left while I was there."

"While you were at Porter-Gaud or any other school that you worked at, when you were hiring teachers, would it have been important to you to know whether a teacher had resigned from another school because of an allegation of sexual misconduct involving a student?"

"I would like to have that information, yeah."

"What about whoever might follow you as the headmaster of Porter-Gaud? Do you think it would be important for whoever followed you at Porter-Gaud to know that this allegation had been made against a teacher at Porter-Gaud?"

"Not in any written form. If they wanted to know why the teacher left, I would probably tell them." His responses were the quintessential "passing the trash" mentality; it is the pattern and practice in the education field of moving bad teachers from one school to another by giving favorable or neutral recommendations for bad teachers in writing, even those who have demonstrated a sexual interest in children. Nothing negative is stated in writing, usually to avoid a defamation lawsuit by the bad teacher, but if a prospective employer calls the prior employer, they will supposedly provide more information about the teacher orally – but not necessarily the truth. It is a practice that has but one inevitable result: children are put in harm's way.

"Are you comfortable today that your decision not to put anything in Eddie Fischer's file about either of these allegations was the appropriate thing to do?"

"Yes."

"Did you ever tell any parents why Ed Fischer resigned from the school?"

"No."

"Why not, same reason as students and faculty?"

"Nobody asked me about it. I didn't want . . . I wasn't going to volunteer the information."

"Did you ever tell the board of trustees why Ed Fischer resigned?"

"No."

"Why not?"

"I didn't have to."

"Did you want to?"

"No. It wasn't any of their business."

"It was none of their business that a faculty member had been accused of sexual misconduct with a student at their school?"

"No, I didn't think so."

He acknowledged, surprisingly, that Fischer did not leave the school the same day in 1982 that Alexander told him about the incident and that Fischer had agreed to resign. Fischer was permitted to finish teaching the rest of the school year, about two weeks. Fischer submitted a letter of resignation after the school year ended. I showed him his letter accepting Fischer's resignation. He explained that he wrote a similar letter to everyone who leaves the school for whatever reason.

"So, if I understand what you're saying, you saw the resignation of Ed Fischer as just a routine matter for the school?"

"Well, it was a resignation, and it wasn't routine because this was the first time we ever had to deal with a sexual allegation brought on by a teacher. It was a different one, obviously. Each one of them is different."

"And even though it was a different reason, you didn't see this resignation as being any different than all the other resignations you had accepted . . ."

"Well, maybe they had different reasons. Some woman is resigning because her husband's being transferred. I mean, there are different reasons for each person leaving an institution or business."

"What did you want to see Eddie Fischer do to make sure that it didn't happen again?"

"Well, I would hope that he would get counseling, psychiatric counseling, whatever these people have to go through to get more or less emotionally cured, away from their sexual proclivities. Obviously, that's what I was referring to."

"Did you ever find out or try to find out if the student needed any counseling?"

"No."

"Was that important to you?"

"I didn't think it was certainly important enough for me to find out what the student was doing. After all, they've got parents."

Grimball then told us about an English teacher he fired because the teacher would "invite students over to his house and drink beer and tell stories. And that's all he did, and he was warned about it, because my feeling was that that just wasn't the thing to do as a faculty member." He fired the teacher in the middle of the school year yet paid his contract through the end of the year.

I returned to the letter. "Referring back to your letter, 'taking positive steps to insure nothing like it ever happen again', do you think it was a positive step for Eddie Fischer to be employed by another private school?"

"That's their business. No one from any of those schools ever contacted me."

"Did Porter-Gaud take any positive steps to insure that nothing like this incident would ever happen again?"

"No."

"You didn't see it as your responsibility or obligation to do anything to see that nothing like this ever happened to a student again?"

"Not at the time, no."

"What about today?"

"Same, no."

Stepp asked for a break because he said Grimball was tired.

After the break, Grimball gave what I thought was one of the most incredible answers I had ever heard in a deposition.

"Do you believe today that it was morally the right thing to do, to recommend Ed Fischer to subsequent employers?"

"Yep."

Not yes or no or maybe or maybe not. There was a pause before the next question because I was truly taken aback by his response.

"Why is it that you allowed Eddie Fischer to resign rather than terminate him?"

"Well, I didn't mean to ruin the guy's career for the rest of his time, assuming that he'd straighten himself out because, otherwise, I mean, his evaluations from the heads of the departments were always positive, his actual work at the school in the academic area and the athletic area."

This statement about Fischer's evaluations was false.

"Do you have children, Mr. Grimball?"

"Uh-huh."

"As a parent, would you want to know if a teacher at one of your children's schools had been accused of sexual misconduct?"

"Not particularly, no."

"What about if it was a teacher that taught a class that one of your children attended? Is that some information that you would want to know?"

"Not unless it would . . . not unless it involved my own children."

"Is it information that would be important to you to ascertain whether it might involve your children?"

"I don't think so." His responses, when read later at trial, caused an audible gasp from members of the jury.

I then asked him some questions about statements he had made to the press at the time Fischer was arrested. He had indicated in one of those statements that, "There has already been one tragedy related to this."

I asked, "What tragedy were you referring to?"

"Mr. Alexander's suicide."

"Do you believe that the molestation of children is a tragedy?"

"Not like a suicide of, I think, a very fine man."

"Do you think that Skip Alexander's death is the only tragedy related to this whole matter?"

"It's the greatest tragedy."

"What other tragedies do you think have occurred?"

"Nothing occurs to me now."

71

The deposition droned on for some time after this, and it was mostly the lawyers arguing and fighting about definitions of words and whether certain questions should be answered. One moment above all others captured the pure arrogance that defined Berkeley Grimball. I was asking him about one of the legal documents filed on his behalf. Stepp instructed Grimball not to answer. While Stepp was speaking, Grimball leaned back in his chair so he was behind Stepp and was emphatically shaking his head at me. So, I asked "You were shaking your head. Is that a no?"

Stepp objected again and instructed him not to answer.

I asked again. "Were you just shaking your head no?"

Grimball said, "Just fluffing up my hair."

"Excuse me?" I was genuinely surprised by the response.

"Fluffing up my hair," he said sarcastically and smiled.

At that moment, I knew we had successfully exposed the arrogance of the school, personified in this man. The only disagreement that Gregg and I had in the litigation was that evening trying to decide which of us was going to cross-examine Grimball in front of a jury. We both wanted him. Unfortunately, he died before we tried the first case.

After lunch, we deposed Gordon Bondurant. We expected more of the same, but we were surprised. Bondurant was very polished, respectful, and seemed to genuinely want to answer my questions. While some responses did seem evasive, we were struck by his demeanor when I began asking about some of the defenses that had been asserted by the school in the lawsuit, including that Fischer's assaults on Kevin were consensual sex between two adults. As I asked the questions, and the school's lawyers objected, everyone on our side of the table noticed that he seemed quite uncomfortable with some of the legal positions that Porter-Gaud had asserted, and he also seemed to be bothered that the lawyers would not let him talk about it. I kept pushing on that topic until, finally, Bondurant said that he "wished some of the defenses had not been asserted."

CHAPTER 11

The next day, Porter-Gaud's lawyers took Guerry's deposition. He was the first person from the plaintiffs' side to be deposed. We expected that. We also expected them to try to intimidate Guerry. From the school's perspective, he was the cause of all their present problems. Bobby Stepp had indicated to Gregg that they might need more than one day to take this deposition, so Gregg agreed in advance that we would see how it went and that we could probably agree to reconvene the unfinished deposition at some later date, if necessary.

We expected the defense lawyers to try to bully our clients. We discussed two ways to deal with this; the conventional way would be to object and push back every time they tried to bully the witness. The problem with this is that it makes the witness appear to be weak and in need of protection. The unconventional method is to allow the lawyers to take their best shots at the witness and not object. This tactic conveys to the other side that the witness is capable -- and more important willing -- to endure whatever is thrown at them to get justice. It is a powerful moment when the lawyer doing the bullying realizes those tactics are failing. Guerry and Kevin both decided to gut it out. Gregg and I would be there if the lawyers got too far out of hand, and there were times I intervened, but we were both pleased and proud that they endured the barrage.

Guerry was nervous that morning but was ready for whatever the defense threw at him. He brought a tape recorder to the deposition because he wanted his own audio copy of what transpired. Of course, the school's lawyers objected and fussed about it until we agreed to provide them a copy of what was on Guerry's tape so they could make sure it was the same as the court reporter's. It was only the first of many insinuations that we would do something nefarious.

We were stunned that Bobby Stepp was not there. He was going to leave the questioning to Robinson. At her side were Bill Craver, Carol Ervin, and Anthony Pisciotti from New York, an insurance company lawyer.

It was clear almost immediately that this deposition was going to take an eternity. Between Robinson's inane questions and Guerry's penchant for starting a new sentence before he finished the last one and his justifiably combative spirit, it was slow going. It also became obvious that Robinson was in over her head.

At one point when she asked Guerry who he had talked to about his deposition, he said the deposition had been a cloud over his life since May. She asked him to explain.

"Because I'm sitting in a chair on one side of the table across from four people who are being paid to cover up and mix and make gray for Porter-Gaud and Mr. Fischer, that just the repulsiveness of what has happened in my life in the last year and I just . . . that is so galling to me, that the idea of Porter-Gaud not working with me but working against me has been the most disillusioning thing in the whole thing."

She alluded to coming questions about his contacts with Porter-Gaud, asking facetiously if he understood that none of the lawyers at the deposition represented Fischer.

"Well . . . but in my mind Porter-Gaud and Mr. Fischer are one and the same."

"Why is that?"

"Because in my mind you all are not interested in the fact that children were raped, you're interested in covering up for Porter-Gaud's mistakes. And if you cover up for Mr. Fischer and you cover up for Porter-Gaud, then you get paid for doing a good job."

She asked if he understood that the deposition was merely to find out what he knows about his allegations against Fischer.

"Intellectually, I understand that. Somehow you don't feel like four fuzzy people who are interested in finding out so you can do something about it."

She spent hours asking about his personal life, why he got a lawyer, and wanted to know about everyone Guerry had ever spoken to about Fischer or Porter-Gaud.

More than *six hours* into the deposition, Robinson asked the first question about Fischer's assaults on him. After describing the first instance in which Fischer molested him, she asked if he had told anyone and if it upset him.

He said he did not tell anyone at the time and then continued. "You know, I . . . I'm going to try to be calm in this because I'm not going to let you upset me. I was a sixth grader. I was innocent. I was naïve, I was a little kid. That was so far beyond my realm of experience and possibilities, and I don't know how to explain that. What upsets me is when people . . . treat it matter-of-factly. Just as you are looking at me dumbfounded. 'Why didn't you tell somebody?' What I don't understand is why people would ask that question. It astounds me that a human being could hear that a sixth grader was touched by some twisted pervert and everybody keeps on writing. It just blows my mind." Guerry was referring to the four lawyers on the other side of the table who seemed to be writing every word he said. "So, you know, no, I don't remember how long I stayed in there or anything. That was the dark beginning of the nightmare and it's real . . . that part's real clear . . . as everybody writes." He gestured at the lawyers. "That just blows my mind. I mean, I know you all are doing your job but, somewhere in there, I've been hoping from day one that somebody would be a human being when they hear such. And that has just escaped people and it just blows my mind."

A couple of minutes later, she asked him to describe again how Fischer had touched him.

"What I remember is lying on the bed with Mr. Fischer rubbing me

saying 'This is what I do to the football team,' in the manner of . . . as he
would if someone pulled their groin, he would massage their thigh. So, it . .
. I mean, it wasn't like he performed fellatio on me. I would tell you he
performed fellatio on me. It was a rubbing me and saying, 'This is what I do
to the football team.' I don't remember going into the room. I don't
remember leaving the room. I remember lying on the bed with Mr. Fischer
rubbing me, this weird psycho guy who I didn't really know. I'm this little
kid out in the country in my own happy little world and this is this massive
intrusion into my reality. It's just this big thing going pain, pain, pain, pain,
pain, pain, pain, pain, painful memory starts here, painful memory starts
here, painful memory starts here. That's it."

"Were you wearing your pajamas?"

"Did you hear anything I just said to you?"

"I heard everything you said to me. Were you wearing your
pajamas?"

She had asked him earlier in the deposition if he was wearing any
clothes when this occurred. He had replied that he didn't remember. "I am
remembering painful memory, painful memory, painful memory, painful
memory, painful memory. I'm lying on the bed." Robinson demonstrably
rolled her eyes. "You can roll your eyes at me, I still don't remember."

"Did he rub your penis?"

"I don't remember him touching my penis. I remember him
touching me and saying, 'This is what I do with the football team.' Up until
that time, I had never experienced anything like that. That was a whole
different experience to catalogue, to describe, to come up with a vocabulary
for, so, you know, the thought process is all somewhat jumbled in that. I'm
trying to convey that to you."

"At the time, did you think he was doing something wrong?"

"At the time, I was a sixth grader. It was so far beyond the pale of
my definable experiences, but I knew intuitively there was something really
weird about it. In the limited vocabulary and scope of a sixth grader's ability
to enunciate, to feel, to know what he's feeling, yes, as I think any sane

person, reasonable person would easily acknowledge."

"Do you remember feeling upset?"

"What I remember is that's the night painful memories started. I'm lying on the bed, he's touching me, he's saying, 'That's what I do with the football team.' You keep asking me for specifics and I'm telling you, you know, when you drop a 20-ton bomb on the parking meter outdoors, it's hard to look for the meter. Big event, I don't . . ."

"So, if I understand what you're saying, you don't remember if you felt upset or not?"

"See, I'm just so floored that you even have to ask the question and I have to answer it 80 times and you still don't . . . you still won't hear what I'm saying and act like I'm not answering your question."

"I believe I've asked you twice were you upset, and I don't think you've answered me yet. And I'll ask you again; do you remember if you were upset?"

"I'm saying I don't remember any feelings other than I knew it was really wrong because that event is of such seismic proportions in the life of a sixth grader, that how do you expect me to describe it in your vocabulary? I'm stunned. If I was one one-thousandth of a million percent as upset then as I am that you all are here asking me this, yes, I was very upset. And I can't imagine that I wouldn't be, so yes, I was upset."

"Why didn't you tell your parents?"

"Can we go through this again? Who was your sixth-grade teacher? Let's think about . . . help me with this."

"Alright, first, let's try to answer the question. Why didn't you tell your parents?"

"I am trying as hard as I can to answer the question."

"Okay."

"I'm saying there is no vocabulary in a sixth grader . . . and I didn't have it in my vocabulary as a sixth grader to describe what I felt or thought or happened, that was so far beyond my scope. And I can't figure out why that's so hard for you all to understand and that just adds frustration which gets in my way and I . . . it's like I am trying to say that the wall is white and you're saying the carpet is blue. I'm saying the wall is white and you keep saying the carpet is blue. I'm talking about a sixth grader being raped and you want to know what I was thinking about, and I don't know how to answer that other than . . . .."

"Let's try to focus on the questions."

"Okay."

"What we're talking about is the first time Edward Fischer touched you inappropriately. Are you with me on that?"

"Yes. We were lying on the bed. Are you with me on that?"

"Yes. And what I'm trying to understand from your earlier description of that event, I'm trying to connect that with what you just said about being raped. Did he rape you on that bed?"

"What do you call it when a teacher touches a sixth grader in the way that I described?"

"I'm asking you Mr. Glover. This is your deposition."

"I say that is . . . it goes beyond appropriate. I mean, I just . . . it drives me crazy when people say, you know, these nice little words, 'Let's make it gray and dress it up,' but a pervert touching a sixth grader is rape. I don't need to gray that up. Whether he put my dick in his mouth that night, I don't need to draw that distinction for it to be rape."

"Again, focusing on that night, where on your body did he touch you?"

"I remember him touching me on my thighs."

"Do you remember him touching any other parts of your body?"

"I remember him touching my thighs."

"I heard you. And what I'm asking you is do you remember his touching any other part of your body?"

"If I remembered that, I would have said I remember him touching my thighs and my toes. You asked the question and I answered the question."

"If he had broken your arm, would you have told your parents?"

"I wouldn't have needed to tell my parents."

"Why not?"

"Well, if I walked downstairs for breakfast and my bone was sticking out of the skin, it would be pretty obvious. I wouldn't need to say, 'Mom, Mr. Fischer broke my arm.'"

"Let's pretend that the bone wasn't sticking out of your arm, it was a small fracture, but your arm hurt, would you have told your parents?"

"If I had a small fracture in my arm, my parents would see that, or I would say, 'My arm hurts.' Or if there was something that I knew in the vocabulary of a sixth grader to communicate, I would do that."

At 5:05 p.m., she was through for the day, but she had only begun to scratch the surface of the incidents of Fischer assaulting Guerry, and she had made it clear that she intended to discuss every single one in detail. We agreed to reschedule the continuation of his deposition for a later date. Guerry was exhausted and angry. But, the most important thing that happened that day was the lawyers learned that they would not, and could not, intimidate Guerry Glover. He was frustrated by their utter lack of compassion, but he learned he could do this.

CHAPTER 12

The next day, Friday, July 3, 1998, it was Kevin's turn. The number of lawyers on the other side of the table had grown to six for his deposition, but the entourage again did not include Stepp. I was beside Kevin, and Gregg and Guerry were further down the table on our side. Kevin had brought a bottle of Gatorade and placed it in a precise spot on the table within easy reach near his right hand. He sat stiffly in his chair very close to the table, interlaced his fingers on the table, and from the beginning stared at a spot on the table right in front of him near his hands. He was a nervous mess, partly because he had seen what Robinson had done to Guerry the day before. But he resolved to endure whatever these lawyers had in store for him.

Robinson again conducted the questioning. She spent the first part of the deposition quizzing Kevin about his background from the time he was a child right up until that day. "I'd like to go over your educational background please. Where did you go to kindergarten?" Gregg and I had attended hundreds of depositions in our respective careers, but neither of us had ever witnessed a more intrusive, humiliating, or intimidating interrogation. Some of her questions included:

"Why did you trust [Fischer]?"

"Why were you praying [while Fischer was molesting you]?"

"When was your first sexual experience?"

"Have you ever had sex with a female?"

"Had you ever masturbated at your house before you met Mr. Fischer?"

"Have you had sex with anyone else besides Fischer?"

"Have you ever had a sexual relationship with [your best friend]?"

"Do you think [your best friend] wants to have sex with you?"

"Have you ever had sex with any of your former roommates?"

"Are you able to have sex?"

"Why did you sue Porter-Gaud?"

At one point, she read into the record some of the names on The List, knowing full well that doing so was a breach of the agreement we had reached about the names on that list; a deposition is considered a public proceeding as if it were in open court. We were incredulous. It was clear almost from the beginning that the defense not only intended to embarrass, harass, and intimidate Guerry and Kevin, but they seemed determined to send a message to any other victim of Fischer that they had better not testify. Every time I tried to intervene and stop a line of questioning, she insisted they needed answers to all of their questions to adequately represent their client. None of the lawyers on the other side representing the insurance company or Porter-Gaud ever tried to distance themselves from her behavior. It was clear to us that her conduct was planned and designed to bully Guerry and Kevin.

Several hours into the deposition, Robinson asked her first question about Eddie Fischer's assaults on Kevin. Almost as soon as she got to the issues involved in the case, the lawyers for the defendants announced that they were going to stop the deposition and come back another day to complete it. They had not asked us about this beforehand like they did for Guerry. Suspending a deposition is a classic ploy utilized by some lawyers to regroup, reload, and come back another day with more questions. It also prolongs the intimidation factor against the witness. The rules of court only allow one deposition of each witness, unless you get an agreement with the other side or permission from a judge to conduct a second one, a luxury that is rarely granted by a court. I told the lawyers that we were not suspending the deposition and it would continue that day until completed. Anthony Pisciotti said he had a vacation planned and that he was going to suspend the deposition and leave at 3:00. Tempers flared; Kevin was shaken. I was furious. The defense lawyers, with one notable exception, insisted that it was their deposition and they were going to suspend it. I told them that they were entitled to leave if they chose, but that we were going to remain in the room and were prepared to stay as long as necessary to conclude the deposition on that day.

The one defense lawyer who wasn't agreeing with the others was Carol Ervin. She asked us to remain in the room and she would go outside where the other defense lawyers were huddling. We witnessed a very animated conversation through the window. When she finished talking to them, Pisciotti came into the room, packed his papers, and left for his vacation without saying a word. The other lawyers took their seats and the deposition continued with no more discussion about coming back another day.

When Robinson finally got around to asking Kevin about the sexual abuse perpetrated by Fischer, the atmosphere in the room was charged. Robinson asked her questions in a very flippant tone; Kevin responded to each of the questions quietly and directly, never taking his eyes off the spot on the table that he had been staring at for hours. His delivery was slow, pained, and compelling. Tears rolled from his eyes to the tip of his nose, where they dripped onto the table and formed a perfectly round puddle. Occasionally, he would reach for the Gatorade, unscrew the top, take a small but quick sip, put the top back on, place the bottle back in the exact same spot, adjust his shirtsleeves, and put his hands back in exactly the same position and find the same spot on the table with his eyes. At one point in the deposition, I noticed that the court reporter was crying as she listened to his testimony. Gregg, meanwhile, sat at the far end of the table quietly stewing over the defense's bullying and working on ideas for how to turn those tactics against the school.

The deposition lasted nine hours. Kevin was exhausted.

The most important aspect of those two days was that Guerry and Kevin showed the defense they would not be intimidated. They had endured all of the bullying, sarcasm, and condescension that Robinson could muster. They knew what she and the school were trying to do, but they emerged from their respective crucibles with their heads held high.

Gregg and I were furious. After saying goodbye to Kevin and Guerry, we resolved to each other that we would make the defendants pay for their treatment of our clients. We began discussing some ideas he had come up with while I was defending the depositions. We began the next day by conveying our outrage to Stepp. We told him that Robinson reading the names on The List into the record and Pisciotti scheduling his vacation in the middle of Kevin's deposition were all going to be shown to a jury someday. The defense apparently got the message. When we reconvened Guerry's deposition in October, it was the polar opposite of his and Kevin's earlier sessions. Stepp handled the questioning. He was professional, respectful, and asked questions in a straightforward manner and did not appear to be interested in intimidating or humiliating Guerry.

CHAPTER 13

One effective tool in discovery is to ask the other side to formally admit certain facts in writing, to avoid incurring the time and expense to prove something that is not reasonably disputed. They are called Requests for Admissions. We decided to use this tactic to narrow the issues we would have to spend time on. One of those was Alexander's signature. Alexander signed the written recommendation form that he had filled out and sent to the Charleston County School District in 1986 on Fischer's behalf. We asked the defendants to admit that it was his signature. Surprisingly, they refused to do so. It seemed silly to us, but we hired a handwriting expert to authenticate the signature. We asked the school for, and they provided, dozens of documents that bore his signature. It was only the first episode of the defense refusing to acknowledge the obvious just to make our job harder.

Another example of their needless obstruction involved their own words. In response to one of our document requests, Porter-Gaud's lawyers had given us a series of faculty manuals for the school. They covered a long period of time and were generally the same through the years. While perusing these seemingly irrelevant manuals, I came across a paragraph stating, "amorous or erotic relationships between teachers and students are always inappropriate." That seemed to contradict their position that the sexual contact between Fischer and Kevin was consensual. I copied the words right from their manual and asked them to agree with that statement. The statement, we naively thought, would force the defense lawyers to abandon their consent argument or contradict their client's own policy as set forth in the manual. It was the first of many traps we tried to set.

On the last day they had to respond, we received one of the strangest responses I ever saw. Instead of admitting or denying the statements in a straightforward way, Porter-Gaud's lawyers did something bizarre; they admitted, on behalf of their clients including the school, that the statement was in the faculty manual, but they would not agree with the statement itself.

Some of their other responses to our inquiries are illustrative of just how far Robinson was willing to go to protect her alma mater. We asked them to admit these statements after Grimball's deposition and after they had a copy of the recommendation that Alexander had sent to the Charleston School District. Robinson signed these responses as being true and accurate.

Admit or deny that Edward Fischer was permitted to resign from Porter-Gaud in 1982 as a result of an allegation of sexual misconduct related to a student.

"Denied as stated. Porter-Gaud objects to the term 'allegation of sexual misconduct' because such terms have not been defined in the context of this litigation and specifically in this Request; therefore, the terms are vague and ambiguous, and Porter-Gaud cannot respond to the Request. However, without waiving this objection, Porter-Gaud responds as follows: Because of his probationary status as testified to by Berkeley Grimball on July 1, 1998, Fischer was placed in the position of choosing to resign or be fired by Porter-Gaud in 1982 because a parent communicated to Porter-Gaud that Fischer had behaved inappropriately with the parent's son. Upon information and belief, Fischer denied any inference that he had behaved inappropriately."

Admit or deny that Porter-Gaud did not inform any student or parent of the true reason for Edward M. Fischer's resignation.

"Porter-Gaud objects to this Request on the grounds that it cannot know Mr. Fischer's reasons for resigning. Porter-Gaud cannot know what was in Fischer's mind nor can it speculate as to his mental state. This Request is improper and incapable of being answered by Porter-Gaud."

*Admit or deny that Porter-Gaud provided a favorable recommendation of
Edward Fischer to the Charleston County School District.*

"Denied. Porter-Gaud is aware of only the document purporting to
be a 'reference form' for Charleston County School District that reflects the
name J. Bishop Alexander which has never been authenticated by anyone
competent to do so. Furthermore, until Porter-Gaud obtained a copy of
this document by means of a subpoena to the Charleston County School
District served after this litigation began, Porter-Gaud was not aware of the
existence of that document, much less whether it was genuine or authentic.
Porter-Gaud also objects to the term 'favorable' because it is a subjective
description that necessarily varies depending on each reader's interpretation
of the document."

Under the rules, we could have asked the court to force them to give
more direct responses. We decided instead to use their own words at trial to
show how evasive and deceptive the school and its lawyers were.

On at least one occasion, Porter-Gaud's legal counsel completely
fabricated evidence in an attempt to distract us from the truth. Robinson
signed the document and based on conversations I had later with the other
lawyers, it became clear to me that she was the only lawyer involved in this
fabrication. In one written response, she asserted that before Fischer was
hired at College Prep, Alexander went to the school and spoke with a 'Ken
Hough'. She went further and asserted that Alexander advised Hough that
Fischer should not be around students. The statement was, and is, patently
false. She never produced 'Mr. Hough' for a deposition in spite of our
repeated requests. She simply made it up. We did, however, find and depose
Thomas Farin, the headmaster of College Prep that Alexander actually
approached to recommend Fischer. Mr. Farin's testimony was decidedly
different than what Robinson had fabricated.

In most cases involving professional misconduct, the plaintiff must
present expert testimony that supports the claim that the defendants did
something that violated the standard of care owed to that particular
plaintiff. We knew early on that we were going to need an expert to talk
about how Grimball's and Alexander's conduct was wrong and harmful to
the plaintiffs. We were also a little concerned that the consent defense in
Kevin's case might resonate with one or more of the jurors. We knew that

age was not an issue, but we needed someone to make that clear to the jury from the witness stand. In accordance with court rules, if we were going to use an expert witness, we had to notify the defense of the identity of any such witness and the topics on which they would offer testimony.

One day as I was reviewing the written transcript of Gordon Bondurant's deposition testimony, it occurred to me that he either said or would likely say all the things that we needed an expert witness to say. It was a risky proposition to use a witness from the opposition as our own expert, but I felt we had sufficiently boxed him in during his deposition such that he would have to say what we needed, whether he wanted to or not. Another fortunate twist of fate was in our favor on this point: we learned that he had retired from Porter-Gaud after his deposition. I felt that having left Porter-Gaud, and thus no longer controlled by its lawyers, Bondurant might say the things that he seemed to want to say at his deposition. I called Gregg and told him my idea of naming Bondurant as our expert witness. At first, he thought I was kidding. But as I laid it out for him, he realized we could probably pull it off. We made the decision to risk it. In accordance with court rules, we sent a written response to the defendants naming Gordon Bondurant as our expert witness and describing the opinions we expected to elicit from him. Over the next couple weeks, we waited anxiously for their response to this unconventional tactic. We expected an objection and a fight; they never commented to us about it until the first trial. We learned why in that proceeding.

The defendants eventually named their own expert witness to testify about liability issues related to school procedures. The gentleman was the superintendent of a public-school district in Arlington, Texas. When we got the response, Gregg wondered aloud how many school districts they had to skip over to get from South Carolina to Texas, and how this guy must be a piece of work. He immediately tried to schedule a deposition. Robinson was less than enthusiastic about getting it scheduled, so Gregg called the superintendent's office one day just to get some available dates. When the 'expert witness' learned who was on the phone asking about his calendar, he picked up the line and spoke with Gregg. He wanted to talk about the case. Gregg answered his many questions and by the end of the call, the superintendent said that there was no way he was going to testify for "that school". We never heard from or about him again.

CHAPTER 14

No one will ever know what made Edward Mein Fischer the monster he was. What is known about Fischer is far less than what is not. By his own account, he began sexually molesting young boys in 1954 or 1955. His first victims were two sons of a friend of his. After graduating from high school, he went to The Citadel, a military college in Charleston, where James Bishop Alexander was his classmate. He began teaching in 1958 at Bishop England, a Catholic high school in the city, and after a couple of years there, he transferred to Sacred Heart, a Catholic elementary school. It is apparently there that he first started molesting students. There are two known victims from this school, and both were molested in the school library during school hours. After two years at Sacred Heart, he abruptly left. He claimed he wasn't making enough money and started selling appliances. We were told but could never confirm, that he was ousted from the school for inappropriate conduct with a student.

From 1963-1967, his whereabouts and activities are largely a mystery. In 1967, he was hired at Rivers High School, a predominantly black high school in Charleston. There are no known victims at Rivers. It was there that he began to be involved in athletics.

In 1970, while he was still employed at Rivers, he began working with the football team at Porter-Gaud as a volunteer trainer and assistant coach. One of his best friends, Paschal Crosby, was the athletic director at Porter-Gaud at that time. He began molesting at least one member of the football team at Porter-Gaud before he was hired as a teacher there in the fall of 1972.

He was an educated, articulate, personable fellow. He seemed to most to be well read, well-traveled, and conversant in any number of topics. He was a gregarious, good looking bachelor who drove a Porsche and seemed to be everywhere in Charleston. He coached basketball and tennis, and was the advisor for various clubs, including the surf club.

After Fischer's guilty plea and sentencing on April 23, 1999, we feared he would not last long in prison. We tried to depose him as soon as possible. It was difficult because there had been other cases filed against Fischer and Porter-Gaud and we were trying to coordinate just one deposition of Fischer to be used in all of them. Now that he had pled guilty and had been sentenced, he could no longer avoid answering our questions by pleading the Fifth. He had been sent to Lieber Correctional Institute, a maximum-security prison near Ridgeville, South Carolina, just off Interstate 26 in a vast pine forest.

After getting through security early in the morning on June 29, 1999, we were escorted to a conference room just off the main dining room where the inmates ate their meals. The room looked like a classroom. When we got there, the court reporter and videographer were already set up. There were three cafeteria tables set end to end, at a diagonal across the room. Fischer and Wells Dickson were seated on the far side of the table. Laura Robinson was seated at the left end near the court reporter, on the same side as Fischer. At the far-right end of the table were two lawyers representing the Charleston County School District in a case filed by Justin Lucey, another lawyer in Charleston.

Lucey and his associate, Sally Phalen, were seated at the left end of the table facing Fischer. Justin had some cardboard boxes with various items in them that he wanted to ask Fischer about. I took a seat in the middle of the assembled tables. Gregg did not attend because he was still on the school board and he was concerned about the appearance of him being present at a deposition in a case in which Lucey's client was suing the school board.

When everyone was settled, Justin Lucey went first and began the long-awaited questioning of Edward Fischer, who was dressed in khaki prison garb. Wells Dickson opened the session with a statement about Fischer's health and aging. He got Fischer to talk about some recent x-rays that showed some areas of concern on his lungs. He also said without offering any support that Fischer had dementia. He seemed to want some sympathy for his client. He didn't get any.

Lucey began with the statement made to the court at Fischer's sentencing involving an illness his lawyer had mentioned to the judge, a reference to his molestation of young boys. "My question to you is what illness is Mr. Lofton addressing in this statement to the Court?"

"That I had needed help, and that I needed further help, and that I had made improvement, and that is about all I can remember."

Justin then moved on to asking about his client, who met Fischer in 1988 in his second year at James Island High School. Fischer testified that he did molest the boy but stopped in 1990.

Justin asked, "Why is that, please?"

Fischer thought for a moment. He began in a halting fashion. He even became a bit emotional as he delivered his response. "I never thought about it, but I will try. I became extremely, I guess the word is caring for him. I looked out for him. I helped him through college. I was more like . . . I didn't want to say a father. I told him I didn't want to be his father. I didn't want to be his brother. I just wanted to be his helper friend. The sexual desire, whatever it was, that went away. From then on it was a relationship of me doing what I could for him. But we never had a social life. He said he wouldn't drink. He wouldn't smoke. He wouldn't do drugs. I said, fine, when you hit a certain age, I will give you x amount of dollars if you don't. But we had a good rapport, a really good rapport. I felt like I had really done something in my life. And that is what I set out to do, and I just cared enough about him that I did it. But we never discussed sex or anything after that. He was very quiet, said very little."

"Were you his mentor?"

"I would say that's a good word."

"You also gave my client an allowance of $50 a month if he

wouldn't drink or do drugs?"

"No. If he wouldn't drink or do drugs, and stayed away from it, on his 21st birthday I think I told him I would give him $1,000, and the way that I would know it is he would come up and tell me I haven't done it."

"Now, another condition of that $1,000 gift at age 21 was that he remain a virgin until he was 21, correct?"

"Now, I didn't use that word. I said stay out of sex. I never used that term. I said if I were you . . . it was don't get hooked up with sex. I was thinking of AIDS, mostly. Don't get hooked up in drugs. Don't smoke, because I knew what I was suffering, and don't use alcohol."

"Did you tell him it would make him a better husband?"

"If he stayed away from sex?"

"If he allowed you to molest him?"

"No. I think I told him he would be a better husband. I think I did make that remark somewhere, that if he stayed away from sex. I don't ever remember using the excuse to molest him."

"You did inform him that he shouldn't associate with women, right?"

"No. I never made that statement."

"He shouldn't have sex with women?"

"Correct."

"It was bad to have sex with women?"

"No. I told him it was dangerous. He had a girlfriend from the very beginning, and he had a succession of them. He always had a girlfriend."

Justin moved to the fall of 1997 when the search warrant was served on Fischer at his home. "Tell me how this all came down in 1997."

"Okay. It was a Thursday, the second of October. I laid down and must have gone to sleep. It must have been about 4:30 [p.m.]. I had a knock on the door. And I went downstairs. I was in my shorts. I peeked out the door and there was a bunch of people. I said excuse me. I ran upstairs and put on a pair of Bermudas and came back. They came in and handed me a search warrant. It really scared me. And I read it, and it said that they were looking for certain things. I said fine. I sat on the couch. They sat a man with me. And for about three and a half hours they went through every stitch of my house. They even went through my computer. They got very little. I didn't know what to do. But there was nothing incriminating. And I just sat down, and I can't hardly remember after that. I think I went to bed. I didn't talk to the media. I knew you weren't supposed to do that, and I told them, 'no, I didn't have anything to say.' And the next morning I got up and I think I walked to mass. I was all out of whack. The next day I think the paper had the first article of Guerry Glover's, and I really, really felt bad. I just . . . and I went to mass, and walked, and stayed at home, and that is what I remember. It was a horrible nightmare."

"Tell me about the incident with the young man known as the 1982 student, please."

"Okay. '82, I do remember that. Somehow, I had gotten close with him, and as best I remember I just said one day . . . I more or less made it pretty clear. He didn't say anything. I said, well . . . trying to say it as best as I can remember because I don't want to be wrong on this because he's a fine person. And we went to my house, and I messed with him. I had really bad regrets there. I don't even remember what I said. But, anyhow, that was on . . . funny how you can remember this, too. That was in May. I do remember that, because it was in May. I think I remember the date, if you want me to take a shot at it."

"Please."

"Tuesday the 18th."

"Tuesday the 18th of May 1982?"

"1982."

"Go on."

"Because this has burnt my whole head for all of these years. And I noticed . . . I knew it was wrong then. I really knew it was wrong. For the first time I really felt terrible. And he was still in my class, and he did well, and he was a great student, but I never . . . we never . . . he sort of avoided me, and I said I don't blame him, and we finished school out."

"Did you show him pornographic magazines while you were molesting him?"

"If you are talking about Playboy that is the only pornographic magazines I had. I can't answer that. I don't know."

Justin spent most of the rest of the day asking questions specifically about his client. He concluded his questioning at 4:21 in the afternoon.

I began my questioning by following up on one of his earlier responses that intrigued me. "You have said a couple of times today that you are not a homosexual, and you said earlier today that you are not a pedophile, or so you have read."

"I didn't believe I was a pedophile because I think if you look at that, that's little children. These people we are talking about were almost as large as me, with a few exceptions. I just never felt I was one, and I took 18 months of treatment and he said you are not one."

When I asked him to describe his sexual orientation, he said that he had never been sexually active until he got to Porter-Gaud. He said he always liked girls, but he could not answer about his orientation. "I don't want to say I'm bisexual because I don't believe in it." He went on, "This may sound ignorant, but I never really felt I was doing wrong, and never thought of arrest when I was doing the things I would, which is pure ignorance." He did say he was always attracted to adult females, but not men or boys. He falsely claimed that the youngest boy he ever molested was twelve.

"Now, from the time you got hired at Porter-Gaud until the time you left Porter-Gaud, how many young men did you have sexual contact with?"

"I have no idea."

93

"Have you ever tried to . . .."

"Never tried, no."

." . . sit down and figure it out?"

"No. I couldn't even think about it, it upset me so bad. You have to understand something. I hate to go through some of this because it just makes me sick at myself. Do you understand what I'm saying?"

"Why?"

"I don't know. Because as I change my life I realize now that what I didn't think was bad was horrible."

"You think now it was horrible?"

"Yes."

"While you were at College Prep, how many young men did you have sexual contact with?"

"About three."

"Were they all students at College Prep?"

"Yes."

"And then at James Island High School, how many young men did you have sexual contact with who were students at James Island?"

"God, I would say four."

"Were there times that you were molesting more than one boy at a time, or were you always sort of exclusive?"

"I was most of the time exclusive, if I can use that term. But there were times, but not often, where there was more than one."

"Did you ever have sexual contact with any female students at any of the schools that you worked at?"

"Never, never. I knew that was a problem."

I asked him a few questions about Alexander's visit to his house after the 1982 family went to the school. "When Skip came to see you at your house, did you admit to Skip that, yes, it was true, that you had done what they said?"

"No."

"Did he ask you if it was true?"

"No. He never asked, and I never answered."

Since one of the defenses that Porter-Gaud asserted was that the sexual assaults by Fischer were consensual sex, freely entered into by the victims, I wanted to get his take on that. "Are you going to contend, or do you contend that any of these young men that you ever had sexual contact with, that they seduced you in any way?"

"I don't know how to take that. I would have to give that some thought."

"Let me put it a different way so you can think about it. Do you contend that any of your victims are responsible for the sexual molestation?"

"Let me stop you there. My being an adult, I was totally responsible. I will answer that. They had no responsibility, either through their young age, being young, and me being an adult. I accept full responsibility."

"And what about your position as a teacher, regardless of what their age was?"

"Yes. What about it?"

"Do you think that that has some effect or some bearing on who bears the responsibility?"

"I think I bear the responsibility again."

"So regardless of the age, if they were a student at a school you taught at . . .."

"It was my responsibility. And even if they were 21, it was still my responsibility. I feel that I was older and more intelligent, and I should have known better. Ignorance of the law is no excuse."

"How would it make you feel if someone were to suggest or contend that the boys were responsible for their molestation?"

"Why would someone say that?"

"How would . . . that is a good question, Mr. Fischer."

"Yeah. I would like an answer."

"I would, too, Mr. Fischer." I looked right at Laura Robinson as I said this.

"Oh, okay. Thank you. Then you know how I feel on some of the questions you are asking me."

I asked about the incident in his first year at Porter-Gaud, "And you said earlier you have no knowledge that Berkeley Grimball had put you on probation?"

"The Hammond allegation was clear that day. It was a one-day clearance. That was it."

I wanted to know what he knew about Alexander's activities with boys at the school. "You said that you knew that Skip Alexander had boys living with him at different times?"

"Yes."

"You also said earlier, 'none of this really hit until I was at Porter-Gaud'?"

"That's right."

"Tell me what you mean by that."

"I didn't get involved in all this until I got to Porter-Gaud, to speak of, as I call an epidemic, a minor epidemic. And then I started . . . I didn't really realize what wrong I was doing at that time. Ignorance of it."

"You said earlier you really couldn't tell me how many victims there were at Porter-Gaud?"

"No."

"Was it more than 25?"

"I don't know."

"Could it be more than 50?" The number of victims who eventually came forward approached 50.

"No. I would say no."

"Let's turn for a moment to what we have marked as Exhibit Number 50, Plaintiff's Exhibit Number 50." I pulled out a copy of The List.

"We are not going to show that." He feared that I was going to put The List on the videotape.

"No, but as you can see, that is a list of names. And as I told you before we went on the record, I want to refer to these gentlemen by number only."

"Suits me."

"And by agreement of counsel we are going to keep this list confidential, alright?"

"Suits me, too."

"Alright. Number . . .."

"One." He seemed eager to get started on the list.

"Young man Number 1, have you ever had any sexual contact with that young man?"

"Yes, I have."

"On how many occasions?"

"Many, but I don't have a number."

"More than ten?"

"Yes."

We then spent a long time with me going down the list of 42 names and I asked for each of the boys whether he molested them, if so, how many times, where it occurred, how old the boy was when it started and how old the boy was when it ended. It was surreal because he discussed very matter-of-factly the molestation of dozens of boys like we were talking about a grocery list. He quibbled with some of the details and some of the names, but for the most part he admitted molesting almost every name on The List, and even added some additional names. He admitted giving drugs to some of the boys and he surprised us by telling us he started molesting Porter-Gaud students when he was a volunteer at the school before he was hired in 1972. Apparently, the Hammond incident that year was not his first attempt to molest a student at the school. I am convinced that he testified truthfully to most of the questions. He refused to implicate the school or Grimball and Alexander. He also maintained that the boys were older when the sexual contact started than the boys say. I think he did this to try to reduce his culpability in others' eyes. There was, however, a moment when he seemed to blame the boys for their own molestation.

"Did you have that feeling with any of the victims at the criminal hearing; that it didn't happen the way they said it happened?"

"Yes."

"Did you feel like the judge didn't get an accurate picture of you or your conduct at that plea hearing?"

"Yes. He didn't know me. Let me . . . can I say something?"

"Sure."

"I realized why they had to write what they wrote. This thing happened in full agreement. But here they are with wives and all now. They have to make me look like the villain and they look like the little saint, which I can understand. I have no problem with that. So that they can say yeah . . . but these people, in my opinion, except for the age and my response, were just as guilty as me, and just as cooperative. But some of them even went to add things that were not true."

"Let me make sure I understand what you are saying. You are saying aside from the age and the fact that you are a teacher, you are suggesting they were cooperative? They were just as cooperative as you were?"

"Absolutely."

"A 12-year-old and a 15-year-old child?"

"Yes, absolutely." He grinned when he said this.

I was livid. I left the room hurriedly, and my rage was apparent to others. It was 6:15 in the evening, and for the first time, Fischer seemed to be blaming the victims, just like Porter-Gaud was. I was walking across the empty cafeteria at a pretty good pace when Wells Dickson started calling from behind me. I didn't turn around. He ran to catch up with me and asked me to stop.

"David, I know you're angry, but he's not saying what you think he's saying. Ask him to explain what he means."

"And give him the chance to blame these boys some more?" My voice was pretty loud.

Wells, in his calm manner, said, "No, that's not what he is saying. What he has described to me is that he did not physically rape any of these boys. He wants people to understand that for whatever reason. That he did not use force. He acknowledges, and has acknowledged today, that it was wrong and that he was responsible, but he just wants you and everyone else to know that these kids were not fighting him off. Now, you and I know that that was out of fear of him, but he doesn't get that. So, I'm asking you to come back in there and let him explain that to you on the record."

I just walked away from Wells. He went back into the room. I took several minutes to calm down. I told myself that just because Fischer said it doesn't make it true. I knew it had been a good day for our side so far, and I should wrap it up before Fischer decided to take some more pot shots. As I was walking back to the room, Wells emerged again. "He's got some more information on one of the victims that he wants to put on the record."

"What is it?" I asked sarcastically.

"He says that one of the names on your list that he denied, if you change the spelling a bit, is another victim. He says he just recalled it. It's number 14. So, ask him about that. Come on David, he doesn't want these victims any madder at him than they already are. Let him explain what he meant."

Ten minutes later, we went back on the record. "Tell me . . . clarify for me your position on the consensual nature, if you will, or the cooperative nature of these young men."

"Alright. I was responsible. I was wrong. And I didn't mean to say that they were cooperative in the sense that they came on. There was no, you know . . ."

"Is what you mean by that that you never physically forced yourself on them?"

"Correct."

"Is that what you mean by that?"

"Exactly."

"But you would agree, though, that your position as a teacher and your position as an adult . . ."

"For that I'm responsible."

." . . that had an influence on them?"

"That's right. Exactly."

"Were you actually trained or instructed while you were at Porter-Gaud that sexual contact with any student was inappropriate?"

100

"No."

"What about at any school you ever taught at? Have you ever learned that?"

"No. I knew better. I guess deep down I realized, yeah, because I hid it. I knew it was wrong."

"That is all the questions I have. Thank you."

"Thank you."

Justin Lucey had a few follow up questions. "You know, sir, I sat down here at the end of the table and listened to David Flowers go through a number of victims with you. Of course, I have already spent all day asking you about a number of things, including victims. Several impressions came to mind. The first one is that the Hammond complaint was essentially the right complaint, maybe the wrong boy but the right complaint?"

"Yes sir."

"And that if, in fact, if the Hammond matter or you had been fully investigated at that time Porter-Gaud may well have learned of your sexual attraction to young boys?"

"I agree with you."

"It also struck me, sir, so many boys, so many schools, so many years. It's just totally disbelievable that your associates would not have had a good idea of what was going on."

Robinson objected, "Object to the form, if there is a question there."

Justin ignored her. "Do you agree with me, sir?"

"I have never given that any thought, to be absolutely honest with you. I just thought it was just a secret."

"Well, here we are, sir, at the end of a long day. We have discussed a lot of victims, a lot of years, a lot of parents that you knew, a lot of schools. Would you agree with me that it's rather disbelievable that your associates did not know what was going on?"

Robinson objected again.

"When I think about it now I can agree with you, yes. But I don't think they did. If they did, they didn't say anything."

"Well, you never said anything to Bishop Alexander about anything he was doing either, right?"

"Never."

"It was the rule?"

Robinson objected again.

Justin tried it a different way, "You didn't talk about other people's private matters?"

"No, I did not."

"So, it's not surprising that they didn't talk to you about yours, correct?"

Another objection.

"No."

I thought these questions by Justin were outstanding. That was the end of it. We all knew that that was probably the last time any of us would ever see Eddie Fischer.

CHAPTER 15

Two weeks after Fischer's deposition, Porter-Gaud's lawyers deposed Carlos Salinas. It was similar to the depositions they took of the other victims: invasive and offensive. Robinson asked him, among other things, for his birthdate and social security number, which are usually provided privately because a deposition is considered a public record. She knew that and asked anyway. She also used the names of many victims that she and the other lawyers had already agreed to keep confidential. At the time, Carlos was a lobbyist for Amnesty International and resided in Washington, DC. He traveled to Charleston to give his sworn testimony and was represented at the deposition by a lawyer other than Gregg and me.

He began attending Porter-Gaud in the seventh grade. He testified he thought he first met Fischer the following year, when he was in the eighth grade. Fischer befriended him and bought him a milk pass, so Carlos could get free milk at lunch. Then in his ninth-grade year, Fischer was his Physics teacher.

When Carlos was in the tenth grade, Fischer approached him in the hall at school one day and told the boy that he had had a dream about him. He wanted to tell Carlos about the dream but couldn't do so at school. Fischer invited the student to visit him at a beach house which Fischer said was his. Carlos agreed to meet with him the following weekend.

While walking on the beach, Fischer disclosed that in his dream, Carlos had asked Fischer to teach him about sex. Carlos was surprised and disappointed because he was expecting the dream to be more profound and life altering. During the discussion about the dream, Fischer also told Carlos that "he ran a group of gigolos, young boys would have sex with older women and get paid for it and that he wanted me to be one of those boys." He offered to train the boy to be part of the group, but it would require them to go to Fischer's house. At the house, Fischer sexually assaulted Carlos. Robinson asked details about the abuse and Carlos answered candidly and confidently.

She asked why he decided to sue Porter-Gaud. His response was remarkable. "I didn't decide to sue Porter-Gaud. We wrote Porter-Gaud a letter in January [1998] saying that we wanted to meet with them and talk about what had happened and to begin a process so that nothing like this would ever happen again. Porter-Gaud never replied. I came down [to Charleston] once in '98, [my lawyer] sent a follow-up letter saying I'm going to be in town, let's talk. Porter-Gaud didn't have the courtesy to reply. That's not how we expected this to happen. By that point we decided to pursue the only remedy that Porter-Gaud seemed to understand. It was considerable time that elapsed between the letters, it wasn't like we sent a letter and then the next week say, oh, well, game's over." Robinson asked what he hoped to accomplish in a sit-down meeting with Porter-Gaud. "I wanted Porter-Gaud to acknowledge that something horrible had happened in their school. I wanted Porter-Gaud to acknowledge wrong to the people that had been wronged, acknowledge the failure, but also to make sure that steps were taken so that something like this could never happen again there. Like bringing in people who know how to troubleshoot this kind of stuff. There's a whole literature, a whole methodology to make sure something like this doesn't happen with child care providers. So, I wanted the school to not just say, 'okay, we goofed', but to say, 'and this is how we're going to move in a proactive direction, this is how we're going to show that we've learned from this'. I also thought it would be important for the school to provide a fund for psychological counseling for people that had been in fact traumatized because of Fischer. I think by then I had spoken with Kevin Dunn and I felt very strongly about the need for good psychological counseling. I hadn't quite realized that I needed to talk a bit, too." She asked if his goals had changed. He replied, "They've become stronger. I see them more clearly. I knew then that it was the right thing to do, I know now that it's very much the right thing to do."

We finally found Thomas Farin, the former headmaster of College Prep School, living in Pittsburgh. Gregg planned to take his deposition at the Pittsburgh International airport. Only Gregg and Robinson attended. The deposition was short because Gregg got right to the point, asking him about his contacts with Alexander at the time Fischer was trying to get hired at his school and the process of hiring him in 1982.

"Can you describe for us the process Edward Fischer would have to go through to apply for and get a job at College Prep?"

"Very briefly, we had a personal interview, he submitted a resume, and I guess the only other thing I can recall is that I also talked with the administrator at Porter-Gaud."

"Do you recall who that administrator was?"

"Skip Alexander."

Gregg walked him through the hiring process and asked what Alexander had to say about Fischer.

"Skip Alexander came to College Prep one day and, please keep in mind this was a number of years ago from my memory, what I remember is that the first thing he said is, could I get a tour of College Preparatory School, that he had never been there before. So, we walked around, and that sort of struck a very casual, friendly tone. I had known Skip Alexander before that time. We talked rather casually. In fact, after he had left, one of the, I guess, remaining feelings I had was that nothing much of substance was really said."

"Alright. Was there any discussion of Edward Fischer?"

"Very briefly, yes."

"And what was the substance of what you recall of him discussing about Edward Fischer?"

"The substance, as I recall it, was he, he being Skip Alexander, talked briefly about the number of years that Eddie Fischer had been at Porter-Gaud, some of the things that he had done and, I guess, basically, that was it."

"Was there any comment favorable or unfavorable in terms of a recommendation?"

"There was, certainly, nothing unfavorable said because I remember not asking him any questions. I just sort of listened to a few things that he had to say."

Gregg then showed him one of the discovery responses we got from the defense and asked for his reaction. "Referring to Interrogatory No. 5 on the second page where it picks up at the top. Right at the end of the first line there, the sentence reads, 'Upon information and belief, the late James Bishop Alexander provided information to Thomas Farin, the headmaster of College Prep School that put him on notice that Edward Fischer was not a good candidate for a position that entailed working with children.'" Robinson had changed the name of the school official and signed this response.

"Do you see that text?"

"I do, in fact, see that text."

"That same substance is repeated in response to Interrogatory 24, and the answer is at the bottom of Page 2 and carries over to Page 3. Is that response is accurate from your recollection?"

"No."

"What did officials of Porter-Gaud communicate to you about Eddie Fischer when you were considering hiring him at College Prep?"

"I guess to be honest, I don't remember anything, specifically, they may have said that may have been neutral or positive, but I know nothing like this was said."

Robinson would not look at either man. She had been caught fabricating evidence again. It was clear she had not spoken to Farin before providing this response to us, which confirmed that she simply made it up.

"Alright. Had something been said that put you on notice that he was not a good candidate for working with children, how would you have factored that in to your decision about hiring him?"

"Simply put, I would not hire him."

"And for what reason?"

"For the obvious reason that he is not in a position to work with children."

"Was there any point at which anyone from Porter-Gaud related to you the circumstances under which Eddie Fischer left Porter-Gaud?"

"No."

"Let me show a letter from Berkeley Grimball to Eddie Fischer. What I want to know is if you have ever seen this document."

"Again, I don't believe. So, I mean, certainly, the language of this would have caught my attention."

"What would catch your attention about this letter if you had it at the time you were making the hiring decision as to Eddie Fischer?"

"Because Berkeley Grimball says he is genuinely sorry that his career has ended the way it did. That is, certainly, one thing. And he also goes on to say, it is my hope that something good will come out of this experience. Positive steps to ensure that nothing like this will . . . no. I have not seen that letter before."

"And had you seen that letter at the time you were making the hiring decision, would you have undertaken any steps of inquiry?"

"Absolutely."

"And what would you have done?"

"I probably would have talked to Berkeley Grimball."

"Would it have been significant for you to know that when he left Porter-Gaud it was under circumstances of him being asked to leave because he had acted sexually inappropriate with a student?"

"It would have been very important."

"In what way?"

"If that had been the case, I would not have hired him."

"As a former headmaster, what you would say about a school giving a job recommendation for such a teacher being well-fitted to continue as a teacher?"

Robinson objected to this question.

"I am trying to be diplomatic and at the same time reflect my real feelings. But I guess the word despicable comes to mind."

"Does it violate any professional standard to give a positive recommendation for a teacher known to act sexually inappropriately with a student and not disclose that?"

Robinson objected again.

"I would say it violates professional, personal, ethical, religious standards."

"As headmaster of College Prep in 1982, could a teacher have kept his job at College Prep if he was known to act sexually inappropriate with a student?"

"No."

Although Farin's testimony was not as strong as we had hoped for, it was still powerful. The jury would hear that Alexander made a personal visit to College Prep within 30 days of Fischer's departure from Porter-Gaud, and that Alexander did not disclose that Fischer was sexually interested in children.

Next, we deposed Ralph Nordlund, a widely respected former teacher at Porter-Gaud. His testimony was helpful enough that we decided as soon as it concluded to call him as our witness at trial.

Gregg and Robinson also flew to Honolulu to depose Ted

Richardson, a former principal at Porter-Gaud. His deposition was notable for two reasons: he was the first person affiliated with Porter-Gaud to admit the handling of Fischer was a mistake, and he said the "probation" that Fischer was supposedly placed on by Grimball was a figment of Grimball's imagination. It is interesting to note that in spite of this "probation", Fischer received annual raises from the school, and Grimball promoted him to the position of disciplinarian of the school. Students who acted up were sent directly to Fischer for punishment by Grimball and Alexander, funneling potential prey right into his clutches.

In spite of the accomplishments thus far, we were constantly frustrated by the fact that so few victims came forward to assist in the civil litigation. We certainly understood their reluctance to thrust themselves into the public eye merely because they were victims of abuse. Survivors of abuse, particularly males, tend to avoid reliving their abuse and the shame they are often left with. We were hoping, however, that more of them would step forward to support Guerry and Kevin. The stories of many of Fischer's victims were similar - in fact almost identical - but one Porter-Gaud student stood out from the rest. Of the 40 or 50 victims we knew of, only one told his parents at the time the assault occurred. Only one. And it was his courageous act that caused Edward Fischer to leave Porter-Gaud in 1982. But he had chosen to not come forward.

Things were going okay in some respects, but we still needed to prove what happened in 1982. The defendants had filed motions to dismiss the cases, and they were likely to be granted if we could not prove what the school knew when they recommended Fischer to the public-school district. We were stymied because we knew who the 1982 victim was, but I did not want to contact him; we needed that victim or his family to come forward. Throughout my career, I had never called a victim out of the blue. As a survivor of sexual abuse, I believe it is the victim's prerogative who he or she tells and when. We believed he didn't even know that we knew who he was.

After waiting for almost two years, I made a decision that would alter the trajectory of the case, and my life.

CHAPTER 16

When I called the 1982 Student for the first time in the fall of 1999, he was shocked and annoyed that I knew who he was and that I knew that he was one of Fischer's victims. I told him who I was and that if he didn't want to talk to me that I would hang up the phone and never bother him again. He paused for a long time before he said he knew who I was and asked what I wanted. I briefly explained to him what we had learned so far and why I was calling him. I told him he and his family were the only ones who could testify about what happened in 1982 and the extent of the school's knowledge when Fischer resigned. He asked what specifically I was asking him to do. I told him sworn statements or affidavits from him and his parents would probably be sufficient, but I could not promise Porter-Gaud would not be drag them into the litigation. He told me he wanted to think about it.

Over the next few days, I got several phone calls from people in Charleston letting me know the 1982 student was asking about me; he was checking me out. Apparently, he was comfortable with the responses he got, because he called me back and said he wanted to meet for lunch. I drove to Charleston the next day, and our lunch lasted more than three hours. He wanted to know what was going on in the cases and what we were seeking to do. I shared with him what we had learned and what we thought we could prove. I explained to him why his family was critical to proving what Alexander knew when he recommended Fischer to College Prep and the public-school district. At the end of the discussion, he said he would help. He offered to draft affidavits and send them to me. He didn't ask any questions about what we wanted in them. I just told him we needed to know what happened in 1982 that caused Fischer to leave the school.

A few days later, I received the sworn statements in the mail. The affidavits laid out in detail what happened in 1982 and the family's attempts to have the school do the right thing. I forwarded the affidavits to Robinson, and she immediately wanted to take the depositions of the student and both of his parents. I called her and told her she really didn't want to do that because the family did not want to be deposed and, as she could tell from the affidavits, it was not in her clients' interests to annoy this family. When witnesses give damning testimony against a party, challenging them or their testimony in a deposition merely gives them an opportunity to expound on their testimony and make the situation even worse for the opposing party. Robinson was so hell-bent on intimidating witnesses and "representing her client" that she could not understand the peril here.

She said it was her right to depose them and insisted on doing so as soon as possible.

The depositions of the student and both of his parents were scheduled for December 7, 1999. We set them all for one afternoon so the family would be inconvenienced as little as possible.

The defense wanted to start with the student. He showed up promptly at 1 p.m. wearing a suit and with his own counsel, an outstanding lawyer named Brian Bevon. Stepp was the only lawyer present for the defense. He began with a very pleasant tone, something Robinson had never used. After several questions about the former student's employment and personal information, he presented the affidavit and asked the witness to verify it.

"This is an affidavit which I prepared, and my signature appears on it."

"What were the circumstances that caused you to prepare this?"

"I spoke with David Flowers, who said that in this case it looked like it was time for me to be deposed, as well as my parents. In lieu of being deposed, I persuaded him that I would prepare an affidavit and my parents would as well."

He then went on to testify about how Fischer had taken him to his house in May 1982, under the pretext of taking the boy to a local college to meet a track coach there. The boy was a freshman who was on the track team at Porter-Gaud. Fischer had already engaged the boy in conversation several times at the school expressing concern because Fischer had heard that an older girl at the school was sending notes to the boy, wanting to date him. Fischer had taken it upon himself to intervene in the situation to warn the boy away from the girl because her boyfriend might beat him up and the girl was far too experienced for the young boy. To Stepp's credit, he did not make this victim recount in detail what happened at Fischer's house that day, as Robinson had insisted on doing with all of the victims she deposed. The former student then testified about telling his mother about the assault. His mother told his father and his parents contacted Alexander to report the incident. Alexander insisted the parents bring the boy to Porter-Gaud so he could question the boy. When he got the opportunity to do so, all Alexander asked the boy was to describe the interior of Fischer's home. When the boy described it in accurate detail, Alexander asked no more questions and was satisfied that the account of the assault was true.

I asked no questions. The witness was credible and, though at times he was very uncomfortable, he answered all of the questions in a straightforward and confident tone. It seemed that he wanted to let the school know he was not going to be intimidated.

Next was the 1982 student's mother. She seemed to be quite nervous when she entered the room. The student's lawyer stayed. Bobby got right to the questioning. Again, after questions about her personal background, he brought out her affidavit. "Did you ever talk to Mr. Flowers about it?"

"No. I don't know Mr. Flowers."

"Okay. But do you know Mr. Flowers now seated over there?"

She looked over at me, smiled pleasantly and said, "Thank you." She held the look longer than expected, conveying that she was grateful for what Gregg and I were doing for our clients

She went on to testify about learning about the assault from her son and the communications she and her husband had with Alexander. She said Alexander told them he would report the incident to the board of trustees, and he would be in touch with them. When Alexander later contacted them, he indicated that the board had held a special meeting about the incident, that Fischer was no longer teaching at Porter-Gaud or anywhere else, and that Alexander would see that Fischer got counseling.

When Stepp was through, he looked like he regretted that this deposition had been scheduled. He knew that this day had not been good for his case. The mother seemed perturbed about being there. She also seemed to me to be uninformed about Porter-Gaud's failure to do what Alexander told her that he was going to do. I decided to ask her just a few questions.

"As you learned earlier, my name is David Flowers. Before today we have never met, have we?"

"No. We have not."

"Have we ever even spoken before?"

"I don't believe so. No."

"In any of the conversations that you had with Mr. Alexander, did he ever tell you that Eddie Fischer was on probation at the school?"

"No."

"Did he ever tell you that the school had information that he had approached a boy inappropriately at any time before what happened to your son?"

"No. He led me to believe that this was new to him. It was shocking to him what we said."

"When you left Mr. Alexander's office and after you had the conversation with him about the board meeting, after you had all the communications with him, were you comfortable that the school was going to handle this in a manner that you thought appropriate?"

"Yes. Yes. As well as it could be done, yes."

"Now, you said you felt they protected your son and you also talked about you always had something in the back of your head about other children."

"Yes."

"Did you feel at that time that what they said they were going to do was going to protect other children?"

"Yes."

"That was one of your interests at the time?"

"Oh, yes."

"Has anybody from Porter-Gaud ever told you that Edward Fischer was not fired?"

"No."

"Has anyone ever told you that he was allowed to resign?"

She had a puzzled look on her face. "No. No."

"Has anyone ever told you that Berkeley Grimball offered to help Mr. Fischer in the future if he needed it?"

"No."

"Would you be surprised to learn that?"

"You mean in the context of teaching?"

"Yes. Anything. If, for example, Mr. Grimball were to say to Eddie Fischer, 'If there's anything I can ever do for you, please call'. Would it surprise you to learn something like that?"

"It would surprise me."

"Now, you said you also learned that Eddie Fischer was working at another school?"

"Uh-huh."

"That was College Prep?"

"I believe it was. Yes."

"As a mother, as a parent, particularly a parent who had taken an issue like this to Porter-Gaud, what would you expect Porter-Gaud to do if another school called to inquire about Eddie Fischer?"

"I would expect them to tell, tell another school about him certainly."

"Would you expect them to put something in Edward Fischer's personnel file about the allegation?"

Stepp objected to this question.

"Yes."

"And for both of those, if a subsequent employer called or something in the personnel file, would those be something to protect other children?"

Stepp objected again.

"Yes."

"Has anyone at Porter-Gaud or anyone else ever told you that within 30 days of you bringing this to Porter-Gaud's attention that Mr. Alexander personally went to College Prep to talk about Edward Fischer with the headmaster there?"

Another objection.

"No."

"Would it surprise you to learn that?"

Stepp tried to break the flow, "Object to the form."

The witness did not pay him any attention, "Unless it was to say what he had done, yes, it would surprise me."

"How would it make you feel if he had a conversation with the headmaster at College Prep and never told him about this?"

Stepp knew these questions were hurting his client, "Object to the form."

"I would be very angry."

"How would it make you feel if he had a conversation with the headmaster at College Prep and never told him anything negative about Eddie Fischer?"

Stepp objected yet again.

"I would be very upset. Yes, I would be very upset." She was, in fact, becoming upset.

"Why is that? Why would you be upset?"

"It would be a betrayal not only to us and our child, but to other children, to the school because they also represent that school, which we believed in."

"Has anyone ever told you about a written recommendation that was made on behalf of Eddie Fischer by Major Alexander . . ."

"No."

." . . to the public-school district . . ."

"No."

." . . here in Charleston County?"

"No, never."

"Would it surprise you to learn that Major Alexander gave a

recommendation in writing for Eddie Fischer to the Charleston County School District?"

"That would surprise me very much."

"How would that make you feel?"

"Angry."

"Why?"

"Again, because it would be a betrayal and it would be . . . we put our trust in the school. This man reassured us. That would make me very upset and it would be terrible."

"Would it surprise you to learn that Porter-Gaud did not do anything to get Edward Fischer counseling?"

Stepp objected again.

"Yes, it would."

"Why?"

"Because they said they would."

"Is that what you expected them to do?"

"What I expected and when I did find out that he was teaching again, that's what I thought happened. I thought he . . . and I didn't know about anyone but my son that this had ever been, and I thought he was being watched carefully."

"And after your conversations and assurances you have from Mr. Alexander, did you ever feel the need to check back with him to see if they had done it or did you feel comfortable that he had done what he said?"

"I felt comfortable he had done what he said. He was very reassuring about it. I believed he had the children's best interest at heart and that school."

"That's all the questions I have."

I didn't think Stepp would want to ask her any more questions, but I was surprised. "You said Major Alexander said that Porter-Gaud would protect other children. When did he say that?"

"In our conversation with him about . . . I mean we felt the school was a good school. We felt the students had a good education and that this was an anomaly, this was something that came up and could be dealt with. We had that much confidence in the school. I had that much confidence . . . .."

"I'm trying to find out . . ."

." . . in what Major Alexander said. Excuse me. I'm sorry."

"I'm trying to find out what he said. Did Major Alexander say, 'we're going to not only protect your son, we're going to protect other children', or is this a conclusion or impression that you had from something different that he said?"

"From what he said, his interest was in protecting not only our son, but other students and that's why Mr. Fischer would be let go. He was very reassuring. Yes. They had it well in hand. I trusted that they did from what he said."

"And specifically, he was talking about other students?"

"Yes. Oh, yes. Oh, yes. This was a concern."

"Well, why didn't you say something about that when you dictated this statement? Why didn't you say somewhere in here that Major Alexander had told you specifically that the school was going to protect other students, if it doesn't? I don't see something to that effect in there. I'm curious as to why you didn't mention that when you dictated this in October."

"Oh, we're talking about it now and I'm telling you as I recall it all. I don't know. But it was a concern."

"Did you have a conversation with your son about those events? Did the two of you all talk about them before you dictated this?"

118

"No. He asked me to recall it as I remembered it in my own words and that's what I did."

"Okay. And did you make your best effort to recall it accurately and completely at that time?"

"Yes. You know, I haven't . . . this is something I kind of put away over the years and I am very proud of the person that my son is, and I felt we had dealt with it and gone beyond it. We had gotten past it. And then all of a sudden there it is, and you are writing it down after 17 years, you know. So that I didn't say that just means I didn't . . . it was so . . . it was an emotional thing even then and as we speak about it now, I can tell you more."

"You said also in your testimony that Major Alexander told you that Fischer would no longer be teaching."

"Yes. Yes."

"Was that important to you?"

"It was important to me that other children . . . this man had a teaching . . . a position of trust from students, children and parents. Yes. It was important. But if he . . . it was his life, also. This is a man's life and if they could deal with it and get him well or get him past whatever it was, good."

"When you realized that Mr. Fischer was teaching at College Prep, did you feel that you had any responsibility to verify whether he had obtained any counseling or been through any treatment?"

"No. I felt that the school had taken care of it. Our son was doing well. We were all doing well. I felt we had dealt with it."

"Did you think you had any responsibility to report your son's episode to the administration at College Prep?"

"No. I thought they knew."

"Did you feel any responsibility to make sure that they knew?"

"No. I trusted. I trusted Porter-Gaud."

"That's all I have." It was pretty evident on Bobby's face that he wished he had not reopened that can of worms.

I could not resist another opportunity: "Did College Prep ever call you for a recommendation or a comment on Eddie Fischer?"

"No."

"Had they called you, what would you have told them?"

"I believe I would have told them the truth. I would have told them what happened. Yes."

She seemed genuinely angry when the deposition was over. She and Brian Bevon left quickly.

Bevon returned a few minutes later with the father. He was fairly stiff, but professional. I think seeing his wife's demeanor in passing upset him. Bobby began the same way, asking about employment and personal information, and the same preliminary questions as he asked the mother about the preparation of his affidavit.

He then recounted the same story that his wife and son did. There were a few moments that differed.

Stepp, with the father's affidavit in his hand, asked, "You say that she, referring to your wife, told me that a teacher, Edward Fischer, had raped our son."

"Right."

"Did she use the word rape?"

"Yes."

"Now, in your second paragraph in the second sentence, you say, 'I told Alexander very specifically and graphically what had happened, and he said, quote, it sounds like things have gotten a little out of hand, but we really don't know what happened, period, close quote.' I mean that's . . .'"

"I mean I was . . . I will never forget that because I was absolutely incensed that here's a man . . . I was telling him of a . . . I mean there were so many unacceptable things from my point of view and, you know, his answer was 'we'll have to look into this. It sounds like things got out of hand.' You know, that's not what I was looking for." The father's anger, even all these years later, was palpable.

"Yes. I mean what were you looking for? What did you expect Mr. Alexander to do?"

"I mean you have to understand, I was ready to go to the legal system. I mean I wanted this man in jail. I wanted him fried, so to speak. I mean, I say that. You have to understand, you know . . ."

"I understand the context of it."

." . . at the time, I mean . . . yes. And I didn't want to hear, 'well, we'll have to investigate this', like questioning the truth of what I told him."

"Well, when you went to see Major Alexander, did you go to tell him that you wanted Fischer prosecuted?"

"Absolutely."

"Sitting here today, do you know that Fischer continued to teach after he left Porter-Gaud?"

"I mean after . . . at that time I didn't know, and I didn't know for some time, but today I know. Yes."

"Well, how did you become aware that Fischer had continued to teach after he left Porter-Gaud?"

"When all this mess became public and I began to read about it in the newspaper."

"You never had any conversations with anybody who told you that he was teaching?"

"I did not."

"I don't have any further questions. Thank you, Sir. Thank you."

Stepp had clearly had enough for one day.

I wanted to follow up because it was apparent that the father also did not know the whole story.

"You said in your testimony that you told Major Alexander that you intended to go to the police."

"I did."

"What was his reaction to that?"

"At this time, I don't specifically remember what his reaction was, but I do recall his general reaction was . . . it was almost blasé, you know. I told him something that was enormous to me and he said, 'well, you know, I need to look into this. Well, this and that', you know."

"Were you comfortable after your meetings with Major Alexander that he was going to look into this?"

"I was comfortable in the sense that if something didn't happen, I knew I was going to go to the police. I mean my son specifically, my wife, I mean this was not . . . you know, these things don't happen and you . . . once you get over the shock, you sit down, and we did this as a family, talked to our son and he expressed his wishes. As I mentioned, he enjoyed being at Porter-Gaud. He didn't want to endanger that. And, you know, if we went to the police, it would be . . . he felt that he couldn't go on at Porter-Gaud. But that was . . . in my own mind, if something didn't happen, the least being that Eddie Fischer was fired, I mean I knew I had the option of going to the police. Just because a week or so passed didn't mean I still couldn't go. In my own mind, that was my option."

"And did you then learn that Eddie Fischer somehow was no longer at Porter-Gaud?"

"That's correct."

"Did anyone from Porter-Gaud communicate that to you?"

"They did not."

"You found it out through the grapevine or something?"

"Specifically, I don't remember how I knew that. I can't tell you. I don't remember. But I do remember that Mr. Fischer was gone, which was my objective, my goal."

"In your meetings with Major Alexander, did he ever tell you that Eddie Fischer was on probation at Porter-Gaud?"

"He did not."

"Did he ever tell you that Eddie Fischer had previously propositioned a young man in an inappropriate way?"

"He did not."

"Is that something you would like to have known as a parent?"

"Absolutely."

"Even before this happened to your son?"

"Absolutely."

"As a parent of a Porter-Gaud student, would you have liked to know if a teacher there was on probation for being sexually inappropriate with a student?"

Stepp objected to the question. The father didn't even hesitate in answering.

"In a school like that, yes."

"Why?"

"Porter-Gaud, because of the nature of the school being in terms of classrooms, smaller classrooms, being more intimate, I think the students on the whole have a wonderful relationship with their teachers. It's a much better . . . at least my perception is it's a much better relationship than some of the public schools, that's why he went there. And consequently, the students and the teachers are much, much closer as peers. My son was with other teachers. And it's a certain closeness in doing projects and obtaining advice about all kinds of things, you know. And, consequently, if the teacher and the student are closer to each other, yes, I would like to know things like that. I think that's very important."

"Had anybody at Porter-Gaud ever told you that Eddie Fischer was on probation at Porter-Gaud?"

"No."

"Had anyone at Porter-Gaud ever told you that he had propositioned a young man prior to 1982?"

Stepp objected again, probably to try to break the rhythm of the moment.

"No."

"Do you know where Edward Fischer went to work after he left Porter-Gaud?"

"I do know. I do know. I remember reading about it in the paper at that time and I said, oh, how awful, but . . .."

"Would it concern you as a parent . . . as a parent generally, but as a parent specifically who was involved in an allegation like this, if someone from Porter-Gaud were to go visit a prospective employer for Fischer . . .."

Stepp objected before I even finish the question.

." . . to talk to them about employing Fischer?"

He reiterated his objection.

"I don't understand your question. I'm sorry."

I restated the question, slower this time, "Having been involved in this situation in 1982, and as a parent generally, if you were to learn that someone from Porter-Gaud went to another school in Charleston and discussed employing Eddie Fischer, would that concern you?"

Another objection.

"Yes. It certainly would."

"If you were to learn that person was Major Alexander, would that concern you?"

"The same way. It certainly would."

"If you were to learn that it occurred within 30 days of you meeting with Major Alexander, would that concern you?"

Yet another objection.

"I would be incensed."

"Why?"

"Well, after the second meeting, I mean it was, to me it was clear what happened and hopefully was clear to Major Alexander what had happened, and the one thing this man had no business in doing was teaching anywhere."

"This man being Fischer?"

"Correct."

"Did Alexander ever give you any indication that he was going to recommend Fischer for employment at any other school?"

Stepp objected.

"He did not."

"Would you consider it appropriate for him to recommend Eddie Fischer for employment at any other school?"

Another objection. This time, there was a hint of resignation in Stepp's voice.

"Absolutely not."

"If a subsequent employer were to contact Major Alexander, what would you have expected Major Alexander to tell that employer or prospective employer?"

"I would hope that Major Alexander or anybody subsequently would tell any prospective employer of Eddie Fischer to say, 'don't do this. There are so many rumors'."

"Don't do what?"

"Employ him. And I would tell them very specifically what had happened."

"If a subsequent employer or someone who is considering hiring Eddie Fischer called you, what would you tell him?"

"I would tell him exactly what I've been saying here, what happened and, in fact, if I had known that Eddie Fischer went to a school, I would have called the school."

"Why?"

"Because I think he . . . you know, I mean, what Mr. Fischer did is . . . I mean it's an awful thing. You trust your children to a teacher. There's an enormous trust involved in that and he betrayed that trust, among other things. You know, I think we all have a responsibility to avoid that."

"And you say had you known that he was applying at other schools?"

"I would call the school up."

"Before this became public and you said you started reading about it in the newspaper, did you know that anyone from Porter-Gaud had ever given a written recommendation to the public-school district here in Charleston on behalf of Eddie Fischer?"

Stepp: "Objection."

"I did not."

"Do you know that today?"

"No."

"Would it surprise you to learn that Major Alexander gave a written recommendation to the public-school district on behalf of Eddie Fischer?"

Another objection.

"I would be very disappointed."

"And going back to 1982, would you have expected the school to put something in Edward Fischer's personnel file about this incident?"

"I would sure hope so."

"Is that something you would expect to find? If you were looking at a personnel file of Edward Fischer from Porter-Gaud School, would you expect to find some mention or some indication of this incident?"

Another objection.

"I would think so."

"No more questions."

Stepp declined any further questions.

I walked the father and the family's lawyer outside and they invited me to a café down the street for a cold drink. As I entered the door, I saw the 1982 student, his mother, and a young woman who I soon learned was the former student's wife. They invited me to join them. They had lots of questions for me about the cases. Apparently, they had heard the story Porter-Gaud was putting out that Gregg and I were making stuff up and grandstanding. As I answered their questions, and told them about the information we had gathered, they became more appalled than they already were. They asked to see a copy of the 1986 recommendation form that Alexander had filled out; they were incredulous when they read it. I told them how many victims we were aware of and how many we believed there might be. When we were finished, they offered to help further if they could; I told them I hoped we would never have to bother them again.

The family's testimony changed the litigation in that it was clear that when Grimball and Alexander allowed him to resign quietly, and when Alexander then recommended Fischer for future teaching jobs, they knew that Fischer not only had a sexual interest in young boys, but that he had sexually assaulted at least one Porter-Gaud student during school hours. It was explosive.

As a lawyer, I thought that their testimony was strong enough that the school, and its insurance company, would have to seriously consider settling all of the litigation. As a human being, I felt empathy for this family, and admiration for their courage.

CHAPTER 17

After the depositions of the 1982 student and his parents, Kevin's trial was looming. In the weeks leading up to it, Justin Lucey and another lawyer in Charleston settled their clients' cases with Porter-Gaud and its insurance company. The other lawyer was Gedney Howe, the same Gedney Howe who had turned Guerry away. After Fischer's plea hearing in April 1999, and after we had survived attempts by Porter-Gaud to have our cases thrown out on the statute of limitations, Howe had sought out clients victimized by Fischer and found two. When he settled their cases in the spring of 2000, he was simultaneously trying to get his young son admitted to Porter-Gaud but did not disclose this fact to his clients. He also didn't tell his clients he made substantial financial contributions to Porter-Gaud while he was representing them. His son was formally admitted to the school within days of the settlement. Howe was also given a seat on Porter-Gaud's Father's Committee shortly after the settlement. Later, Howe would represent Porter-Gaud in a case against its insurance company, and he would assert in legal papers that "everyone knew" these victims' cases were "worth millions of dollars." He chose to not mention in those papers that his two clients received far less in their settlements than any other victim of Edward Fischer, and he never told his clients their cases were worth "millions of dollars."

We wanted to try Kevin's case as soon as we could. When those other cases settled, our cases were the only ones left on the Charleston County court docket. Many lawyers urged us to settle because they thought we could not prevail against Porter-Gaud. Kevin's trial was finally set for May 24, 2000 before judge Daniel Pieper. Pieper was fairly new on the bench and he looked much younger than his 37 years. He was known as a smart and fair judge. Many people believed he was destined for a seat on one of South Carolina's appellate courts. He ran a very tight courtroom and did not suffer lawyers who were unprepared or whose legal arguments were not coherent or well thought out. He genuinely enjoyed legal discourse with lawyers who loved the law as much as he did. Sometimes he would get sidetracked on an issue only tangentially related to the matter before him, but which piqued his intellectual curiosity. We knew of no connection between him and Porter-Gaud. In fact, we knew he had grown up in Hanahan, a blue-collar community close to Charleston situated right next to my hometown of Goose Creek.

On the Thursday before the trial began, a witness named Charlie Bennett was in Gregg's office. We knew he was a friend of Alexander. We were preparing him to testify at the trial. During the conversation, he kept referring, for the first time, to a conversation he had with Alexander the same afternoon Alexander committed suicide. His memory about that event was uncannily precise. I was grilling him in order to prepare him for Bobby Stepp's anticipated cross-examination. When I pushed him on why he remembered that afternoon so vividly, he paused, looked at Gregg, and asked, "What if I pull a tape out of my pocket, if he thinks I'm not telling the truth?" As he said this, he gestured as if pulling something out of his shirt pocket. Gregg and I looked at each other.

Gregg asked, "Charlie, do you have some kind of tape?"

"Yes."

"What's on it?"

"My last conversation with Skip."

He went on to tell us that on the day Alexander drove to North Carolina to commit suicide, he had called Charlie Bennett and said he needed to see him. Charlie thought that because of what was going on with Fischer and Porter-Gaud, he might finally get an apology from Alexander for what he had done to Charlie as a student at Porter Military Academy, where Alexander molested him when he was a child. Charlie wanted a record of any such apology, so he decided to record the conversation.

Gregg and I didn't know what to do; we needed some time to think. We told Charlie we had something we needed to take care of, and we would call him. He left, and Gregg and I walked down the street to a corner café. Over cheeseburgers we discussed the tape, and what to do if it existed. We knew it could be Porter-Gaud's ticket to postponing the trial, which they had been trying desperately to do. We also knew it would be great ammunition to bolster Bennett's credibility and keep Stepp from pushing him around, and it might contain some damaging admissions by Alexander.

Gregg called Charlie and told him to bring us the tape.

Twenty minutes later, we were back in Gregg's office listening to the tape. It was unbelievable. Hearing Alexander's voice for the first time was eerie.

When Charlie had arrived at Alexander's home, they made some small talk, then Alexander got to the reason he had called Charlie over. "Um . . . I don't know if you want me to talk about this . . . these civil cases, and so forth. I don't want to put you in a situation that'd be uncomfortable for you. Nor do I want to bring you into anything. As you well know, they're about money."

Bennett responded, "I think it's about principle, isn't it? More than money?"

Alexander acknowledged this, "Well, part, yeah, yeah."

They chatted briefly about an unrelated matter, then Alexander said, "But uh . . . I am limited in what I can do. And my point in talking with you is that I have a . . . little . . . I have a little bit of cash, and I don't . . . . I could . . . I would like to make it available to you, to get over rough spots and things, uh . . ." He then gave Bennett many thousands of dollars, and went on to say, "Well, it's not something that can be put in writing. It has to be something that is between you and me, so that you don't get yourself in difficulty. Up and call me in . . . you call me to court or something like that. And, uh . . . cause there's possibly if anybody ever knew, and they asked, 'well, why'd he give you money? What's your relationship?' People are not going to understand." This appeared to be the closest that Alexander planned to give an apology.

Bennett interjected, "Alright. Well, I think I get the gist of what you're getting at. You're deeply embroiled in this thing with Eddie Fischer, and . . .."

Alexander cut him off. "I'm not embroiled in it. The . . . other than the fact that I made the terrible judgment of writing two letters. Thinking that it was . . .."

"Understood," Bennett said.

"Yes. Now, the second one, I didn't even remember having done it, but I've seen the thing and it was mine. I wrote it. I didn't write it, what I did was put some checks by it. The name, and his ability, and . . . and is there anything that to your knowledge is there any reason why he shouldn't teach? And I checked 'No', and it was the stupidest thing I have ever done."

Bennett tried to comfort him. "Well, I feel sorry for you, I tell you."

Alexander concluded the conversation with, "And that's the degree of my involvement with Eddie Fischer in the situation. He and I were friends, and poor judgment on my part really led to a horrific situation."

From the grave, Alexander had admitted that he did what we had been saying all along.

CHAPTER 18

The next day, the Friday before the trial began, Judge Pieper held a hearing to resolve all outstanding issues so the trial would run smoothly. He was a good trial judge in that he did not tolerate lawyers wasting the jury's time with matters that can be handled before the jury is ever seated. He routinely conducted hearings on Fridays to deal with such issues prior to the trial.

This hearing was notable for several reasons. First, Gregg was not able to be there because he was in a hearing in federal court, so I would have to handle all of it, including the legal arguments – usually Gregg's area – by myself.

Second, the defense had asked for extra security in the courtroom for the trial; they asserted that their clients were somehow in danger by being in the same courtroom with ours. My initial reaction when I saw their request a few days before this was to object to it, but Gregg astutely pointed out that extra police officers in the courtroom would send a message to the jury that this was a big case. Even though we did not oppose their motion, the judge denied it, saying he didn't see any reason to justify extra security.

Finally, during this hearing, Judge Rawl, the Porter-Gaud alum, came into the courtroom and sat right behind Robinson, his former law clerk, and glared at Judge Pieper. This was not only unusual, it was highly improper. It was clear to everyone present that he was sending a message to Pieper that he was in Porter-Gaud's corner. The feeling we had that Rawl was meddling in this litigation was now confirmed.

On Saturday afternoon before the trial started, Gregg realized that in all the chaos leading up to it, he forgot to have some exhibits enlarged and mounted on foam board. He knew we were in a bind and thought we wouldn't have them for his opening statement or the first few witnesses. It certainly wasn't harmful to our case in any real sense; it just meant the presentation we had planned wouldn't be as clean. Gregg called Susan from his office and asked her if she could run the documents somewhere to get them blown up. She took them to a local Kinko's, but she was told the store was backed up and could not possibly get the exhibits to her before Monday, or more likely Tuesday.

"But these are for a trial that starts Monday," she pleaded.

"What kind of trial?" the clerk asked.

"The Porter-Gaud trial. My husband is one of the lawyers in the case."

"For which side?" a nearby manager asked.

"The plaintiffs."

"We'll have them for you in a couple of hours." They were ready and in Gregg's office by 6 p.m. that evening. We knew the public had been following the case, but this was our first inkling that they were paying attention.

The next day, I arrived at the hotel in North Charleston where I was going to stay during the trial. While checking in, I asked if the staff could provide the local paper each morning so I could follow the local press coverage. The front desk clerk told me the hotel only provided a national paper, either the Wall Street Journal or USA Today. He asked why I wanted a local paper and I told him I was involved in the Porter-Gaud case. A man standing further down the counter, and who was apparently listening to the conversation, asked which side I was on. "The victims," I said.

"I'll have someone get the paper each morning and bring it to your room. Is 7:30 early enough?"

CHAPTER 19

Finally, the fateful Monday in May 2000 morning arrived. Courtroom C, the same courtroom in which Fischer had pled guilty the previous year, was packed with spectators, and the bailiffs had to ask some of them to stand in the hall so there was enough space in the courtroom for the potential jurors. We spent most of the morning picking a jury; the panel selected was made up of 10 women and two men. After lunch, as soon as the jurors were seated, the judge explained to them what opening statements were and then turned to Gregg to give the plaintiff's opening statement.

Gregg smiled at the judge, said, "Thank you, your honor," and stood. He strode over and paused in front of the jury, right next to an enlargement of Alexander's recommendation form. "Ladies and gentlemen, good afternoon. This case is about a school that lied. It lied about one of its teachers. This is the form on which the false information was conveyed. It is a form used by the Charleston County School District to get information about people who apply for jobs at the district. It is addressed to J.B. Alexander, a principal, and the assistant headmaster at Porter-Gaud School. It is signed by J. Bishop Alexander. It refers to a teacher named Edward Fischer.

"Mr. Fischer was a teacher at Porter-Gaud for about 11 years. He first got there in about 1972. In his first semester there, he asked a student to meet him outside of the school, after hours. He said some other things to the student which you will hear, and you will understand how

135

inappropriate they were. The boy's parents contacted the school and spoke with headmaster Berkeley Grimball. Grimball claims that he spoke with Fischer about the incident and also claims that he put Fischer on probation.

Pointing to the recommendation form, he continued, "Four years before assistant headmaster Alexander signed this, he and Grimball had found out that Mr. Fischer had sexually assaulted a student at Porter-Gaud School. One of their own.

"In 1982 some parents reported that Fischer had taken their son to his home and performed oral sex on him. The boy was only 15 years old. The boy reported it to his mom. The mother and father reported it to James Bishop Alexander. Alexander and Grimball let Fischer resign quietly.

"Then in 1986 the same people who made him resign, Mr. Alexander and Mr. Grimball, when they were called upon to give a recommendation for Fischer, they gave him a good recommendation. Overall the general rating is above average here. And it says down here, 'any physical defects or mental peculiarities? None known. In your judgment, is the above candidate well fitted for the above position, the teaching position? Yes.'"

"Based in part on this recommendation, Fischer got a job with the public-school district and went to work at James Island High School. After Mr. Fischer got to James Island High School, he sexually abused my client, Kevin Dunn.

"My name is Gregg Meyers. Seated with me at counsel table is David Flowers. Mr. Flowers and I are both attorneys, and we are handling this case for Mr. Dunn. Mr. Dunn is not here. He will be here, but he is not here now. He will spend as little of his time in this courtroom as he can because he knows that it will be stressful, and he knows what will be discussed in this courtroom are not pleasant events.

"There are other people who are not here. Berkeley Grimball, the former Headmaster of Porter-Gaud School, who was the supervisor of Mr. Alexander is not here. He passed away. We will hear from him by deposition. We took his testimony under oath before he passed, and we will read portions of that testimony to you.

"Mr. Alexander is not here either. Mr. Alexander committed suicide just days before he was scheduled to give testimony under oath. You will hear from a student that went back to Porter-Gaud School a few times, after he was expelled from the school to tell them that he was molested by Fischer and that Fischer is still teaching. He wanted their assistance in getting Fischer out of the education field and away from students. The school declined to help the former student. The school did nothing. And there are some other events you will hear about where the school got more information about Fischer's activities with students and did nothing.

"Kevin Dunn was invited by Mr. Fischer to go to his house when Kevin was 18 years old. He was a senior at James Island High School. Mr. Dunn was a shy boy who is now 29 years old. He didn't have Mr. Fischer for a teacher. Fischer was simply a teacher in his school. Because he was shy and very slight of build, Mr. Fischer targeted him. Fischer contacted Kevin's parents and told them, 'I will help your son come out of his shell and I will help him develop himself physically.' Kevin's parents then allowed their son to go to Fischer's house for dinner one night.

"Nothing inappropriate happened on Kevin's first visit. The second visit turned into a sexual event. Mr. Fischer is a predator. He is in prison, where he belongs for the rest of his life. He is another person who is not here. He has pled guilty to what he did to Kevin and other boys.

"The defendants in this case are the Porter-Gaud School because they knew about Fischer and didn't tell the truth; James Bishop Alexander . . . the estate of James Bishop Alexander because he knew about Fischer and he didn't tell the truth; and the estate of Berkeley Grimball because he knew and while he didn't affirmatively state anything false, he didn't do anything to stop Fischer. He didn't put anything in Fischer's personnel file about the incident in 1972, the supposed probation, Fischer's sexual interest in male students, or the incident in 1982 when he allowed Fischer to resign quietly. He allowed this to happen, and he was in charge.

"The other defendant is Mr. Fischer. Because no one at Porter-Gaud School ever said anything, Mr. Fischer kept using Alexander as a reference. That is how Alexander came to receive this recommendation form from the school district. Fischer was confident that Alexander would give him a good recommendation.

"For years, Kevin never said anything about this to anyone. In the fall of 1997, he heard that Mr. Fischer had been arrested. And you will hear from a former Porter-Gaud student, Guerry Glover, who finally went to the solicitor's office, reported Fischer, and had him prosecuted. He did this with no assistance or support from Porter-Gaud. When Mr. Dunn heard that Fischer had been arrested, he was in Columbia. Kevin feared that if he didn't come forward, Fischer might get off. He contacted the solicitor's office and in the course of the criminal prosecution of Fischer, Kevin met Guerry Glover and found out for the first time in 1997 that Porter-Gaud had known about Mr. Fischer and that the school had recommended Fischer for employment at James Island High School.

"Kevin was not having an easy time. He had been in college. He had done poorly as a student even though he had been a good student in high school. He became confused about whether he was heterosexual or homosexual. He abused alcohol. He abused drugs. He has only recently begun to get his life back together. That is why he is not here. He will come here, and he will testify.

"Kevin was ensnared by Mr. Fischer over a 10-month period, and there were somewhere between eight and 15 sexual assaults. When Mr. Fischer would call him to try to schedule dinner, Kevin would try to avoid him, but Kevin was paralyzed. He didn't know what to do. He didn't think he could tell anybody. He certainly didn't think he could tell his parents, and he told no one. And he went back. And every time, Mr. Fischer would say to him 'it won't happen again' and it would happen again.

"Kevin was a kid. He was 18. He was a kid. Mr. Fischer was in his 60s. Mr. Dunn was no match for Mr. Fischer.

"We are going to ask you at the end of this case for a substantial verdict . . . a substantial verdict. We do not want other students having the problems Mr. Dunn has had. We believe the tranquility and peace of a student is worth a lot, and a young person's life needs to not be changed this way when it is going that way. That is what the case is about.

"We believe we can prove this case to the standard Judge Pieper has just talked to you about, and we will show far more than just a little bit that these events are true. And we would ask for and appreciate your attention and appreciate your consideration for the problems Mr. Dunn has had that were avoidable if the school had done the right thing.

"Thank you very much."

Stepp rose from his chair quickly and passed Gregg between the counsel tables, nodding at Gregg as he passed. "Good afternoon, ladies and gentlemen. My name is Bobby Stepp. I think we met earlier today when you all were seated out there. But I wanted to tell you again who I was, and I want to introduce you to some of the people who are with me at counsel table for the purposes of this case. This is Laura Robinson, also an attorney, who is going to be helping me out.

"Now, we represent some of the defendants in this case, not all of them as I will tell you in a minute. We represent first and foremost the Porter-Gaud School. Now, that's a private school here in Charleston. It is affiliated with the Episcopal Church. And you may or may not have ever heard of it. It is located over west of the Ashley. And you will hear something about the history of that school during the course of this trial.

"I also represented, when this case began, Mr. Berkeley Grimball. As Mr. Meyers has told you, Mr. Grimball is now dead. He died last year in 1999 at the age of 77 years old. Mr. Grimball was the headmaster at Porter-Gaud and had a long history of affiliation with the school.

"Mr. Grimball obviously can't be with us. His estate today is represented by his widow, Mrs. Emily Grimball.

"Also, when this case initially began, I represented James Bishop Alexander. You will hear something about Mr. Alexander. He was sometimes known as Skip Alexander. And as Mr. Meyers has told you, Mr. Alexander is also dead. Yes, he took his own life sometime in 1998. So, you are not going to hear from him during the course of this trial. He will not be here to defend himself. His estate is represented by his brother Tom.

"Now, I appreciate this opportunity to come before you. His honor has already told you and I want to reemphasize that this courtroom is the place where disputes in our civilized society are decided, not on the battle field, not on the dueling ground, not in some joust, not in some tournament, not by fist and not by force, but here in this courtroom by means of evidence and the application of the law to the evidence that you hear. And you play the single most important part in that process.

"Your service as a juror is the highest civic duty that a private citizen can render. And on behalf of my clients, I really appreciate it. I appreciate you being here. I know this is disruptive to you, and it may or may not be a pleasant experience. This is a very emotional case. And you are going to hear about some things that you probably would prefer not to hear about, but they are a part of this case. And we're going to put the evidence before you so that you can ultimately render a fair verdict.

"Now, as his honor said, this is just my opportunity to give you a little preview about what some of that evidence is going to be and some of the witnesses that you are going to hear from.

"One fellow that you have already heard a great deal about is Mr. Eddie Fischer. I don't represent Eddie Fischer. Mr. Fischer is represented by Wells Dickson seated at the end of counsel table. Mr. Fischer is not my client. And as Mr. Meyers has pointed out, Mr. Fischer is not here. Mr. Fischer is in jail. He is serving a twenty-year sentence, and he is not going to be here. And you are going to hear evidence that Mr. Fischer committed a crime and has been punished for it.

"Now, Mr. Fischer was a teacher at Porter-Gaud for ten years, 1972 to 1982. He came there in 1972 which is, what, 28 years ago? And he left in 1982, which was 18 years ago. The last time that Eddie Fischer was employed by Porter-Gaud was 18 years ago.

"During the ten years that he was there, as Mr. Meyers has already suggested to you, two things happened. First, in 1973 a parent reported to Berkeley Grimball that Mr. Fischer had asked to meet that parent's son after school, meet him in front of a drug store after school, off the school grounds. The student was suspicious about that, so he went and told his brother, and his brother went down to the drug store to see if Mr. Fischer came. And, in fact, Mr. Fischer did come, and his brother saw him. No words were exchanged. Mr. Fischer left, and the brother then went home and told the student's parents. And the student's mother called the school and told Mr. Grimball. Now that's the sum and substance of this first episode. There was no sexual contact between Mr. Fischer and this student.

The parents were told. The school was told.

"Now, you will hear from Mr. Grimball's deposition that he confronted Mr. Fischer about that episode, and Mr. Fischer denied any impropriety. He said I went there because I wanted to help this student with his school work. You had Mr. Fischer saying that. You had the suggestion of something improper on the other side. Mr. Grimball told Mr. Fischer, 'if anything happens like this again, you're gone'.

"Ten years go by. 1982, the second episode happens. This one is a lot more serious, I will grant you. It involved actual sexual contact between Mr. Fischer and a student, and that student told his parents. And his parents told the school, and they came to see Mr. Alexander. And you are going to hear from those parents, depositions from the parents. And there is a little bit of conflict between them about what exactly they wanted the school to do. But one thing is clear. They wanted the school to get rid of Mr. Fischer. They wanted him gone from Porter-Gaud and gone he was. He was forced to resign then and there.

"Now, it was Mr. Alexander who was involved in that second incident. I think the testimony will be . . . you correct me if I'm wrong . . . that Mr. Grimball didn't even know about it until after Fischer had resigned. The parents didn't come see Mr. Grimball. They went to see Mr. Alexander.

"Now, four years after that in 1986 . . .

"Gregg, may I?" Stepp wanted to use the blow up of the recommendation form that Gregg had shown to the jury.

"Sure," Gregg replied.

"Mr. Alexander filled out this form. And the only thing he did, as far as we know, are put the marks on here and these words. 1986 . . . we do not know . . . we do not know . . . why Mr. Alexander did that. You're not going to hear any evidence in this case about why Mr. Alexander did that. Mr. Alexander is not here to tell us why he did it, although you are going to be asked to speculate about why he did it.

"Four years later, four years after the check marks were put on this document, in 1989 or '90, sexual contact began between the plaintiff in this case, Mr. Dunn, who is not here, and Mr. Fischer, in 1989 or 1990. That is seven years or eight years after Mr. Fischer had last taught at Porter-Gaud. And the evidence you will hear about that sexual contact is that the plaintiff was a senior at James Island High School and that he was 18 years old, an adult for all purposes of the law.

"And he had this contact with Mr. Fischer at Mr. Fischer's house, not on the school ground and not during school hours, but at night. He would go to Mr. Fischer's house for dinner with his parents' consent. He would drive himself there in his parents' car.

"Now, this went on. The plaintiff has said, and you will hear him say he wasn't sure when it started whether it was in that fall semester of 1989 or the spring of 1990. But it was definitively in the spring . . . at least of 1990, and it continued after the school year. It continued into the summer. And eventually the plaintiff went off from Charleston to Columbia and attended the University of South Carolina and became a freshman living away from home for the first time in his life.

"And you will hear evidence that after he left home and after he left Charleston and after he was in Columbia and after he was in a dorm, he began to change. He began to drink. He began to use drugs. He became estranged from his family. He lost his faith in God. All of these things happened to him while he was at USC while he was in college after he had terminated his contact with Mr. Fischer.

"Now, the plaintiff in this case never told anybody about what Mr. Fischer was doing. He did not tell a friend. He didn't tell another teacher. He didn't tell the principal of James Island. He didn't tell somebody at the Charleston County School District. He never told anybody, nobody. He kept his silence, and he didn't do anything. And he will tell you and you will hear him say that he knew what Mr. Fischer was doing was wrong, and he knew it from the very first day. Yet he did nothing, an 18-year-old man who did nothing.

"Now, there will be some testimony in this case about the damages that the plaintiff claims to have suffered. And you are going to hear from . . . well, first you are not going to hear . . . and my mouth has dried up on me.

I think that's a sure sign of I should be quiet I suppose. I'm almost done.

"You're not going to hear from a physician in this case. No medical doctor is going to take the witness stand and testify about any injuries that this plaintiff has suffered. You will hear from a clinical psychologist who has seen the plaintiff and began to see the plaintiff after this lawsuit was filed who, among a lot of other things, has given the plaintiff what he calls a GAF assessment, a Global Assessment Functioning Test. And you get a score. And what that basically is is how well are you functioning in this world on a scale of 1 to 100 with 100 being perfect and a zero I guess being dead, I'm not sure.

"The plaintiff as he comes to the courtroom for this case you will hear is functioning at a level of 70 which is in the perfectly normal range of coping and behaving. That's the status of the plaintiff as we try this case.

"Ladies and gentlemen, this will be an emotional case. You have already heard the rhetoric from the plaintiff's side of this case.

"I ask you to reserve your judgment until you have heard all of the evidence, and I ask you to approach this evidence objectively and dispassionately and neutrally until you have heard it all. At the end of the case when you have heard all of the evidence, His Honor will instruct you in the law. And only when you have got all of the facts and the law will you be in a position to render a just verdict.

"I look forward to being with you over the next couple of days, and I invite your careful attention to the evidence.

"Thank you very much."

Wells Dickson rose to give his opening statement. "Good afternoon, ladies and gentlemen. I'm Wells Dickson. I can say I'm sometimes the forgotten lawyer in the case. I'm sitting over there in the corner by myself. And as you can already tell, I represent the one defendant that is not forgotten at any time in this case and that's for good reason.

"You see, Mr. Fischer came into this courtroom I believe about this time last year and entered a guilty plea, a guilty plea to molesting a child. The same facts that underscore these civil charges against him in this case, and he was sentenced to 20 years. He is at Lieber Correctional Institute. Mr. Fischer today is 72 years old. He has very little that he can add to this trial. In reality, if you think about it, this is probably a lawsuit between Mr. Dunn and Porter-Gaud and the other individuals that are named.

"There should be very little doubt in your mind that Mr. Fischer has admitted responsibility for this. In addition to the guilty plea, last fall he was deposed at Lieber Correctional Institute. Now, deposed means that his testimony was taken. Many of the lawyers that are sitting in this courtroom today asked him questions, and he answered them under oath as if he were in this courtroom today. You have heard them refer to other testimony coming in by deposition. I suggest to you that Mr. Fischer's deposition testimony will be published to you at the appropriate time by one of the parties. It was also videotaped, so you may actually see Mr. Fischer answering questions.

"Just remember that if I stand up and say something, I'm probably the last lawyer you are going to hear on that particular point. And with that in mind, I'm not going to miss this opportunity to sit down. Someone said don't ever pass that up. So, thank you for your time and thank you for paying attention."

The judge wasted no time in getting the trial started, "Call your first witness, please."

We began the trial with some of the deposition testimony of Berkeley Grimball. Depositions are usually read by a person sitting in the witness box. The lawyer reads the questions, and the reader reads only the responses from the printed deposition. Some lawyers hire actors to read depositions. Most lawyers use a paralegal or staff person from their office. Gregg had arranged for a law student to read it, but she was running late and had not arrived, so Wells Dickson agreed to read Grimball's responses. As he was taking his seat in the witness box, Judge Pieper instructed the jury about depositions, "Alright. Ladies and gentlemen, they are going to read you a deposition. A deposition is sworn . . . is testimony taken under oath. Counsel are entitled to be present to ask questions if they so desire. It is to be treated as any other testimony in case and give it such weight as you may believe it to be entitled. They are going to read to you from this deposition. They are just reading to you what was said. Go ahead."

Generally, reading depositions in a trial can be very tedious and boring. But this deposition was anything but that. In fact, when Dickson read the response about not caring to know if a pedophile was on the faculty at his children's school, there was an audible gasp from some of the jurors. At the end of the transcript, Dickson, who attended only a few of the depositions but not Grimball's, walked to plaintiff's counsel table to return his copy of the deposition to Gregg and me. As he handed it to Gregg, he leaned over and whispered, "You guys have a damn good case."

The judge gave the jurors a break at the end of Grimball's deposition, which was fine with us because we wanted the jurors to have some time to let Grimball's testimony sink in.

After the break, Gregg read a very condensed version of Ronnie Hammond's deposition testimony. We were hoping to have him at the trial, but he was out of town. We did this one a little different. Gregg had selected portions that took less than 10 minutes to read, so he asked to read both the questions and the answers, which the judge permitted to move the trial along. The excerpts were about what Fischer had said to him when he tried to meet him at the drug store.

Next was the deposition of Ted Richardson, the former administrator who admitted that the school's handling of Fischer was a mistake. Again, Gregg asked to read the questions and answers, which was permitted. This one also took less than 10 minutes.

Then we finally called our first live witness, Ralph Nordlund. He was a small, professorial looking man. He testified that he had worked at Porter-Gaud for 35 years as a history teacher and head of the history department. I then asked him about Fischer.

"In your capacity as a department head over the history department, would you have involvement in the evaluation or rating of teachers in that department?"

"Yes sir."

"Now, while you were at Porter-Gaud, did you come to know

Eddie Fischer?"

"Yes sir."

"Mr. Nordlund tell the jury if you ever had an occasion to evaluate Mr. Fischer while he was a teacher at Porter-Gaud School."

"Yes, I did."

"Let me show you what has been marked as Plaintiff's Exhibit Number 20 which is a two-page document. Have you ever seen that document before?"

"Yes sir."

"Would you agree with me that this is an evaluation of Eddie Fischer?"

"Yes sir."

"That appears to be dated in the year 1975?"

"Yes."

"Alright. Would you agree with me that this is a form that you put some information on regarding different abilities or areas with respect to Mr. Fischer during his tenure at Porter-Gaud?"

"Yes sir."

"For example, it asks about professional competency, classroom ability, rapport, contributions to the total life of the school. Those are various categories that you made comments on?"

"Yes sir."

"And the jury can take a look at those. But I want to direct your attention down here where it asks, 'do you recommend continued employment of this faculty member?' Do you see that?"

"Yes."

"And you responded 'yes'; is that right?"

"Yes sir."

"And then you put a comment in here that I want to make sure of . . . tell me if I read this correctly: 'very frankly, I think this of Mr. Fischer. He is not a scholar by any stretch of the imagination and he is lazy in his class preparation. Furthermore, I don't think he is very literate, and I think he is a bit of a confidence man. For these reasons, I would not want him to teach upper level history. However, I do think he has done a good job in teaching seventh graders and that he may do an outstanding job in that capacity in future years if he is given adequate guidance.' Did I read that correctly?"

"Yes sir."

"And you, in fact, signed this document on March 17, 1975?"

"That's correct."

"Now, you referred to Mr. Fischer as a confidence man. Tell the jury what you mean by confidence man."

"I think that he told tall stories. And that is what I meant by it. I didn't . . . in other words, that he was untrustworthy as far as his history classes were concerned."

"Did you want him back in the history department, Mr. Nordlund?"

"No sir."

"That is all of the questions I have. Thank you, Mr. Nordlund."

Robinson now had a chance to question one of her teachers from Porter-Gaud. "Hey, Mr. Nordlund. I'm Laura Robinson. Thank you for coming today. Did any student ever report to you that Edward Fischer had behaved inappropriately?"

"No."

"Did any teacher ever tell you that Fischer had acted inappropriately with a student?"

"No, ma'am."

"Did you have any information that Mr. Fischer had, in fact, ever acted in a sexually inappropriate manner?"

"No, ma'am."

"And is it true notwithstanding your opinions about his personality or teaching abilities that when your own son ran into some disciplinary problems you sent him to Mr. Fischer for help?"

"That is true."

"Those are all of the questions that I have, your honor."

I was quickly on my feet. "Brief follow-up, your honor. Mr. Nordlund did anybody in the administration ever tell you that Edward Fischer was on probation?"

"No, I don't know about that."

"As the department head is that something you would want to know about a teacher in your department."

"Object to the form of that question. It is irrelevant, his opinion as a teacher," Robinson said in front of the jury, which was improper.

The judge didn't agree with her objection, however, "I will allow it. Go ahead."

"Is that some information you would like to know about the teachers that are in your department as department chair?"

"Yes."

"Mr. Nordlund, would you want to know if any teachers in your department had ever been accused of sexual misconduct with a student?"

Robinson: "Object to the question again."

"I'll allow it. Go ahead."

Nordlund spoke right up, "I would want to know."

"Did anybody ever tell you anything like that about Eddie Fischer?"

"No sir."

"That's all I have. Thank you."

We then read a stipulation to the jury, which is just an agreement between the parties about what a witness would testify to if they were called to the stand. We wanted this stipulation because it allowed the 1982 student to not testify in public. I read the stipulation. "That if he was called to testify, a student from the 1982 incident would testify that Edward Fischer performed oral sex on him and that that information was conveyed to James Bishop Alexander."

Gregg rose and read excerpts from the deposition of the 1982 student's father to the jury. There were several looks of incredulity as they heard all the things that Alexander promised to do, but never did. There were some bench conferences with the judge during this deposition, with the defendants attempting and succeeding in excluding much of the testimony.

At the end of the father's deposition, Judge Pieper ended the proceeding for the day. He let the jury go with this standard admonition at the end of every trial day. "Please do not discuss this case in any way whatsoever. If you will, give your pads to the bailiff on the way out. The bailiff will secure those pads overnight. Also, I remind you to try to avoid any exposure to any media coverage or newspaper coverage in the case. And if you do . . . if you are approached by anyone or you do receive any information about this case, you should try to tell the person that you are involved in the case and that you can't discuss it. And if you are accidentally exposed to any information, it would be your duty to report that to me. Again, please avoid any exposure to any media coverage. Thank you very much and have a good night."

CHAPTER 20

The next morning, the trial resumed promptly at 9:15. Pieper had the jury brought right in and began the day with an announcement that court would be abbreviated that day so he could see a dentist to deal with a toothache.

We began the day by calling Dr. Barbara Dilligard, the interim deputy superintendent for personnel at the Charleston County School District. She was in charge of hiring teachers at the public schools in Charleston and was in that position when Eddie Fischer applied to teach at James Island High School. After establishing her credentials, I turned to the hiring process for Fischer.

She described how people interested in positions with the school district would apply to a central office and would be screened by that office before being furthered examined by individual schools if the district determined that they were qualified.

"So, if I understand, it is a two-step process where you clear people for eligibility generally?"

"Yes."

"And then once they are cleared if individual positions come open at various schools, they could apply for those positions?"

"They are free to make contact with the principal for interviews and see if they are suitable for that particular position."

"And if someone does not pass the initial phase of it, are they eligible for any positions in the schools of Charleston County?"

"No, they are not eligible."

"Tell the jury, if you would, what importance, if any, you place on recommendations from prior employers."

"We require recommendations from the past immediate employer or current employer. And we rely on that to give us a history of the person's performance as a teacher or a maintenance worker or whatever the position might be."

"Do you expect prior employers to give you truthful information?"

"Yes, we rely on that."

I showed her the reference blank that Alexander filled out for Fischer. After establishing that it was the form used by the school district, I asked, "Now if, Dr. Dilligard, you received information on a form like this that a teacher had resigned from a school because of an allegation of sexual misconduct . . ."

Stepp cut me off. "Objection, your honor. That is not on that form."

I was annoyed by the objection. "If I can finish the question, your honor."

The judge let me finish, "Go ahead with the question."

"Dr. Dilligard, if on a form that you received there was an indication that a teacher had resigned because of an allegation of sexual misconduct, would they have been eligible for hire by the Charleston County School District?"

"No."

Stepp objected again, only a little late this time, but the judge cut him off, "Go ahead. I will allow it."

I pretended not to hear her answer, and wanted her to repeat it to punish Stepp for interrupting, "I'm sorry?"

"No," she said more emphatically and louder than the first time as she glared at Stepp.

"Thank you, Dr. Dilligard. That is all of the questions I have."

We had established that Fischer never would have been hired at James Island High School if Alexander had told the truth.

Stepp moved quickly from his chair to question her. "Good morning, Dr. Dilligard. My name is Bobby Stepp and I represent Porter-Gaud and the Estate of Berkeley Grimball and the Estate of James Bishop Alexander in this litigation. I appreciate your coming this morning."

"Uh-huh." Her sarcastic tone seemed to indicate that she had already decided who she thought the good guys and bad guys were.

"Now, in 1986 . . . well, let me make sure I understand what you're saying. This two-step process you are talking about your office, if I understand it correctly, sort of serves as a clearing house of information?"

"That's correct. We create the pool."

"You don't actually hire anybody?"

"Other than the people who work directly for me."

"But in terms of a teacher, you don't hire a teacher to work at a school?"

"No."

"The teacher is hired by the principal of the school; is that right?"

"Recommended to the constituent board, yes."

"Right. But then if there are two or three or more candidates for a teaching position, it is up to the principal to decide who he wants; is that correct?"

"Yes."

"Now, you remember Eddie Fischer coming through the system, don't you?"

"Yes, I do."

"Back in 1986?"

"I assume that date is correct."

"If this reference blank is dated in June of 1986, would that refresh your recollection about when Mr. Fischer made the application?"

"Yes."

"Okay. Now, let me ask you a little bit about this form. When this form goes out from the school district, what information is on it, the date?"

"We would generally have the date, to whom it is referred, of course the name of the applicant, address may or may not be there, but the social security number to ensure the person is the same and the position for which the person is applying."

"Okay. Now, the form itself has these places to make check marks. Is that what you are supposed to do?"

"Yes."

"And one of these here are scholarship, personality, character, health; am I right?"

"Yes."

"General intelligence, correct?"

"Yes."

"Personal appearance is a category?"

"Yes."

"Initiative?"

"Yes."

"Tactfulness?"

"Yes."

"Skill in teaching?"

"Yes."

"Student control?"

"Yes."

"Cooperation?"

"Yes."

"Professional growth?"

"Yes."

"Social qualities?"

"Yes."

"And general rating?"

"Yes."

"And so, you expect somebody who receives this to make an appropriate mark with respect to those categories?"

"That's correct."

"And there are choices ranging from superior down to not observed?"

"Yes."

"And right above that is inferior?"

"Uh-huh."

"And then at the bottom there are these blanks, one of which is any physical defects or mental peculiarities; is that correct?"

"That's correct."

"And then the next one is what opportunity have you had to observe the candidate's work?"

"Yes."

"And finally, in your judgment is the above candidate well-fitted for the above position?"

"Yes."

"So, this is one piece of paper, and it goes out?"

"Yes."

"Now, this one that we have here came back with some check marks, a few words down here and a signature; is that right?"

"That is correct."

"Is that the way most of them come back?"

"Most times. They also fill in the remarks that you didn't ask me about."

"So sometimes there might be something here under remarks as well?"

"Yes."

"Now, is that . . . that is not all of the information that you try to elicit with respect to a potential applicant though, is it, Dr. Dilligard?"

"No, the principal is supposed to call the references if a decision about employment is going to be made."

"Okay. Now, Dr. Dilligard, wasn't it the policy with respect to these reference blanks to contact and conduct an oral interview with the reference?"

"Yes."

"And you would not have been the person to have done that; is that correct?"

"No, one of my staff and the principal would have done that."

"And that is what I want to get back to. The person who worked for you . . . his job would have been to conduct an oral interview with all of the references?"

"Not necessarily all."

"At least one?"

"At least the past immediate supervisor."

"The past immediate supervisor?"

"Uh-huh."

"And that is because, is it not, that a lot of times information comes out in an oral interview that is not reflected on the reference blank?"

"That's correct." She was essentially confirming the passing the trash practice in the education field.

"And you learned that over the years and incorporated that into your policy?"

"Yes."

"And you do not know, if I'm correct . . . tell me if I'm correct . . . whether the person in your office conducted any interview with anybody at Porter-Gaud?"

"No, can't say that I do."

"Okay. Now, what we have talked about so far, if I'm correct, is the screening process in what I might call an ordinary or usual case; is that right?"

"Yes."

"Now, if there were issues connected with an applicant even more might be done; is that right?"

"Yes."

"And there were issues with Mr. Fischer's application, where there not?"

"Not that I know of."

"Well, let me ask you then why, Dr. Dilligard, you recall Mr. Fischer's application out of what I think is fair to say are the thousands that have come through your office before and after 1986?"

"I'm not sure I understand the question."

"Yes. You remember this particular applicant. You remember this application?"

"I remember Mr. Fischer's application, yes."

"And that is because there were some red flags in Mr. Fischer's application; isn't that right?"

"I remember Mr. Fischer coming to see me personally which is not usual for a teacher applicant."

"You conducted an interview of Mr. Fischer yourself?"

"Yes, I did."

"And that was certainly not something that happened in the usual case?"

"Well, when somebody is transitioning, I probably looked at that as a need to interview him. But I can't recall anything specific beyond looking at his work history that might have asked . . . begged for me to interview him."

"And in his work history, it revealed that he had been a couple of places not very long?"

"I would rather be looking at the application to answer a question like that."

"Alright. But am I correct that you do recall that you interviewed Mr. Fischer?"

"Yes, I do."

"And that was, at least, somewhat out of the ordinary; is that right?"

"Well, I can't remember if Mr. Fischer asked to see me or whether I initiated it."

"Okay."

"If I initiated it, that would be out of the ordinary trend. If he initiated that would not necessarily be."

"Okay. So, there was at least -- you had some contact with Mr. Fischer?"

"Yes, I did."

"And nothing in that contact caused you to believe that he was unqualified?"

"No, he had good references. None of the past employers had indicated any problems."

"Okay."

"And he wasn't fired." This was an unexpected answer that reiterated Porter-Gaud's decision to let him resign quietly.

He went on to ask her about the process of Fischer being interviewed for the specific position at James Island High School. She did not know anything about that.

"So, all of these steps, if I'm right, is a part of the screening and eligibility process; am I correct?"

"That is correct."

"And so, all of this has to be satisfactory before someone is declared to be eligible; is that right?"

"Yes."

"So, a single reference blank is not the key to whether someone is eligible but rather all of these things that we have talked about?"

"Yes."

"Thank you, Doctor." He ended very abruptly, but at a point which begged for further questioning. So, I decided to oblige.

"Dr. Dilligard, could one reference be the key to *ineligibility* of an applicant?"

"If it has something on it that is a red flag and it is followed up on, yes."

"Would you consider a resignation related to an allegation of sexual misconduct to be a red flag?"

"Oh, yes."

"Mr. Stepp asked about the interview process where the principal contacts the applicant directly. Do you remember that?"

"Yes."

"Prior to the principal even getting the name, if you had known about an allegation of sexual misconduct, would that person have even been in the pool of candidates for the principal to call?"

"No."

"Now, when you send out this form . . . Mr. Stepp asked you a couple of questions about what is on it. And here it says brief description of position to be filled: history parenthesis social studies. Does that indicate they are going to be filling a teacher position in history or social studies?"

"Yes."

"And this would have been on there when Mr. J.B. Alexander received this form at Porter-Gaud School?"

"Yes."

"Is there anything on this form that would raise any concerns to you or give you any indication whatsoever that Eddie Fischer had been accused of sexual misconduct of a student?"

"No."

"Is that something you would expect to find on this form?"

"If that were true, yes."

"If the referring employer believed it to be true, would you expect to find it on that form?"

Stepp objected. "Your honor, he is leading the witness." The judge instructed me to rephrase the question, which I was more than happy to do.

"Would you expect a referring employer to include information about an allegation of sexual misconduct on this form?"

"If that were the case about an applicant, yes, we would expect that person to say that or something that would prompt us to ask further."

"When you interviewed Eddie Fischer, did Eddie Fischer tell you that he had been accused of sexual misconduct with a student?"

"No."

"Would that have been a red flag if he had told you?"

"Most definitely."

"If J.B. Alexander told you, would that have been a red flag?"

"Yes."

"Now, this process that we have been talking about was that the same process that was used in 1986 when this particular form was filled out?"

"Yes."

"And then finally in response to a question from Mr. Stepp you said he wasn't fired. If there was an indication on this form that he was fired, would that have been a concern?"

"Yes."

"Thank you, Dr. Dilligard. That is all of the questions I have."

Stepp rose cautiously, "Just one more, Doctor, is there anywhere on the form where it says reason for leaving employment?"

"Not on that form, no."

"Thank you."

Without taking a break, Gregg went right into reading some deposition excerpts from the 1982 mother. He read the questions and responses again. During this reading, Stepp rose and objected in the middle of it, "Your honor, would you ask Mr. Meyers not to give certain words in the transcript undue influence. I have indulged him to read this, but I object." A couple of the jurors laughed at this objection.

The judge wasn't laughing though. He instructed counsel to approach the bench. At the bench, out of earshot of the jury, he admonished Bobby, "My proper procedure is object, state your objection. Generally, if I want something further, I will let you know."

Stepp was contrite, "I beg your pardon."

Pieper then looked at Gregg, "Please watch your tone."

The plaintiff's next witness was Guerry Glover. The defense raised an objection and argued hard to limit his testimony. Stepp wanted to prevent Guerry from talking about what Fischer had done to him, arguing it wasn't relevant. The judge disagreed.

Gregg rose and said, "Your honor, the next witness is Guerry Glover."

After being sworn in by the clerk, Guerry took his seat. The courtroom was silent. Every eye in the jury box was glued to this man that the community had heard so much about. Gregg began slowly, "Good morning, Mr. Glover."

"Good morning."

Guerry began by testifying about where he lived and his education. He said he started as a student at Porter-Gaud in 1972.

"What year did you first meet Edward Fischer, meaning either how old were you or what was the calendar year?"

"It was the 1976 school year. It was '75, '76."

"How soon after you first met him did Mr. Fischer begin to involve you in sexual acts?"

"Very soon."

"And you were how old then?"

"Nine and 10 years old."

"Mr. Glover, it is true that some sexual acts between you and Mr. Fischer occurred at Porter-Gaud School?"

"Yes."

"And is it also the case that some sexual acts between you and Mr. Fischer occurred after you left Porter-Gaud School?"

"Yes."

"And while you were attending College Prep School?"

"Yes."

"And was that because Mr. Fischer left Porter-Gaud to go teach at College Prep?"

"Yes."

The questions then shifted to his attempts to tell Porter-Gaud officials in 1987 and 1988 about his experience with Fischer at the school.

"I went back and told Maj [Alexander] what had happened to me at Porter-Gaud, that I knew that he knew what Fischer had done and that I knew he had let Fischer follow me to College Prep."

Robinson was on her feet, "Objection, I think we are supposed to be talking about what happened at that meeting."

The judge spoke directly to Guerry, "Yeah, focus on what happened outside of College Prep. Go ahead."

Gregg began again, taking a minute to ask about Alexander's many names. "First of all, let me clear up one thing. How many people am I referring to when I refer to James Bishop Alexander, Bishop Alexander, James Alexander, Skip Alexander and Major Alexander?"

"They're all one and the same."

Gregg asked about what he actually told Alexander in their meeting.

"The thrust of my conversation with Maj was that it was . . . I was made to be the discipline problem and the bad guy, and they kicked me out. But he knew, and I knew why I was trying to get away from Porter-Gaud. And at the same time, I got kicked out, Fischer got kicked out. And I was going back to set the record straight with him and to let him know that I was really angry about that, that how could he have fed me to that and let it keep going while . . . while he knew."

"When you left Porter-Gaud, it was because of a disciplinary situation?"

"Yes."

"And why was it you were trying to get kicked out of the Porter-Gaud School?"

"I was trying to get away from Fischer."

"What did James Bishop Alexander do, if anything, as a result of your communicating that with him in either 1987 or 1988?"

"Maj said, well, there was a time when we didn't talk about these things. And he asked if I had told my parents, and I said no. And he suggested I not do that."

Gregg paused. "He suggested you not do that. Were there any other communications at that time?"

"No."

"After 1987 and 1988, did you go back to Porter-Gaud at any time to speak with any person again about Mr. Fischer?"

"I did."

"Describe when that was. First of all, tell us when that was."

"I went back in 1994. I finished graduate school, and I moved back to Charleston. And when I got back to Charleston, I realized that I needed to go take care of this. My parents' minister and I spoke several times. And he, come to find out, was a member of the board of trustees at Porter-Gaud. And he said, 'Guerry, Gordon Bondurant is the new headmaster. He's a really good guy. Go put this on Bondurant's desk, not on him personally. Go put it on his desk and let him have the responsibility for it. You need to move on with your life.'."

Guerry talked about his first meeting with Bondurant. "I communicated to him that I had been sexually abused by Mr. Fischer, that I had come back and told Maj that I thought there were a whole lot more victims, that they knew that. And I said but I know this is a lot for you to take in. Why don't you take a week? Call Major Alexander, check out my story. Call me back in a week."

Guerry then described the phone call he got from Bondurant in which the headmaster told him that he had confirmed Guerry's story through a conversation he had with Alexander. He said Bondurant told him, "Maj knew that someone had come forward and told that Mr. Fischer had sexually abused him as well, that they had asked for his resignation, that I was telling the . . . that the story I told Bondurant was true."

"What happened as a result of Mr. Bondurant being able to confirm your account? Did anything happen?"

"Well, Mr. Bondurant said that Fischer wasn't teaching at Porter-Gaud anymore. That if I wanted to do something it was up to me."

"What was it you wanted Porter-Gaud to do?"

"I was telling the new headmaster of the school this horrible story of what had happened to me and other people so that he would know. I was thinking that this intelligent man sitting behind this big desk would care enough to do anything."

"As far as you know, did anything happen as a result of . . ."

"No."

"Was there any other attempt you made to talk with Porter-Gaud about the subject of Edward Fischer?"

"So, three years later, '97, I'm working at Rosebank Farms and I get in a horrible argument with a coworker. I take off, and I go flying into town. I'm angry. I'm driving to town. I realize I'm not angry at Mary, at Rosebank or anybody else. I'm angry at Porter-Gaud. I'm sick of this."

"What did you do?"

"From being at River Road in my car, I drive straight to Porter-Gaud. I walk into Mr. Bondurant's office and I say, 'Enough. We've got to settle this. I can't do it anymore. I have talked and talked and talked.' There was nothing left to talk about. I said, 'Talk to whoever you need to talk to. This is going to end.'"

"What was it you were trying to end?"

"Fischer being still in a public-school teaching, everybody acting like it was all wonderful that this child molester was still on the loose."

"What was Mr. Bondurant's reaction?"

"Well, he said he was busy, that he had to go to a meeting. He told me to go take communion. He was not very cooperative."

"Were you able to establish a time to meet with him?"

"Well, he said he couldn't meet with . . . he said, 'I'm busy'. So, I walked over to his desk. I got his desk calendar. I turned pages. It was early May. I got to May 19th. It was empty. I said let's meet for lunch on May 19th. It was empty. I was looking at the empty calendar page."

"So, it was a day you knew he was free?"

"So, it was a day I knew he was free."

"Where was it you proposed to meet him?"

"At the Med-Deli Restaurant."

"Did the May 19th meeting take place?"

"No, it did not."

"What happened?"

"I got a note in the mail from him."

"Can you identify this document?" Gregg asked on his way to the witness stand.

Robinson rose, "I would note our objection to the relevant document."

The judge was terse. "Alright. Overruled."

"What is that note, Mr. Glover?" Gregg asked.

"This is a note dated May 7th, 1997 on Gordon Emerson Bondurant's personal stationery."

"Do you recognize the hand in which that note is written?"

"I do."

"Whose is it?"

"Mr. Bondurant's."

"Read this note very briefly. Read it to the jury."

"May 7th, 1997. Dear Guerry, I shall be unable to meet with you on May 19th. I honestly have nothing else to add to what I have said before. Sincerely, Gordon E. Bondurant."

"What did you decide to do as to how you were going to undertake to report Edward Fischer on your own after you received that note?"

"Well, none of it was absolutely linear. I was stunned that he slammed the door in my face. But it was like raising the stakes. I mean I had gone in '94. I was back in '97. And I knew I couldn't just walk away again. So, I didn't know what to do."

"Did you get another note from Mr. Bondurant?"

"I did."

"Can you tell me . . . let me hand you this document. It's an original of what has been marked as plaintiff's exhibit 9."

Robinson "noted" another objection, "Your Honor, again, I note our objection to that document." She didn't want the jury to see the handwritten correspondence from the school's headmaster.

"Overruled."

Gregg couldn't hide a wry smile, "What is that document, Mr. Glover?"

"This is another note from Mr. Bondurant on the same note paper."

"What does that note say?"

"Dated May 9th, 1997."

"And read the content of that. It's also short."

"Dear Guerry, please disregard my last note of May 7th. Would you be able to meet at 11:00 a.m. on May 19th? I would like to have present a friend who may help bring some resolution to the matters we have discussed. Sincerely, Gordon E. Bondurant."

"Now, he has proposed to meet with you on May 19th but in a different location than what you suggested?"

"Right."

"Tell the jury what your concern was about holding that meeting."

"Well, as a former Porter-Gaud student when you went to the principal's office, it meant that you were in trouble. So, to go to the headmaster's office to meet with him and a friend, I didn't want to get closed up in that office by myself with the two of them."

"Did you find out who the friend was?"

"I did."

"Who was that?"

"Hearsay, Your Honor, we object." Robinson began to sound a little defensive.

The judge seemed a little perplexed by the objection. "The question is did he find out who the friend was. And then he's going to say . . ." He paused a moment, then turned to Guerry and said, "Respond. I will allow that."

Gregg jumped in, "Who was that friend, Guerry?"

"I found out by profession."

"And what was the profession of the friend?"

"He was an attorney."

"Did the meeting of May 19th take place?"

"No, it did not."

"Why not?"

"Well, in between . . . right after I got the May 7th note, Mr. Bondurant called and left a message on my answering machine for me to call him at the school that Saturday morning. I called him and that's when he said, 'I'm going to have a friend'. He said, 'my friend is an attorney'. I said, 'Well, do I need to bring a friend?' And so, then I got nervous, and I wasn't going to go to Mr. Bondurant's office to meet with him and his attorney in his office when the reason I wanted to go to a restaurant was at least I would be in a public place."

"Mr. Glover, the document that is identified as exhibit 13, tell us what that is."

"This is a letter that I typed to the individual board members telling them my story."

"And when is that letter dated?"

"This letter is dated September 30, 1997." This was before Guerry went to the prosecutor's office and before Fischer was arrested.

"And what was your purpose in sending that letter?"

"Well, between May and September, it had all gotten very complicated. And it was getting lost from what I was trying to do so . . .'"

"What was it you were trying to do?"

"To get Porter-Gaud to do something. So, I said if I put this down and I tell board members who know who I am and who know the school and I just tell them my story, surely they will respond as caring human beings."

"And did you get any response to that letter?"

"I got a response from one board member and from [Episcopal]

Bishop Salmon."

"Did you get any response from the institution from Porter-Gaud, meaning from the school or the board as a group?"

"No, I did not."

"Mr. Glover, after that letter, was there any public communications from Porter-Gaud released generally about the subject of Edward Fischer?"

"The school did a press release."

"And tell me if . . .."

Robinson objected again. She didn't want the jury to see her client's false press release. After a bench conference, the judge let Gregg continue with the question.

"Mr. Glover let me hand you what has been marked for identification as Exhibit 14, which purports to be a press release from Porter-Gaud School. Is that the press release you saw?"

"Yes, it is."

It read, in its entirety:

A 33-year-old Johns Island resident has provided the press with a letter addressed to members of Porter-Gaud's Board of Trustees stating that while he was a student at Porter-Gaud in the early 1980's a former Porter-Gaud School teacher sexually abused him. This former teacher has not been employed at Porter-Gaud for over 15 years.

As this letter states, Porter-Gaud has been responding to this matter in the posture of a threatened lawsuit.

At all times, Porter-Gaud has taken both legally and morally appropriate action with the information it had available and will continue to do so. We have previously communicated with and will continue to support and cooperate with the solicitor's office in their investigation and resolution of the issues raised by the former student. We learned information from the letter that we have never known. While Porter-Gaud is receiving a lot of attention from what this former student has said, the school has no direct knowledge of what happened to him or any other former students while the accused teacher was at Porter-Gaud. Without sufficient evidence, the authorities cannot prosecute an alleged child abuser.

We applaud and support the former student's courage for coming forward. We will cooperate fully with the solicitor's office. Members of the media have asked for information about the former student and the former teacher. The contents of a teacher's personnel file and of a student's file are private and we must respect that privacy. Given the likelihood of a criminal investigation, it would be inappropriate for us to make any statements about any of the issues raised by the former student's letter or otherwise. The solicitor's office will have to decide whether to release any of this information in the future.

Gregg continued, "Is there any information in that press release that you know to be inaccurate and you know that Porter-Gaud knew from your own efforts and you informed them was inaccurate?"

Robinson knew it was about to get ugly for her clients. "I object to that question. It's an awfully broad question."

The judge overruled the objection.

Guerry took his cue from the judge, "Well, the glaring falsehood is it says while Porter-Gaud is receiving a lot of attention from what this former student has said, the school has no direct knowledge of what happened to him or any other former students while the accused teacher was at Porter-Gaud."

"Had you taken steps to inform them to the contrary?"

"Absolutely."

"And did that . . ."

"In '94 and '97 and in the late '80s, Bondurant and Alexander."

"Now, there is a reference to the . . . you say to the former student. Who is that referring to, as you understood it?"

"To me."

"Okay. Now, you noted the sentence: 'We applaud and support the former student's courage for coming forward.' Can you describe to the jury every act of support that you have received from Porter-Gaud School since October 1st, 1997 about Edward Fischer? What support did you get for coming forward?"

"Nothing. They have deposed me for hours upon hours upon hours."

Robinson objected again. This time her objection seemed to not only confirm what Guerry had just said but suggested that it was just fine.

Although Pieper sustained the objection, the point was made to the jury, and was reinforced by the objection.

Gregg stayed with the point for one more question, "There are no accounts of support, no phone calls, no letters?"

"Not from the school."

"No other questions, your honor."

Stepp asked for some time to confer with his co-counsel before beginning cross-examination. Surprisingly, Stepp began the questioning of Guerry. It was surprising because court rules provide that only one lawyer per side gets to handle a witness, which means that since Robinson was objecting, she should have been doing the cross-examination of Guerry. Gregg chose not to make an issue of it.

"Mr. Glover, I have a couple questions for you. When you went to see Mr. Bondurant in 1994, how old were you then?"

"Maybe . . . I was born in '65; '65 to '94."

"29, is that right?"

"Uh-huh."

"We have been doing a lot of math in Court."

"I was a history major." Guerry's sardonic tone made a few of the jurors chuckle.

"And you had left Porter-Gaud in 197_ . . ."

"I left Porter-Gaud in 1982."

"1982, so it had been about 12 years since you had been a student at Porter-Gaud?"

"Yeah."

"And you were 29, more or less?"

"Uh-huh."

"You didn't know Mr. Bondurant?"

"Only by the pastor's recommendation."

"Mr. Bondurant was not at the school when you were at the school?"

"No, he was not."

"And Mr. Bondurant was not at the school when Mr. Fischer was at the school?"

"No, he wasn't."

"Do you know the Plaintiff in this case? I don't believe he is in court right now. Do you know him, Mr. Dunn?"

"I met him after this has come out."

"You didn't know him in 1994?"

"No, I did not."

"You didn't know him in 1988 either obviously?"

"No."

"And did you know him in 1997 when you went back to see

Gordon Bondurant the last time?"

"No."

"And the meeting, the May 19th meeting, you canceled that meeting; is that right?"

"It's not entirely correct."

"Well, maybe you didn't cancel it. You said you didn't want to go under those circumstances?"

"I asked Mr. Bondurant to meet me at a restaurant. He wanted to meet me in his office with his lawyer, and I wouldn't do that. But I was perfectly willing to meet him at a restaurant. I was the one that suggested that."

"Thank you. That is all that I have." A very abrupt ending to a very peculiar cross-examination. The whole courtroom expected more.

We had some legal matters to address with the judge, so we suggested to him to end court for the day at that point, which he did. The jury went home with Guerry fresh on their minds.

CHAPTER 21

The next morning it was Kevin's turn; he was our first witness. The jury had not yet seen him, and we kept him in a conference room until it was time for him to testify. As soon as the jury was settled in the box, Gregg told the judge our next witness was Kevin Dunn. Every eye in the courtroom was riveted on him as he entered the courtroom and took the stand. He was wearing khakis and a light button-down shirt. He began his testimony by saying he was 29 years old and a civil engineer.

Gregg did the direct examination. "Mr. Dunn, describe how you came to meet Mr. Fischer."

"It was a gradual process. It was over a period of time at school. I don't remember the first time. He wasn't my teacher so he . . . it is my recollection that he just, you know, he met me in passing like when I was maybe going to lunch, or I was walking in the hallways, he would strike up a conversation with me."

"How did it come about that you first went to Mr. Fischer's house?"

"I don't specifically remember when he invited me over to his house. It's my recollection I was in the office, the school office. I believe I was sick or for some reason my mother was coming to pick me up from school. I don't remember exactly why, and Mr. Fischer was in the office at that time. And, as usual, I mean he would talk to me whenever he saw me.

So, he was talking to me when I was in the office this particular time. And through that conversation, he invited me over to his house."

"And what was the ostensible purpose in having you come to his house?"

"Well, at that time, Mr. Fischer, you know, he would always say how intelligent he thought I was. And, you know, as part of this conversation we were having that day in the office he, you know, wanted to continue the conversation we were having at his home. And, you know, I don't know if it was right then, but, at some point, he was saying, you know, he thought I was very, very shy and, you know, small in stature. He was saying he could help me on those things. He indicated he could help me in various ways. I don't remember all of the things he said."

"When approximately, as best you recall, was it that you first went to his house?"

"I don't remember exactly when it was. It was either in the latter part of '89 or very early '90."

"Can you describe for us any contact he had with your parents to make sure it was okay?"

"Oh, well, yes. He, of course, wanted me to clear it with my parents."

"Did you do that?"

"Yes."

"Now, describe what he did in the first meeting that first evening and how did the evening go?"

"I went over there for dinner. And he was, you know, preparing dinner. He wanted me to help him out, and during that time we just talked and that is basically all that happened."

"The first visit was a dinner and conversation?"

"Right."

"Was there anything established so that there was an agreement to return?"

"Well, I remember before I left his house we had been talking about weightlifting. And he was going to help me because I was small, and I wanted to get bigger. He said he was going to help me out that way. So, he took a Polaroid picture of me without my shirt on that first visit, and he said he would take a Polaroid every time we met so eventually, he could show me the progress. He was wanting to establish a regular time that we could meet. And I remember it as being every Thursday."

"And did anything improper happen in that first evening?"

"No."

"So, your schedule for future visits was supposedly weekly on Thursday?"

"Right."

"And how did that sound to you?"

"It was fine."

"Alright. Did you, indeed, return for a second visit?"

"Yes."

"How did that visit go?"

"It went like the first visit. But at one point, well, he brought up sex. I don't really remember in what capacity. I think he was just asking a question about what is the strongest human emotion or something. I don't remember exactly what he said. He brought it up then. He answered his own question. It was like, whatever. And, we just kept on talking about normal stuff. At some point, we went upstairs. And I had been up there the first time because he had showed me around his house the first time. So, at any rate, we went upstairs. And he had taken me to his library before. He had a library. He had a computer there. It was like a study room. And now I'm not sure if this happened on that second visit, but it may have. I can't remember. He had like a stack of . . . I think it was Playboy in there. And just in talking, you know, he showed me the Playboys. And, I mean, he very casually showed me these Playboys, and I would decline. You know, he flipped through the pages and I was like, yeah, yeah, okay. I had a hurt shoulder or arm. I don't remember what it was. But, at any rate, my arm was hindered because I played a lot of tennis. At some point, he said well he could help me, you know, with that injury. Because he said he was a coach, and he knew all about that stuff. And he had this vibrator, that he said worked and he had used it on other people. And he said it would help my arm. He said it had some kind of thermal thing where it would put heat into the muscle and loosen it up. So, you know, he had me lay down, take off my shirt and lay down on the bed. And he had to put this lubricant on the vibrator he said to make it work. So, he like rubbed it on my arm where he was putting it on the vibrator."

Kevin went on to describe in detail how this led eventually to Fischer sexually assaulting him. In graphic detail he told the jury exactly what Fischer had done. Most of the members of the jury were crying as he described it. There was a particularly poignant moment when Gregg asked him what he was doing while Fischer was assaulting him. Kevin's response caused audible weeping in the courtroom.

"I was laying there perfectly still. I was . . . my hands were by my side. My feet were straight out. I was rigid. I was scared to death. I didn't know what in the world to do. I just laid there, and I just prayed. I prayed and that's the only thing I knew to do."

Gregg continued with the difficult, but necessary, questions, "Can you describe for us any other sexual experience you had had before that night at Mr. Fischer's?"

"None."

"When you came home, did you consider telling your parents what had happened?"

"There was no way I was going to tell my parents what happened."

"Why not?"

"I couldn't even believe what happened myself. I mean I certainly couldn't have told my parents."

"Now, Mr. Fischer had established with you that you would come back, this would be a regular thing."

"I did everything that I could do to keep from going over to Mr. Fischer's house. And the only thing I knew to do was to avoid him at school or not return his phone calls."

"Did that work?"

"Most of the time it did."

"What would you do at school to avoid him?"

"Mr. Fischer's classroom was on the first floor. It was two doors down from my Spanish class. And I avoided that side of the building like the plague. I would not have gone there. I would go, to get to my Spanish class, I would cross upstairs. I would walk down the firewell . . . or stairwell. And it would enter right at my Spanish teacher's class, so I didn't have to go by Mr. Fischer's room."

"Now, you said most of the time avoiding him would work, avoiding his calls and avoiding seeing him at school. What would happen when you were unsuccessful in avoiding him?"

"When Mr. Fischer would get in touch with me by phone or in person, he would want me to come to his house. And when that happened, I just felt I had no other alternative other than to go see him at his house."

"Why not?"

"I just felt I had no other alternative when I saw him. I was that afraid of him. And I couldn't let on to everyone else that something was wrong. I didn't want anyone to know what was going on, and I was just so afraid. And if you're not in that position, I don't think you could . . . anyone else could have done anything else."

"You said you were afraid that people would find out. What was it you were afraid of people would find out?"

"I was afraid that this man that I first thought was pretty cool and that I had talked about favorably with other people I didn't want to let them know he was molesting me."

"You put your first visit to his house in late 1989 or early 1990, and you left for college in the fall of 1990. After you left for college, was there any instance where you went to Mr. Fischer's house?"

"After college?"

"After you left for college in Columbia, was there any other instance where you went to Mr. Fischer's house?"

"No."

"From late '89 to the fall of 1990 is the time period that you are describing that you were trying to avoid him?"

"Yes."

"How many times, as best you recall, when he would catch up to you and you felt you had no alternative did you return to his house?"

"It's difficult to say how many times I was there because every time was so similar. I wasn't counting."

"What is your best recollection?"

"Maybe a half of a dozen to a dozen times. I really don't know."

"So, over that 8 to 10-month period, maybe up to a dozen times?"

"Maybe."

"At any point in that time period in those dozen times, did you tell anyone what was happening to you at Mr. Fischer's house?"

"No."

"Do you recall if you can recall any instance of your parents talking with Mr. Fischer during that time period?"

"Yes."

"Tell us about that."

"My parents had him over for dinner."

"What was your reaction to hearing he was coming to dinner?"

"I didn't want him to come to dinner. I remember the evening he came over. I stayed upstairs in my house as long as I could. My mother, you know, had to come up and say, you know, when are you coming down. I didn't want him there."

"When did you first tell your . . . either of your parents about what had happened to you at Mr. Fischer's house?"

"When did I first tell my parents?"

"Right."

"I first told my mother I think it was in '97. I'm not sure."

"And when was that in relation to when you provided information to the Solicitor?"

"I told the Solicitor in October of '97."

"What prompted you to contact the Solicitor?"

"Well, I told my best friend what Mr. Fischer did. I told him maybe in '93 so he knew about it. I was in summer school and I was working at the State House. And he called me, and he said Mr. Fischer had been arrested and he was arrested for molesting one boy. And I didn't want Mr. Fischer to get off so I came forward."

"To the solicitor?"

"Yes."

"Did you tell your mother before or after telling the solicitor?"

"I think I told my mother in June of '97. And I told the solicitor in

October -- well, October 13th of 1997."

"Kevin, describe for us if you, in any way, found Mr. Fischer attractive."

"I in no way found Mr. Fischer attractive. I was 18. He was in his 60's. I was a student. He was a teacher."

"As you sit here today, can you answer the question of whether or not you are heterosexual or homosexual?"

"I think . . . I don't think I'll ever know."

"Before your experiences with Mr. Fischer, can you describe for us what your attraction was to females?"

"Before Mr. Fischer?"

"Yes."

"I very much wanted and knew someday that I would have a wife and children."

"Before Mr. Fischer, can you describe for us any attraction you had for males?"

"I did not."

"Since your experiences with Mr. Fischer, how do you react to the idea of sex?"

Stepp, unbelievably, stood and asked, "Your honor, may we take a recess?"

The judge looked to Kevin, "Yes. Is this a good time to take a break? Do you wish to have a break, sir?"

Gregg knew this was a particularly difficult issue for Kevin and he wanted to get it over with, "He may want to get past this one question, your honor."

Fortunately, the judge acquiesced.

After a very long and difficult pause, during which he continued to cry quietly, Kevin replied, "If I had a choice, I would rather not have sex at all."

Several members of the jury were also crying, and there were a few pained expressions from them when they heard Kevin's response.

After the break, Gregg tried to get through the tough questions as quickly as he could. "Kevin, since your experience with Mr. Fischer, have you initiated any sexual contact with any other person?"

"No."

"You're not saying you haven't had some sexual contact, you are saying you didn't initiate it?"

"Right."

"When you left Charleston for college at the University of South Carolina, what contacts did you have from Mr. Fischer?"

"Mr. Fischer, he tried writing cards and I . . . well, he did write cards. And at least my roommate says he remembers him calling to see if he could come up but wanting me to call him. And I never returned his call."

"Did you ever respond, in any way, to the communications he made to you?"

"Never."

"Kevin, the twelve or so times you talked about that you were at Mr. Fischer's house where there were sexual acts can you describe for us whether you were consenting to these acts?"

"Absolutely not."

"When you got to college and you were away from Mr. Fischer, did everything settle down for you?"

"No."

"Tell us what it was like for you."

"I mean it was very difficult. After Mr. Fischer, it was always like I was looking for something. I was trying to find out, you know, who I was. So, you know, I went from being a college republican, being an officer there. And just one day I woke up and I started following the Grateful Dead around the country. And I did that for a while. You know, I got involved in drugs and alcohol. And it was very up and down."

"As you look at it, what do you think caused all of that?"

"There is no doubt it is the experience I had with Mr. Fischer."

With no small amount of sarcasm, Gregg asked, "Well, weren't you just a kid off to college for the first time and able to have some freedom?"

Stepp objected to the phrasing of the question, but the judge overruled him and allowed it.

Kevin looked over at Stepp before beginning his response, "Everybody tries to find some feeling of self. And when Mr. Fischer molested me, he took that away from me. And I have always since been searching for who I was. And there is no doubt it was because of Mr. Fischer."

"Before Mr. Fischer, had you been having any confusion about who you were?"

"No."

"Can you tell us how your experience with Mr. Fischer affected your religious life?"

"Well, you have to understand I came from a very religious background. My parents are very religious. I was very religious. That was the most important thing to me. And, you know, I never thought that God would let this happen to me, that I had always trusted God and I always trusted he was going to take care of me. And when Mr. Fischer did what he did, he took that away from me. I was betrayed, I felt, by God."

"Can you describe for the jury what the effect was of Mr. Fischer and his sexual contact with you on your relationship with your parents?"

"I always loved my parents very much, and we were very close. And I always wanted to make them happy. And the last thing I wanted to do was disappoint them. And then Mr. Fischer comes along, and he destroyed that trust, that bond with my parents. He shut off that communication that I had with them. And it has never been the same since."

"Kevin, do you think your parents are responsible for your molestation?"

"No."

"You testified that you had problems with drug and alcohol abuse. Have you been able to stop your involvement in that area?"

"Yes."

"What did you do to stop your involvement with it?"

"I met someone at school who got me off drugs and alcohol."

"When did that occur? When did you succeed in getting off drugs and alcohol?"

"I don't remember, maybe '93, I don't know."

"You said earlier that your friend called you October of 1997 and told you Mr. Fischer had been arrested and that you contacted the solicitor; is that right?"

"Yes."

"When you contacted the solicitor, did you authorize the solicitor to use your name?"

"No."

"For what reason?"

"I didn't want anyone to know."

"Have you ever spoken with the person who first reported Mr.

Fischer?"

"Yes, it was Guerry Glover."

"Tell the jury what you think of Guerry having done that."

Stepp objected, "Your Honor, I object. That is irrelevant."

"Counsel approach." At the bench, the judge determined that it was relevant, and he allowed it.

Kevin asked Gregg to ask the question again.

"Tell the jury what you think of Guerry having done that."

"I was at a virtual dead end, and I probably wouldn't be here today if it were not for Guerry Glover."

"Kevin, let me change the subject now to what other people besides Guerry Glover knew about Eddie Fischer. What did you learn in 1997 about what officials at Porter-Gaud knew about Edward Fischer?"

Stepp objected again and asked to approach the bench.

At the bench, the judge ruled that Kevin could testify about when he learned that Porter-Gaud officials had recommended Fischer for employment at the public-school district. Before getting to that, Gregg wanted to clarify the last point, "Kevin, let me back up to clarify one thing. You said that had Guerry not done that you might not be here. What did you mean by that?"

"I think at some point I would have killed myself."

"Kevin, why have you brought this case?"

"Because I couldn't believe that someone knew about Mr. Fischer when I was approximately one years old and they could have stopped him from teaching at my school and, thereby, I would have never seen Mr. Fischer. I would have never been molested by him. None of this would have ever happened."

"Kevin, what have you done to try to deal with the problems that

Mr. Fischer has presented for you?"

"I have gone to counseling."

"Have you had any physical problems connected to the psychological things you have dealt with as a result of Mr. Fischer?"

"It is difficult for me to explain to you the ways that being molested affects you. But it's like taking your life without killing you. You have to suffer through it every single day. And it affects everything you do."

"Describe for us any physical problems that you have that are affected with that."

"I don't know where to begin. For one thing, it makes me ill. I mean I constantly have diarrhea. It is debilitating in the fact that it just takes so much of your energy. You have no physical drive or anything, always tired. I mean it affects everything."

"Kevin, these events happened in 1989 and 1990. As best you recall, why did you bring no suit until January of 1998?"

"Well, I didn't know anything about Porter-Gaud. I didn't know anything about their involvement."

"Until when?"

"November of '97."

"Your Honor, I have no other questions of Mr. Dunn."

"Alright," the judge said and looked at Stepp to begin his cross-examination.

Bobby got up slowly from his chair. "We met previously. My name is Bobby Stepp. I need to ask you some questions about your testimony. Are you able to answer them for me this morning?"

"Yes."

"Are you taking any medication that would affect your ability to understand my questions?"

"Not at the moment."

"You never attended Porter-Gaud; is that correct?"

"That's correct."

"Did you have any friends in high school who went to Porter-Gaud?"

"None."

"Okay. Have you ever met, or did you ever meet Berkeley Grimball?"

"Never."

"So, I assume you have never had a conversation with Mr. Grimball?"

"Never."

"Prior to the time that you filed this lawsuit, did you ever read any letters that Mr. Grimball wrote?"

"Never."

"Did you ever ask Mr. Grimball to show you Eddie Fischer's personnel file?"

"No."

"When is the first time that you heard the name Berkeley Grimball?"

"It might have been December of . . . I think it was December of '97."

"Within 30 days or so of the date you filed your lawsuit?"

"Probably."

"What about James Bishop Alexander? Did you ever meet Mr. Alexander?"

"Never."

"Never had a conversation with Mr. Alexander?"

"No sir."

"Prior to the time you filed this lawsuit, had you ever read any correspondence that Mr. Alexander wrote?"

"No. No sir."

"I want to show you plaintiff's exhibit number 6, this Reference Blank. When was the first time you saw this Reference Blank?"

"I couldn't give you a specific date. But the year was '98."

"After you filed the lawsuit?"

"Right."

"When was the first time that you heard the name Skip Alexander or James Bishop Alexander?"

"Probably in December of '97."

"About the same time, you heard Berkeley Grimball's name for the first time?"

"Right."

"What about Gordon Bondurant? Have you ever met Mr. Bondurant?"

"Well, kind of. I saw him at a deposition."

"You met him after you filed this lawsuit?"

"Yes sir."

"You had never had a conversation with him before you filed the lawsuit?"

"No sir."

"Had you ever read any notes or letters that Mr. Bondurant wrote before you filed the lawsuit?"

"Never."

"And when did you first become aware of Mr. Bondurant?"

"Probably December of '97 or January of '98."

"When did you first meet Guerry Glover?"

"In person?"

"Yes."

"I don't have a clear recollection of it. But it was maybe the latter part of November of '97, early part of December of '97."

"Okay. And prior to that time, you had never personally met Mr. Glover; is that right?"

"No sir."

"At this point, are you and Mr. Glover friends?"

"Yes sir."

"When was the last time you saw Mr. Glover?"

"This morning."

"I think you testified that you don't really remember the first time that you met Eddie Fischer; is that right?"

"Correct."

"Okay. Was Mr. Fischer ever your teacher, did he ever teach a class in which you were a student?"

"No."

"Now, you have described Mr. Fischer's initial invitation to you to go over to his house. Did you tell anybody about that invitation?"

"I didn't remember telling anyone. But my best friend at the time said he remembered me asking if I wanted him to go with me."

"And he declined to go, is that right?"

"Well, I don't remember, but yes he didn't go with me."

"You just don't have any recollection about that other than what someone has now told you?"

"I don't have any personal recollection of it."

"Alright, sir. Now, you said that this initial invitation was either late in 1989 or early in 1990, is that right?"

"That would be correct."

"And you were 18 years at that time, is that correct?"

"Right."

"You were a senior at James Island High School?"

"Right."

"And you turned 18 in the summer of 1989?"

"Right."

"And I believe you testified that you went over to Mr. Fischer's house as many as a dozen times, is that right?"

"Well, I didn't know. That was a guess."

"And I believe you said you were unclear about that because each visit was essentially the same, is that correct?"

"Right."

"And by that, I mean really after the first visit. The first time you went over there, there was not any sexual contact between you and Mr. Fischer, is that correct?"

"That would be correct."

"But that sexual contact began from the second visit on?"

"Yes."

"And from the second visit on, what happened each time was very similar, is that right?"

"Similar yes."

"I believe you testified that Mr. Fischer wanted you to come over every Thursday, is that correct?"

"That's what I remember, true."

"Okay. And he wanted you to come over for dinner, the last meal of the day?"

"That is how I remember it, yes."

"And when you would go over there, you would have dinner with Mr. Fischer, is that right?"

"Right."

"Now, how did you get from your house to Mr. Fischer's house?"

"I really don't remember. But I have a vague recollection I would drive my mother's car."

"Where did your parents live at that time?"

"On James Island."

"Where did Mr. Fischer live at that time?"

"Downtown."

"It was too far to walk from James Island?"

"Yes sir."

"Did you have a car yourself?"

"I did at one point my senior year, but I don't remember driving it to Mr. Fischer's house. I only remember driving my mother's car."

"Now, did all of the sexual activity between you and Mr. Fischer take place at night?"

"I just remember it being early evening."

"The visits did. Did any sexual activity between you and Mr. Fischer take place on the grounds of James Island High School?"

"No."

"Did Mr. Fischer ever take you from James Island High School to his house in his car?"

"Not that I recall."

"How long did it take you to drive from your parent's house to Mr. Fischer's house?"

"I have no idea. I mean . . .."

"Ten or 15 minutes?"

"Well, I know it takes me 10 minutes now, so I would assume it took around that amount of time then."

"Now, the second time that you went to Mr. Fischer's house is when he offered to massage your arm or shoulder because it was sore from playing tennis, is that right?"

"Right."

"Okay. And you described a vibrator that he used?"

"Right."

"Okay. Would it be accurate to describe that as a massager?"

"I guess."

193

"Now, during that second visit, Mr. Fischer progressively used that massager lower and lower on your body; is that right?"

"Yeah."

"And I believe you testified that you were lying on a bed with your arms straight down beside you and your legs straight out?"

"That is how I always was."

Stepp then asked him questions about the details of the abuse. They included whether Kevin ever protested whenever Fischer was abusing him. Then he asked about the praying, "And I believe you said that, 'all I could do was lie there and pray', is that right?"

"That is absolutely correct."

"What were you praying for?"

"I was praying for a number of things. First, I was asking why this was happening and I was praying that he wouldn't do it anymore. And I was just basically within myself trying to have faith that what was going on was going to stop."

"Did you ask God to make it stop?"

"Yes, I did."

"Did you try to make it stop?"

"The best thing I could do at that time was pray that God would make it stop. I couldn't have done anything."

"Were you physically restrained by Mr. Fischer?"

"I was physically restrained by fear. I mean unless you were there. I was rigid as a board. And I was no other word other than completely terrified, and I was praying, and I prayed, and I prayed, and I prayed that it wouldn't happen. That it would just end."

"I believe you said that that was the most scared you have ever been in your life?"

"I can't think of anything that compared to it."

"After the second visit, did you go back on the following Thursday?"

"I don't recall if I went back the next Thursday or not."

"But you did go back at some point?"

"Yes sir."

"And when you went back the next time, as far as you know, did you drive to Mr. Fischer's house in your car?"

"Yes."

"Now, you testified that after the second visit you tried to avoid Mr. Fischer at James Island High School, is that right?"

"I tried to avoid him every way I could."

"Did you try to avoid him by not driving to his house?"

"Well, you have to understand that at that time, I was confused about a lot of things. I was confused because this person who kept saying, 'I'm not going to hurt you, I will never do anything to hurt you, you have got to trust me, I'm doing this for your own good.' He is doing something I didn't want him to do, and I didn't know what to do about that."

"Did it occur to you not to go back to his house?"

"Mr. Fischer was good enough and persuasive enough that whenever he caught up with me or got me on the phone, whenever he got me in person, I felt there was nothing else I could do but go over to the house, which is why I tried always to avoid him. I didn't want to go over to his house. I didn't like what he was doing to me."

"Did you tell that to Mr. Fischer: 'I don't want to go to your house'?"

"On one occasion, I did."

"And then did you go to his house anyway?"

"Mr. Fischer promised me he wasn't going to do it anymore. He said he was sorry. And he promised me it wouldn't happen again."

"And when you went back, it did happen again?"

"It did."

"And he said the same thing again; did he not?"

"He said, 'I'm doing this for your own good.'"

"And then you went back again?"

"No. Whenever he got in touch with me, yes."

"You knew what Mr. Fischer was doing was wrong; did you not?"

"Yes."

"And you believed that he was hurting you and causing you damage at the time he did it, did you not?"

"Yes."

"You knew where Mr. Fischer was employed?"

"Yes."

"And obviously you knew where he lived?"

"Yes."

"You said after the second visit you went home. And I think what I wrote down you said was, 'There was no way I was going to tell my parents.' Is that accurate?"

"Yes."

"And that was because you thought your parents would be disappointed in you?"

TAMING THE LION TAMERS

"It's because I knew it would hurt them."

"And you did not wish to hurt your parents?"

"I wanted to protect my parents."

"Do you think your parents would have done something if you had told them?"

"That's not what I was thinking."

"I didn't mean to suggest you were thinking that at the time. Do you think that now?"

"When I told my father, he wanted to know if I wanted him to kill Mr. Fischer. So, I think, yes, they would have done something."

"It would have also been embarrassing to you to tell your parents, wouldn't it?"

"Yes."

"Your decision not to tell your parents is a conscious decision that you made at that time, correct?"

"It was the only alternative."

"Well, you could have told them, but it would have hurt them; am I right?"

"I made it through those months by pretending in my head like nothing was going on. I would have never told my parents."

"Okay. But you didn't fool yourself that nothing was going on. You knew something was going on?"

"Mr. . . . . you can do a lot of things when you are scared. And while I was at Mr. Fischer's house, in my mind, I wasn't there. So, when I left Mr. Fischer's house, I tried to pretend like nothing had happened."

"When did Mr. Fischer come to your parent's house for dinner?"

"I have no idea when."

"Was it during the period of time that you were going to his house for dinner?

"It was."

"Whose idea was it for Mr. Fischer to come to your parent's house?"

"It was my parents'."

"Did you tell them that you did not want Mr. Fischer to come over for dinner?"

"I never indicated to them that anything was wrong."

"Did your parents ever ask you about what you were doing at Mr. Fischer's house?"

"Well, Mr. Fischer himself told my parents what I was doing at his house."

"And what did he tell them?"

"He said that he was . . . I don't remember his exact words, exactly what he said. But he was helping me out in some way. I don't remember what, for what."

"Well, I mean did your parents ever ask, you know, how is the weightlifting going or anything of that nature?"

"I don't think he told them that he was helping me lift weights. I just remember him saying something to the effect . . . I mean because I was really shy and kind of withdrawn, he was telling my parents, you know, I was in a shell and he was going to try to help me come out of that shell. I don't remember . . . I mean that is one thing I remember him telling them. I don't think that was the only thing, but that is one thing I remember him saying to my parents."

"Is that something he said at the dinner that he had at your parent's house, or was that previous?"

"Well, I'm sure he spoke with my parents before the dinner. He said things during the dinner that he was helping me out to . . . you know, I don't know exactly when he said those things. I'm sure he said it at the dinner table too."

"How many times did your parents either meet with or have conversations with Mr. Fischer to your knowledge?"

"I'm sure they talked to him on the phone. I don't know how many times, but they had him over to the house once."

"The visits that you made to Mr. Fischer's house continued after you graduated from high school; is that right?"

"Maybe once or twice. I don't . . . it had to have been much less during the summer because it was a lot easier to avoid him."

"The last time that you went to Mr. Fischer's house I believe was right before you left Charleston to go to Columbia for college; is that right?"

"I don't think so. I think what I had said earlier was the last opportunity I had to meet with him was before I went to college, which was in September of 1990. I don't know if I had gone over to his house then or not. I don't remember. I remember the first and second time I went to his house. And all the incidents . . . all other times I don't remember when they were."

"But you know that the last time you went to Mr. Fischer's house was before you left Charleston to go to Columbia?"

"I know that the last time that I could have gone to Mr. Fischer's house was before I went to college."

"That was in 1990?"

"Yes sir."

"At any time before you left Charleston to go to college in

Columbia, did you tell anybody at James Island High School what Mr. Fischer was doing?"

"Before I went to college?"

"Yes."

"No sir."

"In fact, you never told anybody in James Island High School?"

"I never told anyone at James Island High School before I went to college."

"My question now is did you ever tell anybody at James Island High School at any time prior to the time you filed this lawsuit?"

"Who went there?"

"On the phone or in person, wrote them a letter?"

"Obviously, I told my best friend. He went to school with me, and I told a teacher in '98."

"After you filed the lawsuit?"

"Right."

"Did you consult an attorney prior to your being in touch with Mr. Meyers which you talked about a minute ago?"

"I talked to two other attorneys."

"And when was that?"

"I talked to one in October before I knew anything about Porter-Gaud just to advise me on what to do about Mr. Fischer. And then I talked to another after I learned about Porter-Gaud."

"Okay. So, the first time you contacted an attorney would have been sometime in 1997?"

"Yes sir."

"Did you have any belief that you could sue Mr. Fischer for what he did to you?"

"When?"

"At any time."

"It never occurred to me. I mean my main focus was that Mr. Fischer go to jail. I mean I wasn't thinking about anything else."

"So, you did not have the thought until sometime in 1997 about seeking counsel?"

"Right."

"Okay. Were you concerned that a legal proceeding would be a very stressful thing for you to undergo?"

"Indeed, I did."

"And indeed, it has proven to be, has it not?"

"Yes sir, it has."

"I believe that you have said that from the time of Mr. Fischer's first sexual contact with you, you have thought about that every day, is that right?"

"Pretty much."

"Now, when you left Charleston and went to Columbia to go to college, had you ever lived away from home before that?"

"No sir."

"The whole time you were in Charleston you lived in your parent's house?"

"Yes sir."

"Had you ever lived with your family outside of Charleston previously?"

"No sir."

"Did your parents drink or use alcohol at all at your home?"

"My father occasionally drank, but very sporadically and only for social reasons."

"It was not a routine part of your household experiences?"

"Not at all, no."

"Okay. Did you drink when you were in Charleston?"

"No."

"Am I right to say that the first drink then that you'd ever had was sometime after you went to Columbia to go to college?"

"Well, no that wouldn't be correct. You know, sometimes when dad was making himself a drink, I would get to taste it. So, it is not the first time I ever tasted liquor or alcohol. I mean I tasted it before I went to college. I didn't drink until I went to college."

"Okay. After you came to college, I believe you told Mr. Meyers you began to use drugs; is that right?"

"Correct."

"You took LSD?"

"Yes sir."

"You took Ecstasy?"

"Yes sir."

"You smoked marijuana?"

"Yes sir."

"I believe you said you spent some time following the Grateful Dead?"

"I did."

"Are followers of the Grateful Dead known as Deadheads?"

"Yes sir."

"Is it fair to say then that you became a Deadhead for a period of time?"

"Yes sir."

"Did you take time off from college to do that?"

"No sir."

"You just did it while you were going to college?"

"Yes sir."

"Had you ever taken any drugs before you went to college?"

"Never."

"Had you ever been offered any drugs before you went to college?"

"Never."

"And when you got to college, did you go out looking for drugs or were they offered to you?"

"I don't know how that came about. I don't remember the first time. I assume it was just with the people I was with at the time."

"Okay. You were exposed in Columbia to people who used drugs for the first time in your life; is that right?"

"Right."

"Now, did I understand you to say in response to some questions from Mr. Meyers that you feel like you have lost your sexual identity?"

"I think that would be fair."

"And do you mean by that that you are not sure whether you are heterosexual or homosexual?"

"That would be correct."

"You told Mr. Meyers that as a result of what Mr. Fischer did you have become estranged from your family, is that right?"

"I don't know if I would characterize it as estranged. I don't think I said it that way."

"You may not have. Well, tell me what word you would use to characterize your current relationship with your family."

"I would say it is very strained."

"You graduated from USC with a degree in civil engineering; is that right?"

"Right."

"And upon graduation, you went to work?"

"Right."

"As a civil engineer?"

"Well, yes."

"That's all the questions I have, thank you."

Gregg had only a couple of follow up questions. "Were you present in this courtroom when Edward Fischer was sentenced to jail for what he did to you?"

"Yes."

"And Mr. Stepp asked you about Mr. Alexander's completing this form, so Mr. Fischer could be hired when he applied to the Charleston County School District. If you could talk with Mr. Alexander now, what would you like to say to him?"

Probably everyone in the courtroom wanted to hear the answer to that question, except the Porter-Gaud lawyers.

"Objection, your honor. That would be speculative."

The judge sustained the objection."

Gregg sat down. Pieper called for a lunch break.

CHAPTER 22

In preparing for the trial, we compiled our list of witnesses and exhibits and the order in which we planned to present them. One of the biggest decisions was what to do with Gordon Bondurant. We had gone out on a limb by naming him as our expert witness. It occurred to us that one possible reason we never heard from the defense about this was that the defense lawyers might have been setting their own trap. They may have prepared Bondurant to say everything they needed to hurt the plaintiff's case. He was the most credible, likeable, and articulate of any of the witnesses affiliated with Porter-Gaud. We knew from his deposition, however, and his body language during that deposition, that he was not likely to reverse course and say what the defense wanted him to say. We figured that if he attempted to do so, we could discredit him with his own words and do damage control in our closing argument. Gregg and I decided to go with our guts and call him in the plaintiff's case.

After lunch, and before we called Bondurant to the stand, I read some brief excerpts from Fischer's deposition. We wanted him to be a relatively small presence in this trial because we wanted to keep the focus on Porter-Gaud, Grimball and Alexander.

Then it was time to spring the trap. "The Plaintiff's next witness, your honor, is Mr. Gordon Bondurant."

Robinson went into the hall to get him. As he entered, he was dressed in a nice suit, but looked extremely nervous.

I began with a pleasant demeanor. "Good afternoon, Mr. Bondurant."

"Good afternoon."

"You are the former headmaster at Porter-Gaud, is that right?"

"That's correct, yes sir."

"You retired last year?"

"I retired June 30, 1999." It occurred to me for the first time at that moment that was the day after we deposed Fischer in prison.

"And you had been at Porter-Gaud since approximately 1988?"

"1988, yes sir."

"Before you got to Porter-Gaud, you had been a headmaster at various schools in the Southeast for almost 30 years?"

"Now, it's almost 30 years. By then it was about 18 or 19 years. It's 30 years now with the headmastership at Porter-Gaud."

He testified that he attended Davidson College in North Carolina and got a master's degree at the University of Tennessee at Chattanooga. After college he had been employed by several private schools including the McCauley School in Chattanooga, the Darlington School in Rome, Georgia, and Montgomery Bell Academy in Nashville before his hiring at Porter-Gaud.

"Tell the jury what your duties were as headmaster at Porter-Gaud."

"My duties are essentially the same as those of a principal of a public school. Except in a private school, a great deal of time is spent in fund-raising and public relations and that sort of thing in addition to the curriculum, work with the curriculum and work with the student committees, faculty committees. It's those kinds of things. I had responsibility for three divisions: a lower school, a middle school and an upper school that were part of the school community."

"Now, we've heard some testimony already in this trial about a gentleman named Guerry Glover coming to see you about 1994, do you remember that?"

"Yes sir."

"Guerry came to see you and wanted to talk to you about Eddie Fischer?"

"That's correct."

"And he wanted some help from you or the school in getting Mr. Fischer out of teaching?"

"I was not certain what Mr. Glover wanted. I could assume that that potentially was on his agenda."

"But he talked to you about Eddie Fischer, didn't he?"

"Yes sir, he did."

"And he told you that Eddie Fischer was still teaching at public schools, didn't he?"

"Yes sir."

"Now, after Guerry left, you went and talked to Skip Alexander, didn't you?"

"Yes."

"Or you called him on the phone; is that right?"

"I think I saw him. I don't remember calling him on the phone. I think I saw him. He was on the campus though he had retired. He was visiting on the campus."

"But in this conversation with Skip Alexander, you verified that Eddie Fischer left Porter-Gaud as a result of an allegation of sexual misconduct?"

"That's correct."

"Now, after you verified this with Mr. Alexander, did you then do anything to affect the employment of Eddie Fischer at James Island High School?"

"No sir."

"You knew he was teaching there though, didn't you?"

"I assumed that."

"Well, Guerry told you that."

"That's why I assumed it, yes sir."

"After talking to Alexander, did you have any reason to disbelieve anything Guerry Glover had told you?"

"I was . . . I was uncertain, quite frankly."

"Did you go look for a personnel file or anything on Eddie Fischer at this time?"

"No sir."

"Did you attempt, in any way, to find any verification or corroboration as to why Eddie Fischer was let go from Porter-Gaud School?"

"No sir."

"Now, you didn't hear anything again about Edward Fischer for about three years; isn't that right?"

"That's right."

"And then in May of 1997, Guerry came back again, didn't he?"

"That's right."

"And Guerry came into your office unannounced one day?"

"That's correct."

"And he said again that he wanted help getting Eddie Fischer out of teaching, didn't he?"

"That's right."

"And you were busy on that day, weren't you?"

"I certainly was."

"And you told him that you didn't have time to meet with him?"

"That's right."

"And Guerry then went over to your calendar and flipped the pages of your calendar to find an open day?"

"That's right."

"And he found May 19th, didn't he?"

"That's right."

"And May 19 didn't have anything on it, did it?"

"As I recall, it did not."

"And Guerry said let's meet on May 19th?"

"I think that's correct."

"Okay, so, when Guerry left that day, you guys tentatively had a meeting set for May 19th?"

"That's right."

"Okay. Mr. Bondurant, I want to show you what has previously been marked as plaintiff's exhibit number 8 and ask if you recognize that document."

"I do."

"That is a note you wrote to Guerry Glover; isn't that right?"

"It is."

"How about read that to the jury."

"Dear Guerry, I shall be unable to meet with you on May the 19th. I honestly have nothing else to add to what I said before. Sincerely, Gordon E. Bondurant. This is on May the 7th."

"May the 7th of 1997. That's the same day you met with him, right?"

"I think so. I believe that was the date."

"Is that the same day you told Guerry Glover to go take Holy Communion?"

"Mr. Flowers, that was in the context . . . that was taken so out of context in the discussions that we were having about ways of dealing with issues. I think it was taken out of context when it went to the papers. And I feel terrible that it came out just that. There were a lot of other things that we discussed during that time in ways of dealing with issues. And one of the things I said was that when I personally find myself in a problem, I find a great deal of consolation in taking Holy Communion."

"So, you thought Eddie Fischer was Guerry Glover's problem?"

Stepp objected loudly, "Objection. Your honor, that is not what the witness said."

Judge Pieper didn't agree, "You can answer the question, sir."

I repeated the question, "You thought Eddie Fischer was Guerry Glover's problem?"

"I thought Eddie Fischer was Guerry Glover's problem?"

"Right. Is that why you told Guerry to take Holy Communion?"

"No, no. I would take Holy Communion myself."

"Well, Guerry didn't come to talk to you about a problem he was having at his job or anything, did he?"

"No sir."

"He came to talk to you about Eddie Fischer, didn't he?"

"He came to talk to me about his life and Eddie Fischer."

"And how Eddie Fischer had affected his life?"

"How he affected his life, that's right."

"And you told him to go take Holy Communion?"

"In context."

"After that meeting and after you wrote the note to Guerry that said you didn't have anything else to add, you then called a lawyer, didn't you?"

"Yes sir."

"And you then decided that you wanted to meet with Guerry again but only if a lawyer was there? I will help you out. Let me show you plaintiff's exhibit number 9 and ask you if you recognize that?"

"Yes sir."

"Is that a note you wrote to Guerry Glover?"

"Yes sir."

"And in that note, you essentially say I will be happy to meet with you, but I'm going to bring a friend?"

"Yes sir."

"And the friend you wanted to bring was a lawyer?"

"That's correct."

"But you didn't use the word lawyer in that note, did you?"

"But when I talked with him on the telephone, I did use that term."

"After he got the note and called you?"

"He got the note and called me."

"He got the note and wanted to know who your friend was?"

"That's right."

"Guerry had come to see you about Eddie Fischer; isn't that right?"

"Yes sir."

"And in your first meeting on May 7th, he never mentioned going to see a lawyer or any legalities, did he?"

"Mr. Flowers, I don't remember that. I can't say for sure that he did not mention the potential legal problems. I just don't remember."

"But you decided that you were only going to meet with Guerry if you could bring a lawyer?"

"I felt it was necessary. Guerry wanted something, and I couldn't determine what. And if there were actions to be taken, I would probably need some legal counsel."

I approached the witness stand and placed the enlargement of Alexander's written recommendation to the public-school district on an easel right next to Bondurant. "Let me show you what was previously marked as plaintiff's exhibit number 6. Is that a document you have seen before, Mr. Bondurant?"

"Yes sir."

"Do you understand that to be a recommendation blank from the Charleston County School District to J.B. Alexander at Porter-Gaud School?"

"I understand that to be correct, yes sir."

"Now, preliminarily, you would agree with me, wouldn't you, that a principal at Porter-Gaud School has the authority to make recommendations for former teachers at the school?"

"Yes sir."

"Mr. Bondurant, based on your experience in the education field and particularly as a headmaster at several private schools, do you believe that a person who has been accused of sexual misconduct with a student has above average character?" I was referring to the specific check marks that Alexander had put on the recommendation form for Fischer.

"No sir."

"Do you believe that a person who has been accused of sexual misconduct with a student has above average skill in teaching?"

"Objection, your honor." Stepp misunderstood what I was doing. I was trying to get Bondurant to testify in an indirect way how Alexander should have filled out the form for Fischer. "There is no foundation that Mr. Bondurant even knows Mr. Fischer. He's asking him to agree with somebody else's assessment. He doesn't even know the man."

Pieper asked me, "Are you asking in general, or are you asking about Mr. Fischer?"

"In general."

"Alright. If you're asking in general, go ahead."

Bondurant needed no prompting to continue, "No, to answer you, no sir."

"And I guess in a macabre sort of way would you agree with me that a teacher that has been accused of sexual misconduct with a student probably does have superior student control. Would you agree with that?"

"That a student . . ."

"That they would control the student and . . ."

"In a negative sort of way, yes sir."

"Okay."

"I would say so."

"What about social qualities? Do you think that a teacher who's accused of sexual misconduct with a student has above average in social qualities?"

"No, I certainly . . . I'm not sure how to answer that, Mr. Flowers. I would say it is despicable social qualities, if I can put another word in there."

I found myself starting to like this guy. He was giving straightforward answers and was not trying to dodge.

"Okay. And if you were to fill out this form and came to this line where it says any physical defects or mental peculiarities . . ."

"Fill out the form about whom?" Stepp cut me off.

"If I can just finish the question, your honor."

"Go ahead," Pieper said.

"If you were to fill out a form about a teacher that has been accused of sexual misconduct with a student and you were to come to the line that says any physical defects or mental peculiarities is that where you would point out that particular misconduct?"

Stepp objected again, saying it was hypothetical. The judge looked to me for a response.

"I'm just asking him in general if that is an appropriate place."

"I will allow it in. Go ahead."

Bondurant asked me to repeat the question. I was happy to oblige.

"If you were filling out the form, this recommendation form, for a teacher that had been accused of sexual misconduct with a student, would this be an appropriate place to point out that that teacher had been accused of sexual misconduct or . . ."

"If there is not a better place on there."

." . . any physical defects or mental peculiarities?"

"If there would not be a better place on there." Now Bondurant seemed unable to let me finish the question. He was eager to answer.

"Let me ask you, the second one is what opportunity have you had to observe the candidate's work. You never observed Eddie Fischer's work, did you?"

"Didn't know Eddie Fischer, Mr. Flowers."

"And the last one is: in your judgment is the above candidate well-fitted for the above position? Not Eddie Fischer, but as a general sense, a teacher who had been accused of sexual misconduct is that where you might note that they had been accused of sexual misconduct?"

"In no way would he be a candidate to fill a teaching position, which is what the question asks."

"Right. You would indicate to whoever you were sending this recommendation form that that teacher was in no way fitted for the position? Is that what you would have communicated?"

"I would have communicated that."

"If you had information about a teacher that had been accused of sexual misconduct, would you have filled out that form that way?"

"No sir."

"Let me show you another document, Mr. Bondurant." I placed an enlargement of the school's press release on the easel. "Have you ever seen that document before?"

"Yes sir."

"Just tell us what it is briefly, if you will."

"It's the press release that the school issued. I don't remember the date."

"Okay. While you were headmaster at Porter-Gaud, Mr. Bondurant, did Porter-Gaud have a mission statement?"

"Yes sir."

"Tell us generally what a mission statement is."

"A mission statement is the guiding principles of a school."

"Let me show you what has previously been marked for identification as plaintiff's exhibit number 19. Does that appear to be the mission statement of Porter-Gaud during your tenure?"

"It is similar to it if it is not the exact one; I assume it is."

"Mr. Bondurant let's take a look at this one just a second before we look at the press release. The mission statement, which I think you said, was the guiding principles?"

"Yes."

"'The Porter-Gaud School affirms its belief in the sovereignty of God and the dignity and worth of every individual. The school recognizes the supreme importance of the pursuit of truth, the encouragement of scholarship and the promotion of good citizenship.' Did I read that correctly?"

"Yes sir."

"So, at the time you issued this press release, part of the mission statement or the guiding principles of Porter-Gaud School was the supreme importance of the pursuit of truth. Do you agree with that?"

"Yes sir."

"Now, isn't it true Mr. Bondurant, the reason that this press release was created was because of the press coverage related to the arrest of Eddie Fischer?"

"That's correct."

"And you felt the need to respond in a public manner to some of the things that were in the press?"

"That's right."

"And you didn't actually create this, you had a lawyer create it, but you approved it; isn't that right?"

"Final approval, yes sir."

"So, the words that are in this press release are words that were approved by you as headmaster of Porter-Gaud School; is that right?"

"That's right."

"Before this press release was issued, did you do anything to determine whether the allegation against Eddie Fischer in 1982 was true or not?"

"Well, in addition to talking to Mr. Alexander, no sir, I didn't do anything else."

"In talking with Mr. Alexander, you never attempted to find out if the '82 incident was true or not, did you?"

"That's right. I did not pursue it, no sir."

"So, when you issued this, you had no idea whether the allegation against Eddie Fischer in 1982 was true or not, did you?"

"That's correct. They were allegations."

"Did you think that would have been important before you communicated with the public about this?"

"I didn't at the time, no sir."

"Now, you begin this press release with 'a 33-year-old Johns Island resident . . .' would you agree with me that is Guerry Glover; is that who you are referring to?"

"Yes sir."

"'A 33-year-old Johns Island resident has provided the press with a letter addressed to the members of Porter-Gaud board of trustees stating that while he was a student in the Porter-Gaud School in the early 1980s, a former Porter-Gaud School teacher sexually abused him. This former teacher has not been employed at Porter-Gaud for over 15 years.' Where in there do you mention that that former student came to see you twice before this was released and told you about what happened with Eddie Fischer?"

"I don't see it in there. It was not in there."

"You didn't put it in there, did you?"

"No sir."

"Before you issued this press release, you had confirmed with Berkeley Grimball that Eddie Fischer had been on probation while he was at the Porter-Gaud School, didn't you?"

"I believe so."

"Where is that in that press release? Where did you tell the public that while he was at the Porter-Gaud School Eddie Fischer was on probation?"

"I did not feel it appropriate to tell the public personnel information."

"You consider that personnel information?"

"Personal information about personnel."

"But what you did want the public to believe when you issued this press release was that Porter-Gaud didn't have any information about Eddie Fischer; isn't that right?"

Stepp objected and was overruled.

I was once again happy to repeat the question. "When you issued this press release, Mr. Bondurant, you wanted the public to think that Porter-Gaud School had no information about any misconduct about Eddie Fischer, didn't you?"

"I don't think it says that."

"Tell me where in there you mention any bad information that the school had about Eddie Fischer?"

"I didn't put any bad information that the school had about Eddie Fischer in the press release."

"Now, tell the jury, if you would, you mention in there that you support the student. Tell the jury everything Porter-Gaud School has done to support Guerry Glover since he first came forward."

"Guerry, of course, is no longer a student. He's 28 . . . at the time was a 28-year-old adult who was before me. He was not a student at Porter-Gaud at that time."

"Is the answer nothing, Mr. Bondurant?"

"I'm sorry?"

"Is the answer nothing? What did you do to support Guerry Glover after he came forward?"

"Well, I talked with him and counseled with him, but nothing other than that."

"Where in your press release does it say to the public that any sexual contact between Eddie Fischer and his victim or victims was consensual?"

"In the press release?"

"Yes."

"I didn't say anything in there about that. It doesn't say anything about it."

"And, in fact, until this lawsuit was filed, you had never taken the position that it was consensual . . . not you personally but the school?"

"That it was consensual?"

"That it was consensual."

"Not to my knowledge."

"Now, after this was released, you got a phone call from two

220

gentlemen, didn't you? The Hammond brothers?"

"Yes."

"And the Hammonds took issue with this press release, didn't they?"

"They wanted to inform me that there were some other things that had occurred."

"And yet those were things that you already knew about, weren't they?"

"About?"

"About Eddie Fischer being on probation because of his approach to Ronnie Hammond?"

"Yes."

"So, they didn't give you any new information, did they?"

"No sir."

"Did you ever issue another press release to clarify this one?"

"No sir."

"Now, you say in here, 'while Porter-Gaud is receiving a lot of attention from what this former student has said, the school has no direct knowledge of what happened to him or any other former students while the accused teacher was at Porter-Gaud. Without sufficient evidence, the authorities cannot prosecute an alleged child abuser.' What direct knowledge do you need to satisfy you that Eddie Fischer was molesting children while he was at Porter-Gaud?"

"What direct knowledge do I need?"

"That's right."

"Someone who is specifically willing to stand up and face . . . face us with the issue that there is an . . . and willing to go to the legal system to

221

affirm that something had occurred."

"Isn't it true when you issued this you believed that the direct knowledge you were referring to there was that you had to have somebody who was actually present at the molestation before Porter-Gaud could know whether it occurred or not?"

"I don't think that's . . . no, that's not what I meant."

"Mr. Bondurant let me hand you two depositions. Do you remember giving a deposition on May 5th, 1999?"

"Yes sir."

"And you understood at that time that you were under oath, you raised your hand and swore to tell . . ."

"Yes sir."

." . . the truth just like you did today?"

"Yes sir."

"Did you, in fact, tell the truth on that day?"

"Yes sir, I thought I did."

"Well, let's take a look then on page 95, if you will."

"Yes sir."

"And you were asked about this exact same sentence that we were just talking about."

"Yes sir."

"You were asked at that time . . . 'I'm going to reference you to the second to the last sentence on the press release that says the school has no direct knowledge of what happened to him or any other former student while the accused teacher was at Porter-Gaud. Your answer was: yes, ma'am. Question: do you think that sentence is correct?' Your answer was: 'We had no direct knowledge. We had allegations, but no direct knowledge.

Question: what would direct knowledge be? Answer: being present.' Has your position change since May 5th, 1999?"

"It depends on . . . I hate to sound like someone else. But it depends, in my mind, upon direct, quite frankly on the definition of direct. If you mean absolutely direct, yes, I think physical presence is essential. On the other hand, if you mean plenty of evidence weighing heavily, then I would say it's what I had testified earlier is correct."

"The reason I'm confused, Mr. Bondurant, is you chose this word direct knowledge. And I'm just asking what you meant when you told the public you had no direct knowledge?"

"What I meant when I told the public that is that we were not physically present."

"Now, Mr. Bondurant, you are married; is that right?"

"That's right."

"And you have two sons?"

"That's right."

"And you . . . I guess by any account . . . have had a successful, happy life?"

"Very much so until all of this has come up."

"Now, if you could package up that happiness, if you could take the relationships that you have with your wife and children, the success you have in business and you could package that up . . ."

Stepp objected. The judge said, "I have to hear the question first, but where are you . . . go ahead. Let me hear the question."

I continued, "and let's say somebody like Bill Gates wanted to purchase from you in this package your happiness and your life how much would you take for it?" I didn't know if I would get away with this question, but I wanted to plant a seed in the jury's mind that those things are valuable beyond measure.

The judge didn't let me get away with it. "Sustained."

The moment had arrived where we had to decide whether to cross the Rubicon and name Bondurant as our expert witness. I approached the witness stand and moved some of the exhibits in order to buy myself a couple of minutes to think. I liked the responses he had given so far and thought it would work. On my way back to the podium, I made eye contact with Gregg, who gave me a slight nod.

I immediately started qualifying Gordon Bondurant as an expert witness for the plaintiff. I had to elicit testimony that the witness has knowledge or training superior to lay people so that his opinions would be helpful to the jury in determining the issues they had to decide in the case.

"Now, as an administrator, Mr. Bondurant, you have had training in the area of sexual misconduct in the education setting; isn't that right?"

"Yes sir."

"And you also have this almost 30 years of experience as a headmaster at various private schools?"

"Yes sir."

"And, in fact, you've even had experience in your past handling an allegation of sexual misconduct; isn't that right?"

"That's right."

"And you felt like you dealt with that situation appropriately, don't you?"

"Yes sir."

"You dismissed the teacher, didn't you?"

"That's right."

"In that setting, did you ever blame the student?"

"In the previous . . ."

"The previous incident where you dismissed the teacher?"

"No sir, I did not blame the student."

After a long, intentional pause to let that last response sink in, I turned to the judge, "Your honor, at this time, we would offer Mr. Gordon Bondurant as an expert witness on the issue of sexual contact between students and teachers."

Stepp was on his feet. "Objection, and I would like to approach, your honor."

At the bench, Bobby argued that the plaintiff did not identify Bondurant as an expert and that we could not compel him to testify as an expert without compensating him. I offered to pay him and inquired how much he wanted, which annoyed Stepp and made the judge chuckle and Bondurant, who was within earshot, smile. While the lawyers were at the bench, the jury indicated to the judge that they wanted a break. So, after sending the jury out of the courtroom, Stepp and I continued the argument from counsel tables. The judge was as surprised as Stepp, who we later learned had never been informed by Robinson that we had identified Bondurant as our expert witness. He looked at me and with a puzzled look said, "Now, you said you identified him and that you were going to call him as an expert."

"Yes sir, we did last summer. And I will be happy to hand up to the court or I can just read it into the record, if you want me to."

"Alright."

I read from the plaintiff's answers to the defendants' interrogatories, "'The Plaintiff expects to qualify Gordon Bondurant, headmaster of Porter-Gaud, as an expert in the areas of school administration, school policies and school management, particularly in the area of sexual contact between teachers and students. His testimony is expected to be consistent with his prior depositions.' Your honor, we also in another discovery response . . . I don't have the date on it right here . . . 'the plaintiffs expect to qualify Gordon Bondurant, headmaster of Porter-Gaud, as an expert in the areas of school administration, school policies and school management particularly in the area of sexual contact between teachers and students. His testimony is expected to be consistent with his prior depositions.' We put them on notice a year ago. There have not been any motions filed with the court. There has been nothing. We purposely did not retain an expert because we intended to call Mr. Bondurant as an expert, and there is no requirement in the rules that we pay him, that we retain him, that we do anything else other than adequately qualify him, which we believe we have done."

Stepp was reeling. "Your honor, the power of the subpoena goes to fact witnesses. It does not go to expert witnesses. I can't simply subpoena someone and drag them into the courtroom and make them my expert witness against their will. Those opinions are theirs and are not discoverable or producible absent an agreement with the parties. And there is certainly no foundation that Mr. Bondurant has agreed to be the expert for the Plaintiffs in this case."

"Your honor, my reaction to that would be we don't have to get his agreement. As the court is aware, in a medical malpractice case I could qualify the defendant doctor as an expert witness."

"Mr. Bondurant is not the defendant in this case, your honor. They have sued him in other cases, but they haven't sued him in this case."

The judge wanted a break and told us he would give us an answer after the break.

After the recess, the judge still had questions. "Let me ask the plaintiffs, are you seeking to qualify him as an expert to show that they had someone there on staff with expertise in this area and they didn't act accordingly?"

"No sir," I responded.

"That would have been a good theory."

"But he wasn't there during the time, judge. That's the only reason we didn't do that. We are going to use him, though, to establish the standard on sexual conduct between teachers and students in the education field in South Carolina. He has already given abundant testimony that's very relevant to these issues, on the issue of consent and other things."

"Are you going to have someone else on that issue?"

"No sir. We didn't feel like we needed anybody after we took his deposition. Once we took his deposition, we made the decision we didn't need to retain an expert, and we named him as an expert in this case."

The judge looked at Stepp, "I've looked at the rules. I don't see anything in the rules that would prohibit them from doing that. I've checked them. I don't . . . I know it's not the normal procedure, but I don't see any prohibitions to asking that someone be qualified as an expert."

Stepp tried to coach Bondurant with this response, "Well, if he's willing to give him an opinion . . . if he's willing to."

The judge knew what Bobby was trying to do and was clearly annoyed at Bobby's attempt to influence the witness' testimony, "Well, he's here under oath. You know, if he doesn't feel he is capable of giving an opinion when they ask him that question, but I'm going to qualify him. I think he has something that he can offer. Bring the jury in."

Bondurant had been sitting at the witness stand during this entire argument, situated right between Pieper and Stepp. After the judge ruled, he looked at Stepp and didn't seem happy that the defense had attempted to silence him yet again. Then he made eye contact with me and looked anxious for the next question.

When the jury was seated in the box, Pieper took control for a moment. He turned to me. "Now, you wanted to move to have him qualified as an expert in . . . restate the area, please, so we get back up to speed."

I looked at the jury as I responded slowly and clearly. "The area of sexual contact between students and teachers in the educational arena in the State of South Carolina, your honor."

The judge then inquired from the defense, "In regard to what the court has indicated, does the defense wish to contest his qualifications in this regard?"

"Yes, your honor, I do." Challenging the qualifications or

credentials of an opponent's expert witness is a common tactic at trial. It probably didn't occur to Stepp at that moment, but in this case involving sexual contact between a teacher and a student, he was suggesting to the jury that the former headmaster of Porter-Gaud School was not knowledgeable enough about the issue to testify about it. It was a moment that was not lost on many in attendance including, probably, some members of the jury. He wanted an opportunity to ask questions to disqualify Bondurant as an expert witness. "Mr. Bondurant, when did you receive any training in this field?"

"Several . . . two or three institutes back in the early '90s." Stepp knew that these "institutes" were merely training classes provided by the school's insurance company. He did not want to pursue this line of questioning because it gave Bondurant an opportunity to mention insurance to the jury.

"Did you have any . . ."

"Mid '90s, I guess."

"Did you have any training in 1988?"

"No."

"That's all, your honor."

The judge didn't hesitate. "Alright. I'm going to find him to be qualified in that area. Go ahead, sir."

I went right to the questions that we hoped would completely negate the defense of consent. "Mr. Bondurant, would you agree with me that amorous or erotic relationships between teachers and students are always inappropriate?" This was the sentence that was lifted verbatim from Porter-Gaud's faculty manual.

"Unacceptable, yes sir."

"That is because of the difference in power between a teacher and a student; isn't that right?"

"That's what I understand."

228

"And it's the difference in power is always fundamentally unbalanced, isn't it?"

"It is."

"And you would agree with me, wouldn't you, that it is incumbent on the teacher not to abuse or even seem to abuse the power with which they are entrusted?"

"I think that is a fair statement."

"So, you would agree that it is incumbent on the teacher not to abuse or seem to abuse in a sexual nature any student at that school?"

"Absolutely."

"Before you retired in the summer of 1999 did you ever have or find any evidence, at all, that Kevin Dunn consented to sexual contact with Eddie Fischer?"

"Not to my knowledge."

"Did you ever tell the faculty members at Porter-Gaud that students are off limits sexually until they attained the age of 18?"

"No sir."

"You don't agree with that, do you?"

"No sir, I don't."

"Do you agree that even if a student attains the age of 18 or 19, as long as they are a student, sexual contact is inappropriate?"

"I'm not speaking as an expert because I don't know the field that well. But I would certainly feel that a teacher student relationship is a sacred one and, therefore, would prohibit that kind of a relationship."

"Mr. Bondurant, in your training that you received in the area of sexual misconduct or sexual contact between teachers and students, have you ever been trained that the parents are responsible for sexual molestation of students by a teacher?"

"No, excuse me, what? I'm sorry?"

"Have you ever been trained that the parents are responsible for it?"

"No sir."

"I don't have any more questions for Mr. Bondurant."

It would not have surprised us if Stepp had asked no questions. Bondurant had certainly not helped their cause. But he went ahead. "Mr. Bondurant, let me try to go back a little bit. When did you first come to Porter-Gaud?"

"1988."

"And you went there as the headmaster?"

"That's correct."

"Did you replace Mr. Grimball?"

"I did."

"So, you and Mr. Grimball were not at Porter-Gaud at the same time?"

"No sir."

"Was Mr. Alexander at Porter-Gaud when you came there?"

"Yes sir."

"In what capacity did Mr. Alexander serve?"

"He was . . . when I came, he was the upper school principal."

"Well, did he subsequently retire?"

"He was . . . yes, he retired in '94 . . . '93 or '94, I can't remember."

"Was Eddie Fischer a teacher at Porter-Gaud at any time while you were the headmaster there?"

"No sir."

"Have you ever met Eddie Fischer?"

"To my knowledge, I have never met him. I have met a lot of people in this town, but to my knowledge, I don't remember having met him."

"Have you ever had a conversation with Eddie Fischer?"

"Not to my knowledge."

"When you were the headmaster at Porter-Gaud, was Guerry Glover a student at Porter-Gaud?"

"No sir, he was not."

"When Mr. Glover came to see you in 1994, had you ever met him before?"

"Not to my knowledge."

"Did you know who he was?"

"Not to my knowledge, I did not."

"And did you know anything about Mr. Fischer at that time?"

"No sir."

"Did you even know the name Eddie Fischer?"

"I perhaps had heard it in the past, but it had not registered."

"So, when Mr. Glover came to see you in 1994 to talk about Eddie Fischer, did you know what or who he was talking about?"

"Well, other than what he told me."

"Other than what he told, that was it?"

"That's right."

"Now, when Mr. Glover told you something about inappropriate contact, inappropriate sexual conduct by Mr. Fischer, was that the first that you had ever heard of that?"

"Yes sir."

"You never heard anything about that before?"

"No sir."

"Until Mr. Glover walked in your office and told you?"

"First time."

"Why didn't you go to the solicitor's office or to the police in 1994 when Mr. Glover came to see you?"

"I asked Mr. Glover if he would be willing to go to the police, and he said no."

"Mr. Glover was not willing to go with you?"

"He was not willing to go with me."

"Did you think that what Mr. Glover had told you was sufficient for you to initiate a prosecution of Mr. Fischer?"

"I felt very concerned about it; no sir."

"Now, you spoke with Mr. Alexander about the 1982 incident that caused Mr. Fischer to be forced to resign, is that right?"

"That's right."

"Did Mr. Alexander tell you that the names of the people involved in that incident were confidential?"

"He did."

"Did he tell you that was confidential at the expressed request of the parents?"

"He did."

"Did you think you could violate that confidentiality unilaterally?"

"I did not feel I could."

"Did you even know the name?"

"No sir."

"Did Mr. Alexander tell you that?"

"I'm not sure if he told me. I don't remember."

"Do you know the name today?"

"No sir . . . I can't recall if I do. I don't recall it."

"Now, when Mr. Glover came to see you in 1994, did you feel threatened?"

"I felt very concerned."

"Did Mr. Glover subsequently file a lawsuit against Porter-Gaud?"

"Ultimately, yes sir."

"Now, what exactly did Mr. Glover want you to do in 1994 about Mr. Fischer?"

"That I don't know for sure. I wanted him to give me some guidance on what his expectations were for the school's actions."

"And what did he tell you he expected the school to do?"

"He did not tell me what he expected the school to do directly."

"Did he tell you he expected you to go prosecute Mr. Fischer by yourself?"

"No, he did not."

"Did you ask him whether he would be willing to testify if a prosecution of Mr. Fischer were initiated?"

"I don't remember asking that question."

"Now, after Mr. Glover left in 1994, when did you next hear from him again?"

"I think it was 1997."

"So, three years go by?"

"That's right."

"You didn't hear anything from Mr. Glover for three years?"

"That's correct."

"He did not call you?"

"That's right."

"He didn't write you?"

"I don't remember. If it did occur, I have forgotten it."

"When did you first find out that Skip Alexander had signed a Reference Blank to the Charleston County School District?"

"I think probably February of '98."

"After this present litigation was filed?"

"After the litigation was commenced."

"Did you know that at the time this press release was issued?"

"Know the . . .?"

"That Mr. Alexander had signed anything?"

"No sir."

"Did you ever talk with Berkeley Grimball about Mr. Fischer?"

"I think after the litigation . . . or after it became public . . . not the litigation, but after it became public, we certainly did. I don't remember having any conversation, at all, prior to that. Counselor, we may have had, but I just don't recall any conversation."

"Do you know the Plaintiff in this case?"

"Kevin Dunn, no sir, I don't."

"Have you ever met him?"

"I have seen him. I have not met him."

"Did Mr. Dunn ever call you and ask you to do anything about Eddie Fischer?"

"No sir."

"Did Mr. Dunn ever call you and ask you what you knew about Eddie Fischer?"

"No sir."

"Did Mr. Fischer . . . did Mr. Dunn ever call you about that press release?"

"Not that I know about."

"Did he ever call you about that mission statement?"

"Not that I know of."

"Mr. Bondurant, have you ever intended to harm anyone in your handling of this affair?"

"I pray not. I certainly don't want to harm anyone any more than the horrendous hurt that has already occurred to all of the victims and others."

"Thank you, sir."

I rose and asked some questions.

"Mr. Bondurant isn't it true . . . you said Guerry Glover filed a lawsuit. Isn't it true he withdrew that lawsuit?"

"Mr. Flowers, I don't remember that."

"Don't you remember receiving a letter from Mr. Glover where he said I've withdrawn my lawsuit and have instructed my lawyers not to do anything else?"

Stepp surprised me by standing and saying, "Your honor, we will stipulate to that."

I thanked him and turned back to Bondurant. "After Guerry Glover's visits, you could have . . . you couched your earlier answers in terms of calling the police. You could have picked up the phone and called the principal at James Island High School, couldn't you?"

"Yes sir, I could have."

"But you didn't, did you?"

"No sir, I didn't."

"And you . . ."

"And I regret it to this day, Mr. Flowers." No one who saw this man make that statement doubted that he meant it. He had learned that at least one young man was being molested by Fischer after Guerry's visits to him in 1997. The look on his face as he gave this response reflected the anguish it was causing him.

"And eventually Guerry Glover is the one that went to the police, isn't that right?"

"I'm not sure who did."

"Do you have any reason to dispute that?"

"I assume he did, yes sir. Eventually, I know he did, yes sir."

"That is all of the questions I have. Thank you, Mr. Bondurant."

Usually thanking a witness from the other side, especially one that you have sued, is a superficial gesture. With Gordon Bondurant, I appreciated his candor and his willingness to tell the truth even when it did not make him look very good. Witnesses like that, unfortunately, are very rare. While we knew we had him hemmed in on some of the issues, he delivered more for Kevin's case, and the truth, than we could have ever hoped for. At that time, Bondurant was a defendant in some of the other cases we had pending against the school. As a result of his testimony, Gregg and I asked our clients to consider dismissing him as a defendant from all of those cases. Every client agreed without hesitation. It was a tangible demonstration of how important the truth was to these victims.

As the trial progressed, we were rattled by two developments. First, during many of the breaks, Judge Pieper would go down the hall to Judge Rawl's chambers and visit with the senior judge. We wondered if we might be overreacting, so we asked others to keep an eye on it. Many people noticed how much time Pieper spent in Rawl's office during the breaks.

The second was the judge's pressure to settle. It is common for a judge to encourage parties to settle cases, even during trial. Many judges see it as part of their responsibility to encourage settlement. In *John Doe v. Porter-Gaud School*, Pieper had gone the extra mile. Now that Kevin was at the courthouse, Pieper turned up the pressure. He wanted to speak directly to Kevin. Throughout these sessions, the judge constantly said, "I don't want to twist anybody's arm, but . . ." It was always the "but" that was so unnerving, because he made several statements to Kevin indicating that he'd better settle. He never said it directly, but he strongly implied on more than one occasion that he was going to dismiss Kevin's case. He had Gregg, me, and Kevin meet with him in chambers, and even got Kevin's parents to come in.

We only had two more witnesses in our case: Charlie Bennett and Kevin's father. We could have finished our presentation of evidence in less than two hours.

The pressure on Kevin was enormous. He did not want his case dismissed, and Pieper had persuaded him that was exactly what was going to happen. He settled.

About fifteen minutes after the jury was dismissed and the spectators had filed out, Gregg and I finished boxing up all our trial materials and we were alone in the courtroom with Pieper. As we walked by the bench on our way out, I asked, "So what'd you think of us calling their headmaster as our expert witness?"

He looked up, smiled, and said, "Yeah, I was telling Vic about that last night." I didn't stick around to hear the rest of his response. From his own mouth, we now knew Pieper was discussing the trial with Judge Rawl, and apparently even after hours. I was even more angry than I was before I asked him the question.

Kevin and Guerry were waiting for Gregg and me in the hall. The four of us walked downstairs together. As we exited the courthouse, a magical thing happened. Unexpectedly, nine female members of the jury were waiting outside for Kevin. As he walked out, they all came to him and enveloped him in a group hug. Eight of them spent the next hour laughing, hugging, and crying with him. They invited him to dinner. One invited him to come to her church. Another invited him to come live with her. One even offered to adopt him. The despair and guilt that Kevin felt for settling dissipated. They wanted to know all about him and about things they didn't hear in the courtroom, but they suspected; they correctly surmised that Alexander was a pedophile.

They wanted to know about other victims. At first, they had harsh words for Gregg and me for settling the case. One said they "were going to take care of Kevin and his children and his grandchildren." When we explained the possibility of Pieper dismissing the case, they directed their anger at him. They wanted to render a verdict, and the thought that Pieper would even consider taking the case away from them enraged several of them.

One juror who didn't stay the whole time said Kevin's age and the fact that he kept going back to Fischer's house concerned her. She said she wanted to hear more about each of those issues before she made up her mind. While those comments were lost on most of the people still hanging around, they were not lost on Gregg and me.

We knew then we still had work to do in future trials to convince jurors that the boys were not at fault, regardless of their age and how many times they went back.

As the women were finishing with Kevin, Gregg stepped up and asked if he and I could ask them a few questions. They all agreed.

"We were thinking about asking you for damages in an amount of about $10 million. Would that have offended any of you?" Gregg asked.

The responses were similar and surprising:

"Yeah, it would have bothered me because it's not enough."

"I was thinking about $50-100 million."

"Millions? Honey, I was thinking billions."

CHAPTER 23

We knew after the first trial that we would need a new expert witness for the other pending cases. We could not reasonably expect to use Bondurant in the future. At an education-related conference right after Kevin's trial, Gregg was seated next to an employee of the state Department of Education. Gregg asked him if he knew of any school administrator in South Carolina who had dealt with sexual abuse of a student by a teacher. The gentleman immediately said, "I know just the guy for you to talk to."

Dr. Reggie Christopher was the superintendent of a public-school district in the northwestern part of South Carolina. I called his office a few days later. I asked if he would be interested in testifying as an expert witness for the plaintiffs in the cases that were still pending. Reggie said he had never been an expert witness and seemed reluctant. He asked a lot of questions about what it involved. I explained the process and the issues in the litigation that we wanted him to comment on. Initially, Reggie said he found it hard to believe that a school administrator could be as bad as I was describing Grimball and Alexander. I asked if he would look at the depositions and documents without committing himself. He agreed. I delivered copies of several depositions and documents to his office the next morning.

The following week, Gregg and I were at Reggie's office to get his impression of the materials he had read and to discuss his willingness to get involved. He began the meeting by emphatically describing how appalled he was by the sworn testimony of the Porter-Gaud officials. He quoted from memory some portions of Grimball's testimony that particularly bothered him. With no prompting from us, he had identified the crucial issues in the case. We asked him a few questions. His answers were direct, and all had a common theme: the safety of children was the most important issue in every school. It was clear that he was not just reciting administrative policy. He believed it. He told us how angered he got when he reviewed the recommendation form that Alexander had filled out.

While Gregg and Reggie chatted, I got up to look at the plaques and diplomas on his Wall of Honor. I found that the previous year Christopher had been named South Carolina Superintendent of the Year. That would certainly bolster his credibility. At the end of the meeting, he agreed to help.

As we walked to our cars, I told Gregg "I'm in love." We knew Reggie Christopher had the credentials, the experience and demeanor to make a good expert witness. His thick southern accent didn't hurt either. Our only concern was how he would hold up in cross-examination. Porter-Gaud would have to attack him hard to discredit his opinions. He had never been subjected to that, and we wondered how he would do.

During the summer, we also considered a very unorthodox approach to the 11 cases still pending. From the way Judge Pieper treated Kevin, we assumed he was not going to let any of the cases get to a jury. We knew the defendants were not interested in settling, so we would be facing a directed verdict or pressure to settle in every trial. We would appeal a directed verdict. If we ever got to a jury and won, the defendants would appeal. So, we started thinking about whether it was worth all of that for some of our clients. Gregg suggested that we consider losing one of the defendants' motions for summary judgment on purpose in the trial court. If an appeal was inevitable, it made sense to us to get the threshold legal issues resolved -- most significantly the statute of limitations -- by the appellate courts before we put another client through the meat grinder of a trial. If we won the appeal, we would then get a trial without the uncertainties that we were facing in the summer of 2000. We floated the idea to some lawyers we trusted. The lawyers agreed that it seemed to be a risky, but not reckless, strategy given the unique nature of the cases and victims. Gregg was confident he could prevail on an appeal with the facts that we had already established.

While we were formulating, reconsidering, and even questioning this new strategy, we got a big surprise. On August 7, 2000, the Supreme Court of South Carolina issued an opinion in a case Gregg had brought for a sexual abuse victim who had repressed her memory of her abuse. In *Moriarty v. Garden Church of God*, the central ruling turned out to be irrelevant to our litigation, but in its written opinion, the court relied on the case of *True v. Monteith*, a malpractice case against a lawyer. Gregg had been asserting *True v. Monteith* as the foundation of our legal arguments in every case against Porter-Gaud that involved the statute of limitations. The Supreme Court, on its own initiative, had injected the *True* case into the area of sex abuse cases. It was exactly what Gregg had been arguing all along in the cases against Porter-Gaud. Essentially, what the court ruled by citing this case was that a jury would have to decide at least some of the issues in the present cases related to the statute of limitations. Gregg was vindicated, and he and I were ecstatic.

We immediately abandoned the "lose on purpose" strategy. We believed that Pieper could not possibly grant a directed verdict in light of *Moriarty*. Without this threat, we also felt that the judge would not be able to exert the pressure to settle on other victims like he had on Kevin. We thought the victims and their families were finally going to hear what 12 citizens of Charleston had to say about Porter-Gaud and its administrators.

We began focusing on the next trial like a laser beam. We were going to get to the jury.

In September, Pieper summoned all the lawyers involved in the Porter-Gaud cases to Charleston. He wanted to hold a status conference and hear any outstanding motions in all the filed cases. It was clear to all of us that he was now pushing the cases and wanted to either settle them or try another case immediately.

At the status conference Pieper told the lawyers the cases were now on a fast track. He explained that since the parties could not agree on a settlement value for the cases involving Porter-Gaud victims, he wanted to try a parent's case. He said once the jury put a value on a parent's case, which all agreed were worth less monetarily than a victim's case, we might be able to extrapolate a value for the victims' cases. He decided the next trial would be in October and would be *Harold Glover and Maria Cordova v. Porter-Gaud School, et al.* Maria was the mother of Carlos Salinas.

It was apparent to everyone present that Pieper had decided to handle all the cases involving Porter-Gaud. This was somewhat unprecedented because no one had asked him to do so and they had not been determined to be complex cases pursuant to court rules, which would have required them to be assigned to a single judge. We had previously asked two other judges to formally declare the cases as complex, so we could get one judge and wouldn't have to explain the whole case every time we went before a new judge. On both occasions, the judges refused to declare the cases complex. Now, on his own volition, and we suspected with some help from Judge Rawl, Pieper had taken control over all the litigation.

The judge had previously asked both sides to propose a method and schedule to try the 11 cases that were pending on the docket, all arising from the same facts regarding Fischer and Porter-Gaud. We proposed one trial on liability issues to see if a jury would hold the defendants responsible, and if they did, then a series of mini-trials to determine appropriate damages for each individual plaintiff. The defense lawyers proposed separate trials for each case, with a trial being held every month for 11 months. They wanted a war of attrition, which always favors the well-funded insurance companies and big law firms. I'm sure it was just coincidental that the defense lawyers were getting paid by the hour. The judge agreed with their proposal and scheduled one trial a month for 11 months beginning in October. The financial strain that the litigation was putting on Gregg and me was instantly exponentially worse. We worked on a contingent fee basis, meaning we only got paid if we won. We had already advanced approximately $100,000 in litigation costs, which we would likely never recover if we lost.

Also, at this hearing, Porter-Gaud argued that it did not have a legal duty to provide a safe environment for children. The school raised this argument in a brief signed by Laura Robinson. Of all the arguments and legal positions Porter-Gaud advanced in the litigation, this was the most bizarre: a school arguing that students' safety was not the school's responsibility, they were only responsible for providing an education. When the judge confronted Stepp about this argument, he couldn't abandon it fast enough.

Finally, at the September hearing, Pieper suggested he was thinking about bifurcating the trial, splitting it into two distinct phases. The first would be to determine whether the defendants were liable and, if so, how much compensatory damages the plaintiffs would be entitled to. Compensatory damages are intended to compensate plaintiffs for their losses stemming directly from the defendants' conduct. If, *and only if*, the plaintiffs won this phase, the second phase would be to determine whether Grimball's and Alexander's conduct was egregious enough to warrant punitive damages; in South Carolina, punitive damages may not be awarded against an educational institution. Punitive damages are intended to punish or make an example of any defendant who has acted particularly badly. Prior to this hearing, we had not intended to spend much effort seeking punitive damages. Instead, we wanted to focus on the harm to Harold and Maria and their respective families. With bifurcation, however, we could have the best of both worlds. If the plaintiffs prevailed in the first phase, we could really tee off on Grimball and Alexander in the punitive damages phase. Most of the really bad evidence involving Grimball and Alexander would not be admissible in the first phase; we figured this is exactly what Pieper was thinking. At first, Gregg and I were concerned that this might affect our ability to sufficiently paint the full picture for the jury. After thinking it through, however, we realized we could present a good case with only part of the evidence, and that the jury would likely be outraged when they heard the rest of the story in the second phase. We planned for the next trial accordingly.

CHAPTER 24

The trial of *Harold Glover and Maria Cordova versus Porter-Gaud School, Grimball and Alexander* began on October 16, 2000. From the beginning, it was not a good trial for the plaintiffs. Gregg had a death in his family and missed the first day attending the funeral. We had big problems scheduling witnesses; Maria's son, Carlos Salinas, a very strong witness, could not attend because his wife was giving birth to their first child. As the trial progressed, we became dissatisfied with our presentation to the jury.

Some interesting moments came up though. We were only able to get through opening statements and one witness, Ralph Nordlund, on the first day. He was an excellent witness for the plaintiffs again.

The next morning, Gregg rose to his feet and said, "Your honor, the next witness is Charlie Bennett."

Charlie took the witness stand and swore to tell the truth. Gregg began his direct examination establishing who he was, his occupation and other details of his life. The questioning then turned to his history with Alexander.

"Where did you attend elementary school?"

"Porter Military Academy."

"When you began school there, was James Bishop Alexander

working there?"

"Yes, he was a teacher at Porter Military."

"How old were you when you met Mr. Alexander?"

"Approximately 10 years old."

"And how long did you know James Bishop Alexander, from the time you were 10 until when?"

"Up until his demise."

"Please describe any instances in which Mr. Alexander exhibited a sexual interest in you."

"I guess it must've been around the eighth or ninth grade. I spent time over at his house on the Isle of Palms on a regular basis. We would take showers together. There was no such thing as air conditioning, and he insisted that we take naps together in the bed. It was approximately then when he began the oral sex."

"Did you want to have Mr. Alexander as a sexual partner?"

"I told Skipper, Mr. Alexander, on a regular basis throughout the years and throughout the decades, that I was not interested in such a relationship because he was more of a father to me, and I really needed a father figure at that time. But he would never reply to that."

"Did he ever stop his sexual involvement with you?"

"No, he pressed forward over the years."

"For what period of time?"

"'Til his death by suicide."

"How old were you when that sexual involvement began?"

"Well, he died in '98 around late April, and I'm 54 now, so

whatever age I was in eighth or ninth grade. Around 12?"

"All right. Thank you, sir. No further questions."

With that, Gregg sat down. Short, sweet, and straight to the point. The public had now learned for the first time that Alexander, too, was a pedophile.

Now it was Stepp's turn to cross-examine the witness. He strode toward the witness box. "Mr. Bennett, are you confident that you were in the eighth or ninth grade when, according to you, Mr. Alexander first exhibited a sexual interest in you?"

"Yes, I am confident."

"How old were you in the eighth or ninth grade – 13 or 14?"

"I'd have to go back to our yearbook, the Polygon, to be able to figure that out. Maybe the school records would help."

"You don't remember at this point?"

"No, I don't. Not right this moment."

"You didn't skip any grades?"

"No, I didn't."

"So, are you testifying that your sexual relationship with Mr. Alexander continued right up until his death?"

"That's correct."

"And did you ever call the police?"

"Concerning?"

"Your sexual relationship with Mr. Alexander?

"No, I didn't."

"Did you ever call the solicitor's office?"

 "No, I didn't."

"Did you ever call anybody in his family?"

"No."

"Did you ever tell anybody before the time of Mr. Alexander's death?"

"Yes, I did tell a friend. We talked about it on a regular basis."

"You told one person in all of that time?"

"Yes."

"But you never made any public statement about it, correct?"

"That's correct."

"Not until Mr. Alexander is dead and can no longer deny it, right?

"That's right."

"So now with Mr. Alexander dead, you can say whatever you want to about him, can't you?"

Charlie shook his head. "I don't know. Is that the case?"

"You tell me, Mr. Bennett."

"I don't know. You're the lawyer."

After a long pause, Stepp said, "That is all I have, Judge."

Gregg rose to ask a few questions on redirect since Stepp had suggested Charlie was being less than truthful.

"Mr. Bennett, have you recounted anything that is not true today?"

"I have told the truth."

"And do you find these details somewhat embarrassing to relate?"

"Very."

"Nothing further, your honor," said Gregg. He knew exactly when to stop.

Pieper looked back at Stepp and said, "Anything else?"

Stepp shook his head. The existence of the tape had apparently accomplished what we hoped. Stepp knew if he attacked Bennett's credibility too much, the jury might get to hear the tape of Alexander admitting what he had done.

We next played some portions of the video of Eddie Fischer's prison deposition. The members of the jury were riveted to the screen. They heard Fischer say it wasn't the kids' fault. That was followed by some deposition excerpts from the 1982 student's mother and father describing exactly what they told Alexander and what he told them he would do. We ended the morning session with some videotape of Gordon Bondurant testifying at the first trial.

The next witness for the plaintiffs was going to be the 1982 student. As we broke for lunch, Stepp came over and told me he was no longer agreeing to let the 1982 student use a pseudonym. I angrily reminded him that it had already been agreed upon. He responded that he did not agree anymore and that "if he's gonna testify, he's going to use his real name." I was furious.

I had arranged to have lunch that day with the 1982 student. He had arrived in the courtroom just before the proceedings broke for lunch. He saw the heated exchange between Bobby and me. As I walked toward the door, the 1982 student approached and said, "What's wrong?"

I just said, "Come on."

We walked down the stairs and out of the courthouse. As we were crossing the parking lot, I said, "I told you the first time I ever talked to you that if this ever got too heavy that you could just walk away, no hard feelings."

"What's going on?" He was very nervous.

"They're not going to let you use a pseudonym." I recounted to him exactly what Bobby had said.

The 1982 student looked down at the ground and was silent as we took another ten steps or so. He then said quietly, but firmly, "Fuck him."

"What?"

"Fuck him, I'm testifying."

At that moment, I knew we needed to do nothing to get this man ready to testify. At lunch we talked about everything but his testimony.

When we returned from lunch, I told Stepp the 1982 student would testify using his real name. Stepp then changed his mind and said he could use the pseudonym. I was instantly even madder than I was before lunch, because Stepp's change of heart proved he was merely trying to intimidate the witness.

When the jury was seated, I called the 1982 student to the stand. He calmly told the jury his story of the assault and his meeting with Alexander. He did a remarkable job. He also handled Stepp easily on cross-examination.

The 1982 student was followed by another of Fischer's victims, who provided one of the few genuine surprises during the trials. The parties agreed to refer to him as John Doe. Gregg and I had only recently discovered him during Kevin's trial when he had called Gregg during that trial to ask some questions. During lunch that day, while I was with the 1982 student, Gregg was having lunch with John Doe. John Doe had made a comment to Gregg that was to have a huge impact. Gregg was to do the questioning. As he got up, he announced to the court John Doe was the next witness and then he leaned over to me and whispered, "A nuclear bomb is about to go off in this courtroom." I had no idea what he was talking about.

Gregg turned to the witness and elicited testimony from him about his identity and his experiences as a Porter-Gaud student in his youth. He met Fischer during his freshman year of high school.

"Can you describe for the jury the first occasion when Mr. Fischer did something that was odd with you?"

"Well, I guess it was close to the end of September, beginning of October. And at that time a lot of the boys at the school wore their pants kind of hanging low on their waist. And he commented how funny he thought that was and how he thought it would be a great idea if he made up some kind of a costume where he would sew a shirt to a pair of pants, and it would just be ridiculously low. He thought that would be really funny, he told me. And I didn't really think anything of it. He asked me to bring a pair of pants and a shirt and I met him in his teacher's office at the school."

"So, you understood you were to bring a pair of pants and a shirt to school. You met with him. What happened then?"

"I went to his office. I removed all of my clothing and stood there in my socks while he brushed his hand against my penis and told me how remarkable that was and different things of that sort."

"This was in the course of trying out the costume?"

"That's exactly right."

"Now, was there anything . . . other than what you have described, was there anything overtly sexual about that, beyond what you have described?"

"He seemed to get quite excited and just . . ."

Stepp objected. "Objection as to what he seemed."

The witness continued, "He was visibly excited . . ."

The judge had not yet ruled on the objection, so he interrupted the young man, "You can state what you observed."

He literally took guidance from the court with his answer, "I observed that he was physically excited and kept commenting how great he thought it was that I had an erection and how remarkable that was."

"And this took place where?"

"This was in his office at the Porter-Gaud School."

"And when was it in relation to the school day? During hours, after hours?"

"It was during hours of the school."

"Now, this is when you are a freshman?"

"That's right."

"Did there come a later time when Mr. Fischer began to be sexually involved with you?"

"Yes. At a later time, he had suggested to my parents that he could really help me with my school work and help me in other ways. I was having maybe some problems at home, as a lot of adolescents might, in that my mother might say I want you home at 8 o'clock and I would say no, all my friends are staying out until 9 or 10. So things were not terrible at home, but there was tension. And I had relayed that to him, and he said, 'Well, I can help you with a lot of these problems at home.' And the next thing I know he had called up my mother and had suggested that . . ."

Stepp objected again to any statements that Fischer might have made. The judge cautioned the witness not to say anything that Fischer said, and the witness continued his answer, "The next event was I went over to his house for dinner and he offered me alcohol and marijuana. And I think that was maybe the first Friday night. And the next Friday night after that he had offered me alcohol again and had given me a sleeping pill. He had given me a sleeping pill and I was pretty out of it by that time. And he set up a movie projector and started showing pornographic films. And then he started to fondle me. He said, 'Why don't we go in the bedroom?' and I said, 'No, I think I should go home.'"

Gregg tried to make it easier, "And let me ask you, just . . . I think we are beginning to get into details."

"Yes."

"But for purposes of today, is it fair to say that a sexual . . . Mr. Fischer began to sexually exploit you?"

"He did, yes."

"And this was in the fall when you were 14?"

"Yes."

"For what period of time that you attended Porter-Gaud School did that exploitation continue?"

"The whole entire time I was at Porter-Gaud."

"Alright. Was there any time that you talked with any school official about what Mr. Fischer was doing with you or attempted to talk to a school official?"

"Yes, the principal of the school was Major Alexander, who was also my college advisor. And on two separate times, one time most in particular, we were going over my college selections. And I had told him that there were things that Mr. Fischer was doing that were inappropriate. And he didn't really want to hear so much what I was saying. His comment was along the lines of, 'Well, what are you saying? Why are you saying this? This man has helped you so much. The type of things that you are saying can get him in trouble.' And I never really said that he sexually molested me. But it was implied based on other events of which Major Alexander was present and aware of. And that's why . . . did I need to say what exactly was happening? No, I did not because he was aware of what was happening. And when I tried to tell him about it . . ."

Stepp objected because he did not know what the witness was referring to, "Objection, Your Honor, to what Mr. Alexander was aware of."

The judge sustained the objection and instructed the jury to disregard what Alexander was aware of.

Gregg responded to the judge, "I think we are going to get to that."

The judge seemed surprised, "If you can get to that, fine."

"Mr. Doe, can you relate in time when this meeting was, when you had this conversation with Major Alexander?"

"That would have been in my junior year, probably the fall of my junior year."

"And if your junior year was the '79-'80 school year?"

"That's right, it was in '79."

"Now, what was your phraseology when you tried to communicate with Major Alexander what was happening to you with Mr. Fischer? If you didn't say I'm being sexually molested, what did you say to him?"

"I said there were things that he is doing to me that are not right, that God would not approve of; that was the basic gist of it."

"Is there any point in time in which he asked you to be specific about what you were saying?"

"He didn't say be specific. He said, 'What are you talking about?' followed by, 'These type of things can get him in trouble. What you are saying? Why would you want to hurt somebody who has helped you so much?'"

Then Gregg lit the fuse on the bomb, asking if anyone else from the school was present when Fischer molested him.

John Doe answered with an incident from the 1978-79 school year.

"There was a time when I was at Mr. Fischer's house when I was upstairs in his bedroom. And I had probably had a few sleeping pills and probably smoked marijuana and probably drank something. And I remember kind of waking up and seeing Major Alexander and Mr. Fischer looking in at me in the bedroom. And Mr. Fischer was in his underwear and Major Alexander appeared to be clothed."

You could hear a pin drop in the courtroom. Until, that is, the weeping started from the gallery. Several people were crying for this young man because of the collective realization that Alexander was more culpable than anyone had imagined. Those who weren't weeping looked furious. Some of the jurors were visibly angry.

"So, that's after you spoke to Major Alexander in the fall?"

"That was before I had spoken to him. I might have the dates wrong but that had happened before I spoke to Major Alexander, which is why when I tried to further impress upon him what was going on that I felt that he knew what was going on."

"So, in the situation you were at Mr. Fischer's house unclothed?"

"Yes."

"And Mr. Fischer was wearing his underwear?"

"Yes."

"That's what Mr. Alexander saw?"

"That's right."

"No other questions."

Stepp could not conceal his anger as he rose to cross-examine. "Let me ask you a couple questions if I might, sir. When you went to see Mr. Alexander, I believe you said in 1979, is that right?"

"It was the '78-'79 school . . . oh, '79, yes."

"And you went because you wanted to tell him what Mr. Fischer was doing to you?"

"Yes."

"And so, when you went to tell him that, you didn't think he knew that then, did you?"

"I felt like he did know that."

"Why would you need to go tell him if he already knew it?"

"Because I wanted it stopped."

"What exactly did you say to Mr. Alexander in 1979?"

The witness paused for a moment and looked at Stepp as if he wondered if Bobby had been paying attention. His answer was delivered with a sarcastic tone. "I think I was a little bit clear, but I will repeat it. I said that there are things that are happening that are not right. There are things Mr. Fischer is doing to me that would not be right in the eyes of God."

"And Mr. Alexander said to you, 'Well, what are you talking about?' Is that correct?"

"That's correct."

"To which you responded at that time, 'Well, I don't know,' isn't that right?"

"Can you ask that again?"

"Yes sir. During that conversation with Mr. Alexander, he looked at you at one point and said, quote, 'Well, what are you talking about?' Correct?"

"Correct."

"To which you responded to Mr. Alexander, quote, 'Well, I don't know.'"

"That could have been what I said but I probably . . . that's what I said in a deposition sitting next to my wife who went there to help me get through it. And I was very nervous. And I was probably on drugs at that time."

"You were on drugs when you gave your deposition?" Stepp seemed genuinely astonished.

The witness responded sarcastically, "No, I was not on drugs when

I gave my deposition."

"You were on drugs at the time you visited Mr. Fischer?"

"Yes. But I do remember sitting with Major Alexander after he had witnessed me . . . viewing me laying naked on a bed over at Mr. Fischer's house with Mr. Fischer standing around in his underwear and him looking at me. And I sat with him and I told him that things were happening that were not right, and that Mr. Fischer was doing things to me that were not right and that God would not approve of. And if he said, 'Well, what are you talking about?' Maybe I had a hard time coming out and saying that I was being sexually molested by that man."

"I can understand . . ."

"I felt like he knew what I was talking about."

"You would agree with me that you did not come out at that time and say that Mr. Fischer was sexually molesting you?"

"No, it was not needed."

"Now, this incident that you have described today about being at Mr. Fischer's house and seeing Mr. Alexander there, you said you had had something to drink and taken some drugs, is that right?"

"That's right."

"Yet you have a clear memory of it?"

"I have clear enough to know that it happened."

"Did you, when we took your deposition only a week ago, did you have a memory of that at that time?"

"I had a memory of it. I didn't say it."

"You did not tell us anything about that when we took your deposition a week ago?"

"No."

"So, you are saying that for the first time today?"

"I am saying that for the first time today. I did say a week ago that I had been over at Major Alexander's house or his mother's house on Gibb Street when Mr. Fischer went to visit him. And I had been there several times, probably as many as ten times, when I waited out in the car and he went inside and the two of them were together, not knowing exactly what they were doing."

"That's all I have, your honor." The cross ended very abruptly.

Gregg asked only two questions on redirect.

"Mr. Doe, you were what age when the sexual contact began?"

"I was 14."

"And when you gave your deposition, were you asked the question that I asked you, 'Did Mr. Alexander ever witness anything?'"

"No."

"No other questions, Your Honor."

We then read into evidence some excerpts from Harold Glover's deposition. When we were done, the judge sent the jury to their room for their afternoon break.

Guerry was the first witness after the break. He was magnificent in his very direct and heartfelt way. He talked a lot about his father and their relationship.

Because Carlos was not able to be present, Gregg read excerpts from his deposition. It was not the best presentation because Carlos is a very compelling and credible witness. His statements always seem to be measured and well thought out but are delivered with no small amount of gravitas and sincerity. His live testimony would have added much to the proceeding.

I then called Dr. Reggie Christopher as our expert witness. It was his first time testifying as an expert, and he also did a superb job.

Having put on the best case we could under the circumstances, we rested the plaintiffs' case. The judge sent the jury out and we prepared to respond to the expected motion for directed verdict. It is a motion made in every case asking the court to dismiss the case; the argument is usually that the plaintiff has failed to prove their case. Stepp surprised everyone by making a motion for a mistrial. We didn't think much of the motion and I whispered to Guerry not to worry about it.

The motion was based on the introduction of the testimony of the 1982 student and his mother. Guerry left Porter-Gaud in the first few months of 1982; Fischer assaulted the 1982 student in May 1982. Eddie Fischer was allowed by Grimball and Alexander to work until the end of the school year in June. Prior to trial, the judge had ruled that the testimony of the 1982 student and his mother was only admissible if there was evidence that Guerry was molested between the date of the assault on the 1982 student, which Fischer had pegged at May 18, and the end of the school year. In the pretrial hearing, we informed the judge that Guerry could testify that he was molested on a weekly basis from 1975 until 1986, which included that specific time period, but he could not definitively give any date on which it happened during the relevant time period.

When Stepp first made the motion, we were surprised and more than a little amused. As the argument dragged on, however, the judge began suggesting that the plaintiffs had not fulfilled a commitment that we had made to him at the pretrial hearing. We became concerned that the judge was considering granting the motion. The judge accused me of misrepresenting what we intended to prove. I insisted that I represented at the pretrial hearing that we would prove what we did prove. It got quite heated, especially when the judge began suggesting I had lied to the court. It was difficult holding my temper in check. The judge reviewed, and ordered the lawyers to review, the transcript of the pretrial hearing. In the end, the judge agreed that Gregg and I proved exactly what I said we would, but that he had misunderstood what that proof would be. The judge said the 1982 evidence should not have been admitted. He granted the motion for a mistrial.

In an attempt to have him reconsider his decision, Gregg offered to have Guerry get back on the stand and ask him a few questions to cure the alleged deficiency. The judge agreed to let Guerry get back on the stand, out of the presence of the jury. During lengthy questioning by Gregg, Stepp and the judge, Guerry testified that he was 90% sure that he was molested between May 18 and the end of the school year in 1982. The judge stated that he believed Guerry's testimony was sufficient to support the introduction of the 1982 incident.

Incredibly though, he was not going to change his mind on the mistrial. The trial was over.

It was difficult to believe that this was unrelated to Pieper's visits to Rawl's chambers and the other shenanigans we had witnessed.

The Porter-Gaud lawyers smiled when the judge granted the mistrial. A reporter noted their reaction and it was the lead of the next morning's story in the local paper.

Remarkably, no one on our side was upset. We were frustrated that we would have to do the same thing all over again, but everyone realized this trial had gone poorly from the outset. It was a relief in a way.

As we were packing our bags, one of the bailiffs, who are supposed to be neutral in all cases, passed by our table and in a barely perceptible whisper said, "Don't you let them get away with this. You guys keep up the fight." It was the perfect elixir for the day's events.

The judge scheduled a settlement conference the next day in the courtroom. Settlement conferences are rarely held at the courthouse, and even more rarely ordered by a judge. Everyone attended, but it was unsuccessful because we had asked for some nonmonetary concessions from Porter-Gaud as part of any settlement and the school was unwilling to even consider them.

We were headed for trial again. The judge was not inclined to schedule the next trial that day, but I pleaded with him to give Harold his day in court as soon as possible. Harold was gravely ill, and his family believed he was hanging on just to see the outcome of the case. The judge finally relented, and set Harold's case only for the following Monday, just a weekend away. It appeared he was trying to put us in a bind, but we were thrilled.

TAMING THE LION TAMERS

That afternoon, as we were at Gregg's office preparing for Harold's retrial, one of the jurors called his office. She wanted to know why and how the judge ended the trial. Gregg explained the mistrial to her. She was really angry. He asked her if the jurors talked at all after they were dismissed and she said they did, so we decided to pick her brain a little bit. Gregg asked how she or the other jurors felt about rendering a verdict against the estates of Grimball and Alexander since the men were dead. She said the jury was outraged at the school's conduct and were particularly angry at those two men. She said even though they had not yet been instructed by the judge, it was her sense that the jury was going to return a very large verdict against all three defendants.

On the drive home that evening, I began to think about an argument I could make to the jury on punitive damages. As I was driving up I-26, I mulled over a few basic points. When I got close to home, after about two and a half hours driving and thinking, I called Gregg and left a message on his voicemail: "I know this is going to sound really, really, really crazy, but if you get us to the jury, I'm going to get $100 million in punitive damages."

That weekend, while preparing for Harold's retrial, I realized we could try the case without introducing the 1982 family's evidence in the initial phase. I called Gregg and we carefully walked through all the other evidence and decided to proceed without it. To be safe, we decided to put in all the foundation evidence leading up to it and use it at the end only if we absolutely needed to in the first phase, but we agreed we would definitely introduce it in the punitive damages phase, assuming we got that far.

261

CHAPTER 25

On Monday morning, knowing Pieper would likely pressure Harold and his family to settle, Gregg left his home much earlier than usual, so he could drive to the Glovers' home on Johns Island to see Harold.

He spoke candidly. "Harold, the judge is going to want to know what you want to settle."

Harold, with little strength remaining, told Gregg in a barely audible voice, "You tell him that I'll pay them a hundred dollars to let me hear what the jury says."

Gregg was ecstatic but knew instantly that Pieper would not be happy. As he drove to the courthouse, he tried to focus on his opening statement. He was distracted, however, because he knew the judge was going to pressure Harold to settle. He had no idea just how far Pieper would go.

Even before we started picking the jury, as expected, Pieper called us into chambers and asked about settlement. When Gregg told him Harold's position, the judge was visibly annoyed. He had no choice but to begin the trial.

In selecting a jury, lawyers generally try to select people who could easily identify with their clients. Having had input from members of the two previous juries, we knew we didn't need elderly white tomato farmers to decide Harold's case. We had only one criterion: parenthood. We wanted 12 people who either had children or were planning to. Moms and dads from all walks of life would decide this case.

Because of the publicity surrounding the first two trials, it was more difficult to seat a jury in Harold's case. Some people said that because of what they heard in the press, they didn't think they could be impartial. We knew we were losing some favorable jurors in this crowd.

In an interesting twist, we kept a man on the jury whose stepchildren attended Porter-Gaud. We knew it was risky because he might want to protect the school, but Gregg pointed out that once this gentleman heard the evidence, he would likely be even more outraged than those who didn't have children at the school.

The trial began after lunch that day. Following the opening statements, we read some excerpts from Grimball's deposition and Ronnie Hammond's deposition. The first live witness was Ralph Nordlund. His testimony was identical to the previous trials.

The next witness was John Doe, who had dropped the nuclear bomb in the courtroom the week before. He again recounted the incident where Alexander witnessed him naked in Fischer's bed and Fischer standing beside Alexander in his underwear. Stepp again tried to rattle him on cross-examination using the exact same line of questioning.

"And you did not tell him on that occasion 'I'm being sexually abused by Eddie Fischer'?"

"No, I did not. I said what he is doing to me is not right and God would not approve of what he is doing to me."

"To which he responded what are you talking about, isn't that right?"

"Yes, that's right."

"And you told him I don't know; is that correct?"

"That might have been what I said."

"Well, that's what you said when we took your deposition, was it not?"

"If that's what it says on the piece of paper, then that is what I said. Is it not a recorded document? Have you ever been through anything like this? Have you ever been sexually molested? I mean . . ."

The judge cut him off, "Hold on, sir. I understand what you're indicating, but you're not going to ask the questions here, sir. Thank you."

Stepp asked to approach the bench, where he asked for another mistrial. "Your honor, I move for a mistrial on that basis he is . . . all I'm trying to do is cross-examine."

Pieper was firm in his response, "Not on that basis, I'm not going to grant it." The judge then addressed the jury, "Just disregard all of that, ladies and gentlemen. As you have heard throughout the presentation of this case, and I think some of the attorneys made reference to the fact, you will be exposed to various emotions as testimony is being presented. Those emotions are not what you will be basing this case on. You will hear the testimony and evidence in this case. You will take those facts as you find them to be, apply the law that I will give to you and make your decision. We all understand the emotions that everyone is experiencing in this case, but those emotions will not be determinative to your decision in this case." He directed Stepp to continue.

"Let me give you a transcript of your deposition. Did you review that before you came in here today?"

"No, I did not."

"Well . . ."

"I had it with me last time I was here, and I looked through it."

"Okay. Look with me now at page 69, if you would. And you see in the middle of your statement there on page 69 you say quote, 'and then finally looking at me and going,' you're talking about Mr. Alexander quote, 'Well what are you talking about?' And I said quote, 'Well I don't know'. Do you see that?"

"Yes, I do."

"Okay. A little further down the page, did you quote Mr. Alexander as saying, 'What are you trying to say?' To which your response was 'Well I just . . . I don't know, I don't know.' Is that correct?"

"That is probably what I said, yes."

"So, it would be correct that you did not . . .'"

The witness did not wait on Stepp to finish. "I was sitting in a deposition with my wife. I was very nervous. I have never been deposed before. I have never talked with anybody about what happened to me. Does it come out crystal and clear? I remember sitting there very clearly with him and I remember talking to him and I remember knowing that he knew what I was talking about having seen me with Mr. Fischer and seen me laying naked on his bed. And so, did I feel like I could even say it? I have a hard time saying it even now, what happened to me and discussing it."

Stepp knew this was not going very well for him. "Your honor, can I ask you to please to admonish the witness simply to answer my questions and not make these speeches."

The judge politely said to the witness, "You answer the question, sir. If you need to explain after you answer the question, you may do that." It wasn't what Bobby was looking for and he gave up a few minutes later.

The next witness was Charlie Bennett, who recounted his childhood experiences with Alexander.

That afternoon, during a break, Judge Pieper told us that he wanted to talk to Harold. We informed him that Harold was at a dialysis clinic and was expected to be there all afternoon. Incredibly, he instructed us to call the clinic and get Harold on the phone. We started to protest, but he cut us off and told us to make the call.

Reluctantly, Gregg made the call. After explaining why he was calling, he was put on hold. After several minutes, a nurse picked up the line. He explained again why he was calling. Her response was not what we expected, but we liked it. She told us, "You tell the judge that Harold Glover is hooked up to a dialysis machine. He is not in any condition to talk to a judge. I will not put him on the phone. If the judge doesn't like it,

265

you tell him that he can call me." She gave Gregg her name and phone number.

When we conveyed her message to the judge, he seemed to distrust what we were telling him. Gregg gave him the number to the clinic and the nurse's name. We expected him to call, but as far as we know, he never did. Harold's children were justifiably outraged. Little did any of us know, Pieper was not through trying to reach Harold.

The next morning, Gregg called Reggie Christopher to the stand. After the usual preliminaries, including Reggie's background and qualifications, he got to the heart of the case. "Dr. Christopher, in the field of educational administration, have you ever been qualified to give an expert opinion in a court of law?"

"Yes." This would have been the previous trial.

Gregg got him to discuss the differences in administering public and private schools. After acknowledging that there are some slight differences, Dr. Christopher said, "In my training, there is no differentiation whether you go into private or public schools. And as administrators of children in public or private schools, our goal is the same, and that is to ensure the very best possible education in a safe and healthy environment."

The judge then qualified him as an expert witness.

Gregg began eliciting his opinions by following up on the last point. "As a result of your education and training, do you have an opinion about whether the standard of care for an educational administrator in 1973 for protecting students from a pedophile teacher was any different from a private school or a public school?"

"No sir, in my opinion, it is no different. When you talk about sexual misconduct, it doesn't matter whether it's in a private school or a public school. It's the same."

"And what is your opinion based on?"

"Well, my opinions are based on my experience over the years, what I have seen and read, cases I have read as well as knowing that the administration of a school is basically taking care of children."

"Is the standard any different today on this topic in public and private schools?"

"No sir, I would not think so."

"For an educator acting with due care, what is the proper priority of student safety compared to all of the other obligations the school has to its students?"

"Well, first and foremost, parents want to know that their child is going to be safe at school, and their children are going to be safe at school whether it's private or public. If you ask any parent out here, they will tell you we want to make sure our children are safe."

"So where does that rank in the priority?"

Stepp objected and argued to the judge that this question sought an opinion that he was not advised would be elicited. He claimed surprise. The judge ruled that it was within the general opinions that we had notified the defense about.

Gregg stated it again. "Dr. Christopher, I believe the question was for an educator acting with due care, what's the proper priority of student safety compared to all of the other obligations an educational administrator has?"

"Student safety is a top priority. Children cannot learn in a state of chaos or where there are things going on that are inappropriate, so that is the first priority."

"As a result of your education and training, do you have an opinion about whether there are any circumstances in which it is alright, as a matter of educational administration, for a teacher to be sexual with a student?"

"No sir, there is none."

"As a result of your education and training, do you have an opinion about proper view for an educator to take about a teacher's responsibility for sexual involvement with a student regardless of the student's age?"

"The teacher as an adult in the situation is always the one that should take proper care with a student. It is up to the teacher, the adult in the situation, to make sure proper care is taken of students. And if that is breached in any way in a sexual manner, then it is inappropriate and it's sexual misconduct."

"Does your opinion change based on the age of the student . . . if the student is over 18, for example?"

"As long as that student is in the school's care, then the teacher has that responsibility."

"As a result of your education and training, do you have an opinion about whether Berkeley Grimball and James Bishop Alexander acted within the course and scope of their duties as administrators of the . . ."

"In reading the deposition and looking at what transpired according to Mr. Grimball, I don't believe that he handled the situation correctly in dealing with the 1973 incident."

"Well, one moment. Before we get to the meat of how he handled it, the question is, is handling that within the course of the duties of the headmaster?"

"Yes sir, he should have handled it."

"And with respect to principal Alexander, describe for us if that is within or without the scope of the duties?"

"That was within both of their duties."

"Now, as a result of your educational training, do you have an opinion about whether Berkeley Grimball complied with the proper standard of care in investigating the 1973 Hammond report?"

"When the report was brought to Mr. Grimball by Mr. Hammond, the father of the student, Mr. Grimball had an obligation to investigate that thoroughly, the accusation, for two reasons. One is to protect the student. That is first and foremost and to find out whether the incident was true or not, and the second was to protect the teacher -- but first and foremost to protect the student. He should have investigated it thoroughly. Now, he did talk with the parent and he did talk with the teacher, Mr. Fischer. He never talked with the student. And Mr. Grimball said that, I believe in his deposition, that in a sense he put Mr. Fischer on probation. Well, you can't put a teacher 'in a sense' on probation. They are either on probation or they are not on probation. I also recall that he indicated that if it happened again that it would . . . he would be dismissed or asked for his resignation, which indicates it is a more serious nature than the way he handled it. If it had just been a meeting after school to help with homework or something, then he certainly would not have said if this happens again, I will dismiss you if nothing was going on."

"Dr. Christopher, as a result of your education and training, do you have an opinion about whether Berkeley Grimball complied with the proper standard of care in deciding to place Edward Fischer on probation in 1973?"

"I do not feel like, in my opinion, Edward Fischer was ever placed on probation. And the reason that I have come to that opinion is because in a situation like that, if a person is placed on probation there is something documented, written documented, that the probation is in effect and what it covers. For instance, he would have been written up, a copy would have been given to him; a copy would have gone into his personnel file. In that letter, it would indicate that he was on probation. It would indicate also that he could . . . the limitations, for instance, being alone with students on campus, off campus, things of that nature. And there is no indication that was ever done as far as a written documentation."

"As an educational administrator, do you have any quarrel with his decision to put Mr. Fischer on probation assuming he had done it correctly?"

"No sir, I don't have a problem with that."

"Can you tell us as a result of your education and training do you have an opinion about whether Berkeley Grimball complied with the proper standard of care in making a record of Edward Fischer's probation?"

"He did not comply with the standard of care, because he did not make a record."

"And what is your opinion . . . what fact is your opinion based on?"

"Because if there is no indication, we don't have anything. If he would have made a record, we wouldn't be talking about this now."

"As a result of your education and training, do you have an opinion about whether Berkeley Grimball complied with the proper standard of care in deciding who should know about Edward Fischer's 1973 probation?"

"No sir, I don't believe that he did."

"And what is your opinion based on?"

"I believe that he should have not only let Eddie Fischer know that he was on probation, he should have let Mr. Alexander know because he was his immediate supervisor, and then the department head who was evaluating Mr. Fischer."

"Assume this fact: a parent comes to Berkeley Grimball and says this teacher is getting too intimate with my son. In your opinion, what is the proper response by an educational administrator with that information?"

"When a parent comes to an administrator -- whether it's the headmaster, the superintendent, the principal -- with information that a teacher has been too intimate with a son or daughter or whoever, that is a serious incident and should be investigated thoroughly. In my professional opinion, Mr. Grimball dropped the ball. He was indifferent to the situation and never did live up to his professional responsibilities in protecting children."

"Now, what is your opinion as to the actions of James Bishop Alexander on that same subject with respect to him complying with the standard of care?"

"Well, Mr. Grimball basically took it out of Mr. Alexander's hands when he told Mr. Alexander that he would handle it. He informed him of what happened. But as headmaster, he had the authority and the right to tell the principal I will handle it, which he did. So, he basically took it out of Mr. Alexander's hands at that time."

"As a result of your education and training, what is an educational administrator's proper standard of care about the foreseeable risk when the teacher has a sexual interest in the student?"

"Let me say this: Mr. Grimball compromised his position as headmaster when he did not thoroughly investigate this matter or take proper precautions to make sure that it wouldn't happen again. If you have a teacher who does a serious breach of conduct, in this case being sexual misconduct, and you don't address that situation, then as administrator you have compromised your position as far as what you expect from teachers. So therefore, the standard of care is not met."

"Dr. Christopher, let me ask you to shift your attention to 1979. Please assume the following facts: Mr. Alexander, a principal, is at the home of Edward Fischer. He sees in Mr. Fischer's home a student of Porter-Gaud. He is naked upstairs in a bedroom. Mr. Fischer is wearing his underwear only. Do you have an opinion about the proper standard of care for a principal in that situation?"

"Yes sir, I do. First of all, Mr. Alexander should have notified the police or legal authorities. If a principal came into a house and saw what you just described, then the principal should call the police and then take measures to remove that person from employment at the school. Again, what the principal did in this situation was compromise himself. There is no way that after that incident that he could discipline this teacher whatsoever in any matter. So, I mean this particular incident is . . . I mean it is just totally unacceptable."

"Dr. Christopher, assuming a principal took no action, did the principal in your opinion comply with the standard of care?"

"No sir."

"Your honor, I have no other questions of Dr. Christopher."

Stepp began his cross-examination slowly by asking a lot of questions about Dr. Christopher's own school district and its policies about contact between teachers and students outside of school. Then he moved to the substance of this case.

"Now, your testimony is, I believe, that Berkeley Grimball did not adequately investigate the 1973 incident?"

"Yes sir."

"Do you understand that he talked to both of the student's parents?"

"And I think I stated that he talked with the parent or parents, yes sir."

"And you understand that he talked to the teacher?"

"Yes sir."

"Alright."

"But he did not talk with the student."

"And it is your opinion that he should have dragged the student in even after talking to both of his parents?" One of the jurors furrowed his brow at this question.

"Yes sir."

"Now, I think you said that Mr. Grimball should have let Skip Alexander know that Eddie Fischer was on probation, is that right?"

"Yes sir."

"And I believe one of the things you said in which Mr. Grimball failed was he didn't let Skip Alexander know?"

"As his supervisor, yes sir."

The questioning then turned to Dr. Christopher's district policy manual, and discussion about the district's policy on probation and documenting probation. Stepp was trying to establish that the things Dr. Christopher testified about were not required by his own manual. His response was that the policy manual contained broad guidelines and that reason and common sense had to be utilized in implementing the policies. Stepp concluded his questioning by getting Dr. Christopher to agree that a teacher's personnel file is not a public document.

We showed a brief excerpt of the video of Fischer testifying, and then took a lunch break.

After lunch, Pieper summoned Gregg and me to the visiting judge's chambers, an office used by circuit court judges from other parts of the state when they presided in Charleston. The room was large, with a desk in the center, a large table in one corner, and a few chairs against the opposite wall. Pieper was the only person in the room when Gregg and I entered. He was sitting behind the desk as we entered the room. It seemed odd to both of us that he had summoned us there and not to his own chambers, just down the hall. It was also unusual that the other lawyers were not there. When we entered, the judge said, "I want you to call your client. I want to talk to him."

Gregg started to protest. "Your honor . . ."

"Call him. I just want to talk to him." The judge slid the phone toward Gregg and got up from the desk.

For a long moment, Gregg and I just stared at each other. Gregg went around the desk to make the call. As he dialed the number, I reminded the judge that Harold was heavily sedated and near death. The judge would not even look at me as I spoke. He was watching Gregg dial the number.

After he finished dialing, Gregg turned his back to the judge. I could sense he was trying to figure out what to say to Evelyn when she answered to convey that he didn't want Harold to get on the phone. Suddenly, an awful look came over his face. It wasn't Evelyn who answered the phone. "Harold?"

Judge Pieper moved quickly toward Gregg, reaching for the phone. Gregg didn't hand him the receiver. The judge put the phone on speaker.

"Mr. Glover, this is Judge Pieper, how are you doing?"

"Alright, I guess." Harold's answer was barely audible.

"Well, good, good. Listen Mr. Glover, $250,000.00 is a lot of money, don't you think so?"

There was no response. Gregg and I exchanged a glance in which we mutually conveyed "*What the fuck?*"

The judge pressed the point. "Don't you think that's fair?"

In an almost inaudible voice, Harold said, "Well, judge, if that's what it is, I guess so."

"Well, it is a lot of money. You've accomplished what you wanted to. Don't you think it's fair?"

There was a long pause. We didn't know if Harold was thinking about it, had nodded off, or something far worse.

Judge Pieper bored in, "Mr. Glover, don't you think that's fair?"

Again, barely audible, Harold said, "Well, judge, if that's what it is, then that's what it is."

Pieper looked at Gregg and me and said, "I'm going to speak to the defendants."

Gregg picked up the handset to talk to Harold. As Pieper headed for the door, I stepped in front of it, blocking his path. The judge's momentum brought his face within inches of mine. Our eyes locked.

Trying to contain my rage, I said, "Your honor, I protest in the strongest of terms. You know that the court has great weight in the eyes of lay people, and you know that this man is heavily sedated and is dying."

Pieper's response was terse. "Are you accusing me of doing something improper?"

I paused longer than I probably should have, but never broke eye contact with the judge. Slowly, and with as much disdain as I could muster,

274

I replied, "Not . . . at . . . this . . . time."

The judge reached around me, opened the door, and left. After a moment, as Gregg continued talking to Harold, I went to the courtroom to get the Glover clan.

As I entered the courtroom, they could tell that something was wrong. I motioned for all of them to follow me. They sprinted across the courtroom. I didn't begin speaking until we were all in the chambers where Gregg was still talking to their father. Guerry and his siblings stood very close together, some holding on to each other. As Gregg kept Harold on the phone, I explained to them what just happened. Guerry's oldest sister, Leize, reached for the phone, "Let me speak to daddy."

She didn't hide her anger, even from Harold. "Daddy, how could you do this?" The others in the room could not hear Harold's response, but Leize was angry with her father. However, she quickly determined that Harold was confused. He thought the judge was calling to tell him the jury's verdict.

When he realized it wasn't the verdict, he told Leize that he did not want the money, and he did not want to settle. When Leize conveyed this to us, I immediately ran out to find the judge. I found him in his own office with the Porter-Gaud lawyers. I heard laughter inside the room as I knocked and entered without waiting for a response. I cut my eyes toward the judge.

"No deal," I said. "Your honor, I need to see you." Pieper's face flashed anger. The lawyers looked surprised and angry. As Pieper rose from his chair, I turned and walked back down the hall to the visiting judge's chambers. In the hall, the judge asked me what was going on. I ignored the question.

I arrived at the door to the visiting judge's chambers first. I opened it and held it open for the judge to enter. I noticed that Gregg was back on the phone, sitting at the desk. Guerry and his sister Ethel were in opposite corners of the room. Lee and Leize were beside each other in the middle of the room, in front of the desk. As Pieper entered, Lee and Leize advanced on him simultaneously in a very aggressive manner. Pieper stopped suddenly and put up both hands, signaling for them to stop. They halted their physical advance but unleashed a verbal one.

"Who the hell do you think you are calling our father at home?!?"

"You know he's dying!"

"He's a very sick man!"

"You know that he wants to hear what the jury has to say!"

It was clear that contempt of court was not on their minds. As Lee and Leize continued their joint tirade, Ethel began praying aloud in the corner. Guerry, glaring at the judge, lobbed sarcastic comments into the midst of his siblings' very pointed attacks.

After a few minutes of very heated comments, Pieper put his hands up again, stopping the comments, and said, "You want a verdict, I'll give you a verdict."

He shot Gregg a quick glance, then me, and left the room.

As the door shut, Gregg and I shared a look and we knew intuitively that we were both thinking the same thing: directed verdict. We believed at that moment that the trial was over. We tried to delicately prepare the Glovers for that and even talked about an appeal. We knew we would have to somehow make an official written record of what just transpired, which would include allegations of improper conduct by the sitting judge, but before any of that, we had to go back into the courtroom and finish the presentation of our case.

Back in the courtroom, we were prepared for the worst. Incredibly, just the opposite occurred. Judge Pieper seemed more empathetic to the plaintiff's positions and even ruled our way on several questions the rest of that day. That led us to believe that he was merely trying to appear balanced, before directing a verdict for the defendants.

Guerry testified that afternoon. He was confident and calm, but his testimony was still powerful. Many people in the gallery, and a couple in the jury box were weeping as he detailed for the third time from the witness stand the assaults by Fischer, his attempts to get away from Porter-Gaud, and the horror he felt when he learned that Fischer was at College Prep. His most poignant testimony came when he talked about his father. He described to the jury the gulf that existed between him and his father for 22 years. He also described what a decent man his father was.

We concluded the plaintiff's case in the initial phase of the trial with some very brief excerpts from Harold's deposition. We wanted the jury to hear from him, even if he could not be there. It took less than 5 minutes. "They broke our hearts, and we will go to our grave with it." Some of the jury openly wept when they heard that testimony.

Gregg rose and informed the court that "the plaintiff rests." We chose to not present any of the 1982 student evidence in this initial phase of the trial. Immediately, Stepp knew he had been snookered. He had mentioned this evidence in his opening statement and now he was in the position of either introducing it himself or leaving the jury wondering why he talked about it. It is a cardinal rule in trials not to promise the jury anything you will not deliver.

At this point everyone expected Stepp to make the motion for a directed verdict. Instead, he made a motion for another mistrial. His argument was that we failed to introduce the very evidence that caused the mistrial the week before when it *was* introduced. He reminded the judge that he had mentioned it in his opening statement, and he was concerned that the jury would think he promised something that he didn't deliver. Pieper pointed out that he could introduce the evidence when it was his turn to present his case. Stepp tried to make Gregg and me look bad, accusing us of misconduct. His anger was obvious, but it was much ado about nothing.

When we got a chance to respond, I informed the judge that we had placed the 1982 student evidence at the end of the plaintiff's case in the event we chose not to use it. I also agreed that Stepp could introduce the evidence himself. We knew he wouldn't do it.

Pieper, by then genuinely confused about Bobby's argument, denied the motion for a mistrial.

Stepp then made his motion for a directed verdict. Gregg responded, paying particular attention to how the written record would appear on appeal because he and I still expected the judge to grant this motion. To our astonishment, Pieper also denied the motion for directed verdict.

Then, when it was finally Porter-Gaud's turn to tell the jury, and the community, its side of this horrible story, the defendants decided to call no witnesses and present no evidence. Whether Porter-Gaud's lawyers felt comfortable that we had failed to prove our case, or they feared the cross-examination of their witnesses, only they will ever know. To observers in the courtroom, the decision not to present any evidence was an admission that everything we had presented was true. No rebuttal was no disagreement. Of course, no one could predict how the jury would interpret it, but it looked like a monumental mistake.

Gregg and I were not surprised. We understood the position Stepp was in. Any witness or evidence the defendants presented would probably be turned against them and a bad situation would be made worse. Also, by presenting any evidence, they would open the door for the plaintiff to present still more evidence in rebuttal.

After the presentation of all the evidence, the judge conducted what is known as a charge conference with the lawyers to decide what legal instructions he was going to give the jury. It can be quite mundane or quite lively, depending on the case. In the matter of *Harold Glover v. Porter-Gaud school, et al.*, nothing had proven to be mundane. Gregg had prepared heavily for it. The defense team tried to do some damage control by limiting what the jury would be told but didn't have much luck.

The most interesting moment came when the judge inquired about the defense of comparative negligence. The defendants argued that even if they were negligent, Harold was too, and his negligence should offset any of the defendants' bad conduct. The judge asked Stepp if there was any evidence at all that Harold was negligent. Stepp argued that Harold knew something was wrong with his son and didn't ask enough questions to find out that Guerry was being molested by his teacher.

When the judge turned to us for a response, I rose and said, "Your honor, we invite the defendants to argue that Harold Glover was responsible for the molestation of his son." We believed this defense to be so offensive, so repulsive, that it would anger the jury.

"Are you sure?" the judge was surprised by our position.

"Yes sir."

"Okay, I'll charge it then." We really didn't expect the defense lawyers to suggest it to the jury, especially after we invited them to.

Before closing arguments, someone in the gallery pointed out to us that Laura Robinson was festooned in Porter-Gaud's school colors: a burgundy business suit with a yellow and white scarf. If she was nothing else, she was loyal to the end.

Closing arguments are an opportunity for lawyers to summarize the evidence, discuss the law, and persuade the jury to agree with their client's side of the case. In South Carolina, the plaintiff begins the argument. Then, the defense responds. Finally, the plaintiff gets an opportunity to reply.

I delivered the plaintiff's first argument. Briefly, I reviewed the evidence with the jury and expressed my genuine indignation that they were blaming Harold for what happened to Guerry, and then moved across the room and pointed to the very spot on the carpet where Eddie Fischer had stood when he pled guilty and said the teacher had accepted responsibility for his role in what happened, and now Porter-Gaud, Grimball and Alexander refused to accept their own responsibility. I used the analogy of a lion and a lion tamer. I characterized Fischer as an animal. "If you take your kids to the circus and a lion gets loose and attacks your child, who do you blame? The lion who is only doing what comes naturally. Or do you hold the lion tamer responsible, whose job it is to make sure that the lion does not get an opportunity to attack children?"

In an intangible injury case, it can be difficult to get a jury to value injuries that are not quantified by medical records, bills, and other documents. We had offered no records or bills to support Harold's injury. I asked the jury to imagine that the case was about a pick-up truck. "The truck goes off a cliff, and the evidence shows that the defendants' negligence caused it to go off that cliff. If the evidence is that the value of the truck is $5,000, you would not hesitate to award $5,000 to the plaintiff.

Now, let's put some cargo in the truck, say eggs. Five Hundred dollars' worth of eggs. Same truck, same cliff, same negligence. You would not hesitate to award $5,000 for the truck and $500 for the eggs. Now change the cargo. Put a thoroughbred racehorse in the bed of that truck. Secretariat. What is that worth? $1,000,000? $10,000,000? Same truck, same cliff, same negligence. Again, you would not hesitate to award $5,000 for the truck, and the value of the horse." I paused for several minutes to let the concept sink into the jury's minds. "Now, let's put something intangible in the truck. A work of art, say, the Mona Lisa. What's that worth? $50,000,000?" I paused again. "Harold Glover would give ten Mona Lisas to have this taken out of his life. The relationship between a father and a son is worth more than any work of art. But what is it worth? You decide. Tell this school and these men what that relationship is worth."

Stepp told the jury that the plaintiff was only appealing for sympathy. He said the school and its administrators, Grimball and Alexander, exercised reasonable care in 1982 by allowing Fischer to resign quietly. He also placed the blame for what happened to Harold and Guerry squarely at the Glovers' feet; he said they were a dysfunctional family that didn't communicate well, and that if Harold had just asked more questions when Guerry was having such a tough time as a teenager he would've found out about the molestation. When he discussed damages, he told the jury, "Harold Glover doesn't have a broken bone or a scar, so let's be reasonable."

When it was the plaintiff's turn for rebuttal, Gregg leapt to his feet. He was visibly angry at Stepp's remarks. In an uncharacteristically loud and stern voice, he told the jury, "Harold Glover doesn't want your sympathy. He wants a cold, calculated award from you that will demonstrate to this school and these administrators the value of the relationship between a father and his son. They don't get it. Harold wants you to tell them what that's worth."

Once the arguments were over, it was time for the jury to go to work. Normally when a jury deliberates, they decide all questions at one time. However, because of the effect of the charitable immunity statute, and the implication it may have on other issues, the judge chose to let the jury decide the question of gross negligence first. The South Carolina Charitable

Immunity Act prevents punitive damages from being awarded against any charitable organization, like churches and private schools. The policy reason behind the statute is to prevent such an organization from being financially wiped out by a single large jury verdict. However, it provided further that if a plaintiff could prove gross negligence, a higher standard of culpability than regular negligence, against an individual employee of a charitable organization, punitive damages could be awarded against that individual.

The judge proposed to pose two preliminary questions to the jury on a single sheet of paper:

"Do you unanimously find that the employee, James Bishop Alexander acted in a willful, reckless or grossly negligent manner?"

"Do you unanimously find that the employee, Berkeley Grimball acted in a willful, reckless or grossly negligent manner?"

A finding of gross negligence would allow the jury to award punitive damages against the estates of Grimball and Alexander. As a general rule, it is entirely appropriate for a judge to separate the issues. Here though, there was a huge problem.

Pieper had excluded from the first phase of the trial the really bad evidence, the evidence of gross negligence that would support an award of punitive damages, like Alexander's recommendations of Fischer to other schools.

It was only to be admitted in the second phase of the trial if Harold Glover won the first phase. At this point in the trial, we had not yet been given a chance to prove gross negligence, but the judge was asking the jury to determine if we had proved it. I argued this point angrily to the judge, but either Pieper did not understand the problem, or he was intentionally doing it. Either way, we believed he would be reversed on this point by a higher court if we lost the case. Despite this obvious problem, Pieper decided to submit the two questions to the jury before anything else.

The jury room in courtroom C directly adjoins the courtroom. The only way in or out of it was through the courtroom. Whenever a jury was deliberating, a bailiff was posted at the door to prevent anyone from entering or leaving without the judge's permission. Whenever jurors needed to communicate with the judge, they would knock on the door from the inside and the bailiff would crack the door slightly and have a whispered conversation with whoever knocked.

Generally, a quick verdict is a defense verdict. So, we were quite alarmed when the jury knocked on the door after only *seven minutes* of deliberation. The bailiff cracked the door, spoke quietly with someone on the other side, and then closed the door. He turned to the courtroom and announced, "They have a verdict."

Judge Pieper gave a stern lecture to all present that he would not tolerate any displays or reactions when the verdict was announced. He threatened to cite anyone who did so with contempt of court. He did this because the jury would still have work to do regardless of their response to those two questions. He didn't want the jury to be influenced by any outburst. Extra security personnel were brought into the courtroom. He then instructed the bailiff to bring the jury into the courtroom.

The answers to the first two questions would have a major impact on the rest of the trial. If the jury answered no, it meant jurors were not outraged at the conduct of the individual defendants. If they answered yes, it showed they were angry and would likely come down hard on the defendants.

The jurors filed in at 3:10 p.m., all with very serious expressions. They took their seats and looked only at the judge.

"Madam foreperson has the jury reached a verdict?" Pieper inquired.

"Yes, we have your honor."

"Please give the form to the bailiff." The bailiff took the single sheet of paper to the bench. In an age-old maneuver, the clerk took the form and passed it immediately to the judge. Judge Pieper took a long time reviewing two check marks and the signature of the foreperson. After holding everyone present in extended suspense, he handed the form back to the clerk. "Alright. It appears that the form has been properly executed. If the clerk would please publish these decisions."

The tension in the courtroom was supercharged. The clerk stood and read the verdict, "In the matter of *Harold Glover v. Porter-Gaud School et al.*, case number 98-CP-10-613, the jury answers the questions as follows: Do you unanimously find that the employee, James Bishop Alexander, acted in a willful, reckless or grossly negligent manner? Yes. Do you unanimously find that the employee, Berkeley Grimball, acted in a willful, reckless, or grossly negligent manner? Yes."

The courtroom was filled with a palpable silence.

After a brief bench conference, the judge addressed the jury. "Ladies and gentlemen, in response to your decisions about the preliminary questions, I'm now going to give you a series of verdict forms that I need you to answer. Again, remember your decision as to each of these must be unanimous." He explained the new forms to them, then sent them back to the jury room to deliberate. They began at 3:30 pm.

One hour later, there was a knock on the door. This time, after the whispered conversation, the bailiff turned toward the parties and merely nodded his head.

The jury returned to the courtroom at 4:33 pm. Upon receiving the verdict forms from the jury, the judge had a question about something that was scratched out and initialed on one of the pages. After clarifying that, Judge Pieper took the unusual step of reading the verdicts himself.

"Alright. As to the claim for loss of consortium, we the jury unanimously find for the plaintiff as to the claim against Porter-Gaud, for the plaintiff as to the claim against James Bishop Alexander, for the plaintiff as to claim against Berkeley Grimball."

"As to the claim for breach of fiduciary duty against Porter-Gaud School, question one: do you unanimously find that Porter-Gaud School breached a fiduciary duty to Harold Glover? Answer is yes. Question two: if you answered yes to question one, do you unanimously find that such breach proximately caused injury to Harold Glover? The answer is yes. In response to those two same questions as to James Bishop Alexander and Berkeley Grimball, those same responses were given to the court. Yes and yes as to both defendants."

"On the negligence verdict forms as to the claim against

Porter-Gaud School: do you unanimously find that Porter-Gaud School was negligent? Yes. Do you unanimously find that such negligence proximately caused injury to Harold Glover? Yes. Do you unanimously find that Harold Glover was negligent? Yes. Do you unanimously find that such negligence proximately caused injury to Harold Glover? Yes. In response to the question about allocating percentages, the jury allocated 20 percent negligence to Harold Glover, 80 percent negligence to Porter-Gaud School. As to James Bishop Alexander: do you unanimously find that James Bishop Alexander was   negligent? The answer is yes. Do you unanimously find that such negligence proximately caused injury to Harold Glover? Yes. Do you unanimously find that Harold Glover was negligent? No. Do you unanimously, thereby the answer to question four is not necessary. And no allocation was necessary in regard to the claim against James Bishop Alexander. As to the claim against Berkeley Grimball: do you unanimously find that Berkeley Grimball was negligent? Yes. Do you unanimously find that such negligence proximately caused injury to Harold Glover? Yes. Do you unanimously find that Harold Glover was negligent? Yes. Do you unanimously find that such negligence proximately caused injury to Harold Glover? Yes. Thereby requiring an allocation of percentages to which the jury allocated 20 percent to Harold Glover and 80 percent to Berkeley Grimball. I believe I have covered three causes of action; is that correct?"

All the lawyers nodded their heads at the judge. No one said a word.

"And then finally the last page: if you have found for the plaintiff on any of the causes of action, please state the total amount of damages sustained by the plaintiff, to which the jury has awarded 15 million dollars."

The judge looked right at the defense lawyers when he read the amount of damages.

Stepp asked the judge to poll the jury, a process whereby the judge asks the jurors individually to state whether they agree with the verdict. When that was done, the judge addressed the jury again.

"Alright. Ladies and gentlemen, that does not complete the presentation of this case. There is another phase coming up next. You have focused on an award of damages which we called actual damages. There is

284

also a concept called punitive damages, and you will hear testimony on the issue of punitive damages in the next phase of the trial. I'm going to send you back to the jury room at this point, so I can coordinate with counsel how we are going to proceed insofar as the next phase of the trial. Do not discuss this case in any way. Thank you very much."

When the jury was back in their room, the lawyers had a brief discussion with the judge about how many witnesses were to be called in the next phase of the trial. He decided to let the jury go home for the day and start the next phase in the morning.

That evening, we tried to make our presentation as succinct and as powerful as we could. We didn't want to be too heavy-handed, but we wanted the jurors to be sufficiently angry at Alexander and Grimball that they would send the message we wanted them to send.

The only evidence we presented to the jury the next morning was excerpts from the depositions of the 1982 mother, Thomas Farin (the former headmaster of College Prep school), Edward Fischer, and Berkeley Grimball. Each took less than 10 minutes. We also introduced into evidence Fischer's resignation letter, Grimball's letter to Fischer after the resignation, and Farin's letter to Fischer offering him a position at College Prep. The jury heard all of this for the first time. We then rested Harold's case. It was very short, but it was devastating. If the jury wasn't mad enough before, we thought they would be incensed now that they learned that Grimball and Alexander had advanced Fischer's career at College Prep.

The judge declared a lunch break after the plaintiff's presentation. We thought the timing was great. The jury could spend the lunch hour stewing over what they just learned. I hoped that the jury would recall Stepp's argument the day before that the school had acted reasonably in 1982.

During the lunch break, a bizarre incident threatened to derail the trial. Harold's oldest son, Lee, was standing in the hall outside the courtroom. One of the jurors, as he was returning from lunch, walked past Lee, and said, "Pretty warm today."

Lee politely said, "Yeah."

The juror kept walking past Lee.

At that precise moment, Bobby Stepp rounded the corner. He was too far away to hear what was said, but he said he saw a juror talking to Lee. He also said it appeared to him that they were engaged in conversation. Stepp was duty-bound to report what he saw to the judge. He first approached Gregg and told him. He made it clear that he was not accusing Lee of misconduct, but thought it was serious enough that it should be addressed. Gregg was stunned. He knew that if the judge believed that a member of Harold's family had intentionally accosted a juror, a mistrial would be declared again.

Gregg went directly to Lee, who explained exactly what happened. While Gregg reported back to Stepp what was said, I tried to calm the family members and other people in the gallery. It was a serious matter, and it was completely up to the judge how it was to be handled. When the judge returned from lunch, Stepp told the judge's law clerk that he had a matter to take up in chambers. In Pieper's office, Stepp related what he had seen. The judge was shocked. Gregg quickly explained what Lee said happened. The judge then spoke with Lee, who explained exactly what happened. Hearing this, the judge excused Lee from the room, then turned to Stepp and said, "I don't think this is grounds for a mistrial. If you want me to, I will bring in the juror and ask him what happened." The defense lawyers asked for a few minutes to discuss their options. While they were out of the room, the judge told Gregg and me to explain very clearly to the family and anyone else on our side that any further contact with a juror, intentional or otherwise, would result in a mistrial.

The defense lawyers came back in and said they did not want the juror questioned, because they feared he would think Stepp was accusing him of doing something wrong. The judge explained that without further inquiry, he was not going to grant a mistrial. We had dodged a huge bullet.

In civil lawsuits, punitive damages, also known as exemplary damages, may be awarded to punish a defendant who has acted particularly badly, or to make an example of that same defendant to deter others who might be in the same position from acting in a similarly bad manner. In spite of a popular misperception fostered by insurance companies and large corporations, they are rarely awarded. In the punitive damages phase, the defense lawyers did mount a defense. It was not a defense to the merits of the case, but it was something.

After arguing in each of the trials and many pretrial hearings that the plaintiffs were merely seeking sympathy, the defense made a rank appeal to elicit sympathy from the jury.

They called only one witness: Emily Grimball, Berkeley's widow. She got on the stand and wept and talked about what a great man Grimball was. They introduced a photograph of him and one of his extended family. The purpose of the family photo was not clear to us at the time.

That was it. Their entire presentation to the jury in this case was the grieving widow and a couple of pictures. Nothing to dispute the plaintiff's evidence. We were surprised.

Without a break, the judge moved right to closing arguments. For this argument I put enlargements of three documents in front of the jury: Fischer's resignation letter, Grimball's acceptance letter offering to assist Fischer in the future, and the letter from College Prep offering Fischer a job after Alexander's visit, less than 30 days after he left Porter-Gaud.

"May it please the Court, ladies and gentlemen, yesterday you were told that in 1982, as soon as they had sufficient information about Eddie Fischer they acted reasonably."

"Objection, your honor. This is not about the school." I was genuinely surprised by Stepp's objection. It is unusual for a lawyer to object during another's closing argument.

I directed my response to the judge. "The individuals, your honor, are who I'm addressing."

The judge let me continue, "Alright. You focus on the individuals, sir."

I turned back to the jury. "You were told that James Bishop Alexander exercised care the first time he had information about Eddie Fischer. Now, I want to tie something together. This is Eddie Fischer's resignation letter from Porter-Gaud. You are going to have an opportunity to see this. I want you to notice the date, May 31, 1982. This is Mr. Grimball's letter accepting that resignation that you just heard some deposition testimony about: 'Let me know if I can ever be of any help in anything.' June 10, 1982. This is a letter from Mr. Tom Farin, the headmaster at College Prep dated July 6, 1982. You just heard the deposition testimony. Within 30 days, within one month, of promising the 1982 mother that he was going to do everything he could to protect kids to make sure that Eddie Fischer wouldn't be teaching, James Bishop Alexander made a personal visit and recommended Eddie Fischer for employment at College Prep. Mr. Stepp also made much yesterday of . . ."

Stepp objected again. "Your honor, I object to my argument yesterday. This is a different phase of the trial. That is simply not relevant."

I loved the fact that he was objecting to me using his own words against his clients.

The judge instructed Stepp and me to approach the bench. At the bench, Stepp argued that he was being prejudiced by me using his own words, a ridiculous argument. The judge overruled his objection but told me to move on.

I went back to the jury box, paused, then said what I came that morning to say.

"Ladies and gentlemen, I will be really brief because the evidence that you just heard of the lying, the cover-up, the corruption, needs no explanation, no argument, no embellishment. It is clear and convincing evidence of a willful, wanton, reckless, conscious disregard for the rights and safety of parents and children everywhere. As the judge is about to instruct you, in this phase of the trial you can award punitive damages. Punitive damages are also known as exemplary damages, to make an example. Harold Glover is not asking you to punish Berkeley Grimball or James Bishop Alexander; you can't do that. They're dead. But what you can do is make an example of them. You can send a message, not only to the current administrators over on Albemarle Road or the administrators of the schools in South Carolina but you have an opportunity and I would submit to you an obligation . . . an obligation . . . to send a message to every school administrator from South Carolina to New York, Seattle, Anchorage,

Honolulu, Los Angeles, Dallas, Miami and everywhere in between, to send them a message. When they sit down to watch the news sometime soon, let them know that a jury right here in Charleston, South Carolina had a message for them. And that message ought to be 'you better be doing everything you can to make your schools safe for kids.'"

"Now, what is that going to take? What is it going to take to get that message out? 100 million? 200 million? 300 million? You decide. But when you decide the number, you make sure that the message is loud enough and large enough to make headlines not only here in Charleston, but in The Wall Street Journal, The New York Times, all the way to the Podunk Daily News in Nowheresville, Nevada. You make sure that every administrator, every principal, every assistant principal at every school in this country pauses and reads your message. And you make sure they cut that article out, take it to work with them that day, and before they do anything else, they pick up the phone and call their legal advisors or they call their consultants or whoever and say, 'how about come over here as soon as you get a chance and let's take a look at our procedures and policies and make sure we won't ever have to deal with a situation like they had to deal with in Charleston, South Carolina'."

"Margaret Mead, a famous anthropologist, once said 'never doubt that a small group of thoughtful committed people can change the world. In fact,' she said, 'it is the only thing that ever has.' Today you 12 have an opportunity to change the world. Help us make it safer for kids."

Stepp rose slowly and looked beaten down. "Ladies and gentlemen, I appear before you this afternoon on behalf of my two clients. As his honor has told you, Porter-Gaud is not a part of this phase of the suit. You may not award punitive damages against Porter-Gaud. That has been decided, so I'm here in front of you today for two clients only. They are the estate of Mr. Grimball and the estate of Mr. Alexander. Now yesterday when you retired to that room and came back out and you announced a verdict against those clients, you judged their conduct. You judged it harshly. We have heard you . . . we have heard you. Now today, you have the power to punish. You have the authority, if you see fit, if you find based upon what Judge Pieper tells you the law and the elements necessary for you to do have been met, if you find that they have been met by clear and convincing evidence, then you will have the power to punish. Because, of course, that is what punitive damages are all about. They are called punitive because they are intended to punish, and they are intended to deter a person who did something wrong, and that also Judge Pieper will tell you. But the question we are confronted with in this case is who will you punish and who will you deter? I don't know what you think about what Berkeley Grimball did. I'm not going to argue with you about that. I gather from your verdict yesterday some of what you think. I'm not here to dispute that or to argue with you about that when you decide this verdict. But Berkeley Grimball is not here. Berkeley Grimball is dead. Berkeley Grimball can't be punished. And the same thing is true of Skip Alexander. Whatever you may think, whatever judgment you might seek to pass, you cannot punish him because he is not here. He is dead. He is beyond judgment, as is Mr. Grimball. All we have left here today is Mr. Grimball's and Mr. Alexander's family. That is all there is left for you to deter. Whatever you may think, whatever you may now decide about Mr. Grimball and Mr. Alexander, these people have not done anything to warrant the wrath or warrant punishment at your hands. Justice does not require that they be punished, not even retribution requires that they be punished. Now, Mr. Flowers has asked you to let your verdict send a message. Haven't you done that? Didn't you send a message yesterday? You sent a message to me, and I heard it. You sent a message to my clients, and they heard it. Isn't that enough? Your verdict yesterday was in support of the plaintiffs. Does justice today require that you vote against two families? I hope not. I hope that is not the way you feel. Justice, I think, doesn't require that. You have the power. You also have the discretion as to how you will use it. Judge Pieper will tell you that it is entirely up to you whether to award punitive damages and, if so, in what amount. That is within your discretion. Having the power and having the discretion, what I hope and pray on behalf of my clients is that you will exercise that power wisely and justly and that you will use your discretion under these circumstances to return a verdict that is fair and that is not punishable to these families."

Usually, Gregg does the plaintiff's reply argument, but I spontaneously put my hand on Gregg's shoulder, keeping him down in his seat, and rose.

"What the Judge is going to tell you, I think, is that the purpose of punitive or exemplary damages is not just to deter the wrongdoers in this case but they are also intended to deter similar conduct of other actors in other places in the future. Harold Glover heard your verdict yesterday. And as the judge told you, and as Mr. Stepp knows, that verdict was to compensate Mr. Glover for his loss only. It was not to send a message. That is not what you were instructed to do, and I'm sure that is not what your intent was. Today is the opportunity to send that message and that is what Harold Glover is asking you to do, not to punish a man, not to concern yourself with where it comes from or where it goes to. What you should concern yourself with is 'how are we going to make this world safer for kids?' That is what you should focus on. This is your opportunity to change the world."

The judge then gave the jury some further instructions about punitive damages. They began their deliberations at 2:20 pm. While the jury was deliberating, Gregg and I went to a nearby cafeteria to get lunch. While in line, a customer in front of us recognized Gregg from the press coverage. He walked over and said, "Aren't you the guy handling that case against Porter-Gaud?"

Gregg looked at me and said, "We are."

"I just want to shake your hand and thank you for doing what you're doing." He then shook our hands. Several of the other customers came over and shook our hands as well. To Gregg and me, it was confirmation of something we had felt all along: if we could just get any 12 people from the community to listen to the case, they would get it.

At 4:35, the jury returned to the courtroom with its verdict. Pieper seemed exceptionally serious when he addressed the panel. "Madam forelady, I understand the jury has reached a unanimous verdict as to each of the questions that were proposed to you, is that correct?"

"That is correct."

"Please hand it to the bailiff." For the third time in about 26 hours, the bailiff retrieved the verdict form and handed it to the clerk who handed it to Pieper. After looking at it for much longer than it takes to read the few words on it, he looked right at the defense lawyers for a few seconds before he said, "Madam clerk, publish the verdicts, please."

The clerk took the form and read it aloud. "Case Number 96-CP-10-613. Do you unanimously find that the conduct of the defendant James Bishop Alexander was willful, wanton, or reckless? Yes. We unanimously find for the plaintiff in the amount of 45 million dollars punitive damages. Do you unanimously find that the conduct of the defendant Berkeley Grimball was willful, wanton, or reckless? Yes. We unanimously find for the plaintiff in the amount of 45 million dollars punitive damages."

As the jury was polled yet again, Gregg leaned over to me and whispered, in mock seriousness, "You said $100 million. You keep screwing up and I'm not going to let you do the closing anymore."

The judge spent some time thanking the jurors and then discharged them.

After the handshakes and the hugs, our thoughts were about Harold. We hurriedly packed our things and drove to Johns Island.

The family members had beaten us to the Glover home, where there were tears, hugs, and handshakes. I went into the den to see Harold. He was sitting in a recliner with an IV in his arm. I went and spoke some now forgotten words to him.

Then, Gregg walked into the room. As Harold saw Gregg, tears filled his eyes. Gregg said, "Well Harold, we did it."

Harold's reply demonstrated the essence of this remarkable man.

"Well, I just hope it helps the others."

EPILOGUE

Immediately after the verdict, several things happened in sequence and simultaneously. As a result of Judge Pieper's scheduling order, issued in accordance with Porter-Gaud's request, the next trial was scheduled to start in about three weeks. Laura Robinson tried several things to delay it, arguing that they needed more time to prepare for the trial which was silly because the next trial was going be the exact same trial as the one we had just completed, the only difference being that it was on behalf of a victim, not a parent. One of the few things that both sides agreed on in this litigation was that the verdict in a victim's case would be substantially larger than a verdict in a parent's case. She also filed a motion seeking a change of venue, arguing that Porter-Gaud could not get a fair trial in Charleston. Her argument was that due to the adverse press coverage of the Glover trial and verdict, potential jurors would be biased against the school. Gregg and I were amused that all the press reported was the truth, which the school and its agents had been trying to keep hidden for years. She included an assertion that survey data would be forthcoming to prove the publics' bias against the school, but no such data was ever produced.

Porter-Gaud's insurance company approached us about settling not only Harold's $105 million verdict, but all of the remaining cases as well. We didn't think they were serious, but we decided to meet with them. Gregg and I chose to divide our efforts, at least for a couple of days. He stayed in Charleston, preparing for the next trial, while I met with the insurance company representatives in Greenville, where I lived about 200 miles away from Charleston. The settlement conference started out at the Greenville county courthouse and lasted all day. I derived no small amount of fun every time we hit a stumbling block by saying, "That's okay, we don't have to settle, we'll just see you in the courtroom next Monday." At the end of the day, we seemed to be making some progress, so we continued the conversations at my office. During the discussions, they kept asking us to agree to postpone the next trial to give everyone more time to prepare and continue the settlement talks. I refused. I kept reminding them that they are the ones who put themselves in the bind by insisting on one trial a month for eleven months. Finally, about 10:30 pm, we reached a tentative settlement after the insurance company representative, Sally Johnson, assured us that they had no more money to offer. Church Insurance Company was a relatively small insurance company that mostly handled entities affiliated with the Episcopal Church around the country. There was a genuine risk that the company would file bankruptcy, which would halt all of the other cases. The reason the insurance company was facing such peril is due to a well-settled principle of law in South Carolina known as the *Tyger River Doctrine*. This is a case that held that if an insurance company unreasonably refused to settle a claim against an insured, the insurance company itself might be responsible for the full amount of any verdict, even if it exceeded the limit of the insured's policy. So, the Church Insurance Company's own assets were potentially at risk to satisfy the enormous verdict. Later, we learned that Johnson had allegedly lied in her representations about the company's ability to pay the judgment, which spawned further litigation.

Our clients opted to settle because our main goals of exposing the school's arrogance and defeating it and exposing the truth had been met. Gregg and I knew the verdict would be difficult to defend if we continued. Judge Pieper had the authority to reduce the verdict if he chose to, and due to the number of novel legal issues we had used in the case, any appeal was fraught with uncertainty. Also, there was a chance that Pieper would stay, or freeze, all of the other cases while the verdict in Harold's case was appealed. Appeals in South Carolina generally take 3-5 years and we did not want to put our clients through that much uncertainty for that long. In the end, all of our clients agreed. A global resolution was effectuated, and we thought that was the end, until more victims came forward. Many more.

Porter-Gaud and its insurance company eventually settled the claims of dozens of Fischer's victims. And it was not just about money; the victims demanded and got nonmonetary concessions that would provide help for other victims, including a fund to provide free therapy to Fischer's victims who had not yet come forward and a hotline for students at the school to call if they felt they were victims of sexual misconduct.

While all of that was happening, Porter-Gaud's spin doctors shifted into high gear. Their administrators and lawyers tried to persuade the community that Porter-Gaud was a victim of its insurance company and its lawyers. The school's new administration met with the editors of Charleston's Post and Courier newspaper to assure the public that enrollment and fundraising had not been affected by the litigation. The school also sued its insurance company, alleging the company's refusal to settle harmed the reputation of Porter-Gaud school. In their lawsuit, the school disclosed the identities of some of the victims which they had previously agreed to keep confidential. At least one of these victims who was publicly identified committed suicide a few years later. The school pocketed hundreds of thousands of dollars from a settlement of that suit. After the verdict, Porter-Gaud named the headmaster's house on the campus after Grimball, its Fine Arts Center was already named after him, and continued to give an annual award in his name to a top student. The school even called one of its fundraising levels the Grimball level.

Porter-Gaud still didn't get it.

Harold went back into the hospital. On November 30, 2000 he passed away.

On December 2, he was buried in the small graveyard of an Episcopal church on Johns Island, where he was born and lived his entire life. Hundreds turned out for his funeral, from all walks of life. Even people who didn't know him, but who knew what he had done for the community, attended. Some words were spoken about his stand and the unselfish way he offered himself to help his son and the other victims. He had finished his work, and he was laid to rest.

Shortly after the verdict in Harold's case, Gordon Bondurant wrote to Gregg and asked if Guerry would be willing to meet him for lunch. Guerry agreed. Bondurant apologized to Guerry for not helping him to protect students by ending Fischer's career when he had a chance.

During the litigation, a non-profit organization was created to help raise awareness about child sexual abuse. Anne Lee, herself a sexual abuse survivor, started Darkness to Light and it became a voice for victims everywhere. Because of Anne, Darkness to Light was the only institution in Charleston that publicly supported Guerry and the other victims during the lawsuits. Other groups, even other child advocacy groups, were too fearful to criticize Porter-Gaud.

Within a year after the verdict, the South Carolina legislature revived a dormant bill that Gregg had drafted years earlier to change the statute of limitations to make it easier for victims of childhood sexual abuse to file claims. The bill passed both chambers and was signed by the governor in 2001.

Fischer died in prison on July 6, 2002.

After the verdict, I became good friends with the 1982 student. I admired his courage and willingness to step forward and help the other victims. He was also just a really good guy. Several years after the verdict he, like so many other Fischer's victims (more than a dozen), took his own life. I felt responsible because I made the call that dragged him into the litigation and compelled him to talk about his experience with Fischer. His death started a downward spiral for me that lasted for years and seemed to have no bottom. I quit practicing law, my marriage disintegrated, and I spent weeks and months at a time in the woods, where I found a small measure of solace. I gave away most of my worldly possessions and wandered the country for several years and eventually ended up on the island of Kauai, where I had previously done volunteer work restoring wilderness areas. I went there to work in the wilderness for the rest of my life, planning on no human contact except for my children and people employed at the local post office and grocery store. While there, I began a process of healing which continues today. I will forever miss the 1982 student, and I will never forget him or his courage.

In 2018, Paige Goldberg Tolmach, a Porter-Gaud alum, released a documentary film about the school's handling of Eddie Fischer after learning how many male alumni of the Fischer era had committed suicide. *What Haunts Us* received universal critical acclaim and was nominated for an Emmy in the Exceptional Merit in Documentary Filmmaking category. More importantly, the film informed decades of Porter-Gaud alumni about the true story of the school's complicity in and support of Fischer's reign of terror in Charleston. Graduates of the school had been lied to for years. Many of them were outraged when they learned the truth.

It is my hope that my life's work bringing cases such as these to light will someday help to end the seemingly bottomless capacity of school officials, clergy, politicians, and others to harm those with no power to stop them, especially the children.

ABOUT THE AUTHOR

David Flowers is a recovering attorney who spent his career representing the victims of sexual abuse in civil litigation. He also represented crime victims *pro bono* in criminal proceedings to ensure their constitutional rights were protected. Although he no longer practices law, David continues to advocate for abuse victims and welcomes any chance to educate and raise awareness about issues related to this crime that is far too prevalent in our society. He lives with Natalie in the mountains of North Carolina.

He can be reached at davidflowersauthor@gmail.com